MADISON
AVENUE
U.S.A.

MADISON AVENUE U.S.A.

Martin Mayer

NTC Business Books

a division of *NTC Publishing Group* • Lincolnwood, Illinois USA

Library of Congress Cataloging-in-Publication Data
    Mayer, Martin
        Madison Avenue U.S.A./Martin Prager Mayer.
            p. cm.
        Includes index.
        ISBN 0-8442-3247-5
        1. Advertising—United States. I. Title.
HF5813.U6M3   1991   91-20059
659.1′0973—dc20

Published in 1992 by NTC Business Books, a division of NTC Publishing Group
4255 West Touhy Avenue
Lincolnwood (Chicago), Illinois 60646-1975, U.S.A.
©1958, renewed 1986 by Martin Prager Mayer. All rights reserved.
No part of this book may be reproduced, stored in a retrieval system,
or transmitted in any form or by any means,
electronic, mechanical, photocopying, recording or otherwise,
without the prior permission of NTC Publishing Group.
Manufactured in the United States of America.

1 2 3 4 5 6 7 8 9 0 VP 9 8 7 6 5 4 3 2 1

FOR
my parents, who have borne a great deal over the years;
not least, recently, this book; with love

CONTENTS

"Let's follow it and see what it eats."

Runic inscription (rough translation)

". . . the student must avoid the error so frequently made of assuming a simple cause-and-effect relationship between advertising and change in the consumption of a brand or product."

Advertising Text and Cases, *by Neil Borden*

A NOTE FROM THE AUTHOR

The nicest thing about *Madison Avenue, USA* was its reception. Cleveland Amory hailed it as the most damaging attack ever on the advertising industry, and David Ogilvy acclaimed it as the most effective defense of the industry ever written. "It reports what is *really* happening in most of the top agencies today," Ogilvy wrote, "with blazing indiscretion and uncanny accuracy." My friend and mentor Richardson Wood, formerly managing editor of *Fortune*, wrote that "It does for the 'Madison Avenue' of the Eisenhower Age much what the *Canterbury Tales* did for Southern England of the late Middle Ages." Honest, he did; we printed those words on the jacket. Orville Prescott gave it a rave in the daily *New York Times* on publication day, and the New York bookstores alone put in almost three thousand reorders before the sun set. We were on the bestseller list (my first time ever) within three weeks and stayed there for months.

This was my third book, following a novel which had also been published in England and a reportorial book entitled *Wall Street: Men and Money*. Fred Warburg of Secker & Warburg had published the novel in Britain but had not wanted the Wall Street book. Max Rinehart of The Bodley Head was shown the manuscript of *Madison Avenue, USA* on a visit to its publisher, then known as Harper & Brothers, and vowed he would have it. Told that I considered myself under option to Warburg (George Orwell's publisher and Angus Wilson's employer, who had given us a wonderful time in England, and was to be the publisher of my wife's book *The Dandy*), Rinehart promptly bought the English rights to *Wall Street*, which meant he could option the advertising book. I then did a new 1959 edition of *Wall Street* for him (footnotes to update, rather than changes in the text), which Harper brought out in the United States as a revised edition, and Collier Books kept in print for another fourteen years. Fallout.

xi

Madison Avenue, USA was a Pocket Book in America and a Penguin in England, and was translated into Japanese, German, Spanish and French (ten years later, when I told the lady from Hachette that it was rather out of date, she said, "That's all right; so are we"). It provoked one lawsuit, which probably should not be invited again. I credit the then famous slogan "You'll wonder where the yellow went/ When you brush your teeth with Pepsodent" to "copywriter and jazz hobbyist Don Williams," who had been the copy group head for Pepsodent and had both written and performed the musical end of the jingle. But he had not written the words, which had been penned by a young woman named Therese Macri, gone from the agency and suing it for something or other when I came round to interview. They were not going to mention that name, so I never heard it, and the paperback reprint (the statute of limitations had run out on the original edition) was sued for "libel by omission." *Macri v. Mayer* got into Prosser's Restatement of the Law of Torts for the American Law Institute. The New York Court of Appeals (the highest state court) ruled that there was such a cause of action, but only for demonstrable damages. At this point Harper and I each kicked in $100 and settled the case.

As I noted in 1991 in *Whatever Happened to Madison Avenue?*, my return to the subject after 33 (!) years, the book's importance was that it gave the first public prominence to the four men I chose as exemplars of the schools of advertising: Bill Bernbach, Norman B. Norman, David Ogilvy and Rosser Reeves. And to several of the researchers, especially Alfred Politz. It also, which was unusual in those days, took the subject itself rather seriously. I also, which was not unusual in those days, took myself rather seriously in the last two chapters.

Though the business has changed in many ways, much of what is here remains true—especially, perhaps, Rosser Reeves's statement that his function in the first political radio spots, which he wrote for Eisenhower, was "to apply the mechanics of advertising to the expenditure of money." The description of the planning of the campaign for the Edsel may also have continuing value, as testimony of how hard and how well people can work without knowing theirs is a lost cause.

Fifteen years after the publication of this book, I gave a lecture on some other subject—I think television—at a midwestern university. As I walked across the campus with my hosts to lunch, a young Japanese man who had been in the audience came running up to me with enormous excitement, having just enjoyed an epiphany. "I know you," he said enthusiastically. "I know you. You have written a *crassic*." For a book a generation old, *Madison Avenue, USA* still gets mentioned surprisingly often, and people tell me it's still fun to read. Like some other *crassics*.

Martin Mayer
September, 1991

PREFACE

"So you're writing a book about advertising," they said, dozens of them, as their visitor took out his notebook and pencils. "What's your angle?"

And I would say, "I don't know that I have any angle."

They stiffened a little, and then relaxed, resigning themselves to their fate, certain that they were about to get clobbered in print, once again. But they answered questions openly and thoughtfully. Of all the people I saw in preparing this book, I owe the greatest debt to these men who gave their time and intelligence to a project which, they felt, could do them nothing but harm.

Madison Avenue, U.S.A. is a reporter's book about advertising—specifically, about the national advertising of branded products in general media of information and entertainment. The bulk of it is devoted to showing advertising men at work in those areas where manufacturers compete with each other primarily by means of advertising—groceries, soaps, drugs and toiletries, cigarettes, automobiles, alcoholic beverages and beer. Most of the money and most of the skill in advertising are spent here. Concentration on such advertising is unfair to the industry in one way, because it virtually eliminates any presentation of advertising's genuine informing function. In another way, however, it is more than fair. Heavily advertised products draw to their service the best talent in the industry, and because this book is concerned with product advertising it is almost entirely about able people.

The media section of the book deals largely with newspapers, local radio and television stations, consumer magazines and network television, slightly with billboards and network radio, scarcely at all with the other advertising media. I regret the omissions, mostly because I had the material; but it was my aim to make the book reasonably short and continuously interesting rather than complete. I have also tried to discuss only those concepts and methods which are central and permanent, eliminating certain currently popular peculiarities of procedure and certain aspects of contemporary advertising which strike me as nothing more than side reflections of high corporate profits taxation.

Except in the last two chapters, which are avowedly editorial, I have generally avoided expressions of my own opinion. This restraint proved especially difficult in the sections on advertising research, where salesmanship and science have been ingeniously interwoven and everyone must separate the strands his own way. Where there is controversy, I have attempted to give both sides of the argument, though I have made no great effort to hide my own sympathies—when I have any. The neutrality which so becomes a reporter was natural to me, because I have never worked in advertising and I have no stake in the success or failure of any individual, organization or theory. I recognize that nobody is so thoroughly objectionable as the man who has no axe to grind because the stiletto he carries is quite sharp enough; and I have tried to avoid *that,* too.

The book represents about sixteen months of work, which included nearly four hundred interviews, a reading program of little less than thirty thousand pages, and what seemed to my wife and friends an interminable stretch of talking-the-subject-out. Most of the books from which I have drawn important background or information are mentioned somewhere in the text, but three of them are not—Otto Kleppner's *Advertising Procedure,* Irving Graham's *Advertising Agency Practice* and James Webb Young's *Diary of an Ad Man.* The luxuriant trade press of the advertising business was a great help to me from the beginning, and virtually every periodical publication in the field made some contribution to the fund of knowledge from which this book is taken.

I would be remiss in an obligation, however, if I did not acknowledge a special debt to *Advertising Age*, the liveliest and, taking the rough with the smooth, the least inaccurate trade magazine I have ever seen.

I am obliged to all those who gave up their time to help me, and particularly to those heads of organizations whose words, by accident, found no place in these pages—to Archibald Crossley, Matthew Culligan, Roy Durstine, Earle Ludgin, Pierre Martineau, Lawrence Valenstein and others. I am indebted to personal friends and friends of friends, who helped me fill in background material—to Robert Brody, Sidney Dean, Helga Dudman, Ann Foster, John Goodwillie, Joel Raphaelson and Jim and Olivia Trager. And I am grateful to those senior men who did me the kindness of reading the whole book in manuscript form before the type was set—to William Bernbach, Sherwood Dodge, David Ogilvy, Alfred Politz, Rosser Reeves, Richardson Wood and James Webb Young.

At least thirty advertising men read manuscript or galleys on all or part of this book, and caught a considerable number of errors, too. I was not bound to accept their suggestions for alterations, however, and in many cases did not; any blame for inaccuracies must rest on my shoulders alone. For the record, I should like to say that most of those who read the book displayed an unusual and generous desire not to complain about good stories, even though the stories displayed their subjects in an undignified, even unflattering, posture.

Final acknowledgments are due also to Cass Canfield, who suggested the book; to Henry Wolf, art director of *Esquire* Magazine, who designed the jacket; to Ellen Thurneyssen, who typed the manuscript in short takes while I was fighting an unusually ferocious deadline; and, as always, to my wife, for her invariably intelligent and pointed critical comments.

MARTIN MAYER

Part I | INTRODUCTION

CHAPTER I

THE ADVERTISING MAN:

Habitat,
Functions
and History

From three men, anonymous for good reason.

One, a senior vice-president of an advertising agency, formerly an account executive:

"My first job was in a promotion department, working from seven-thirty to four P.M. I was seventeen years old. One day my boss called me in and said, 'Your problem is that you don't have any selling experience. If you want to get ahead in this business, you'd better put your belly against a counter and sell.'

"I went out and got a job from six P.M. to midnight, first at the McAlpin Liggett's. The job was for Saturday and Sunday, too. I had Friday night off; Friday nights I took a course at NYU. I learned pretty quickly that I wasn't much smarter than anybody else. But I was willing to work a little harder.

"Where I sit now, part of my job is to talk with the messenger boys and the boys in the production department who want to get into client servicing, they want to be account executives. They come up here to me and say, 'I'm a salesman, I want to sell.' I ask them, 'Where does your wife do her shopping, at what supermarket?' And they don't know. I say to them, 'Do you ever hang around a gas station, and find out what people ask for when they drive in?' They look at me as though I'm crazy.

"Even today, on Saturday, up at my country home, I'll put on some old clothes—nothing shabby, you understand, but not the sort of thing I would wear to the office—and I'll go over to one of the local grocery stores. They all know me by now. I'll ask for a chance to wait on customers, without salary, and if they don't want to let me do that I'll ask permission just to stand around the store. I'll go over to the dessert counter. When a woman picks out a package of Jello and puts it in her cart, I'll step over to her and I'll say, 'Excuse me, madam. I don't work for the store, and I certainly don't work for the Jello company, but I was wondering if you'd tell me why you chose Jello rather than some other dessert . . . ?' "

Two, an executive vice-president of an advertising agency, formerly a copywriter:

"I come from a professional family; at the age of three I was going to be a doctor. When I got a little older I was going to be a lawyer, then a writer. At the age of fourteen I rebelled; I ran away to sea. They brought me back, I went to college and I couldn't finish. In my family that was like venereal disease, not finishing college.

"In my twenties I had what I guess was a nervous breakdown. Then I worked as a shipping clerk for a while, I was the worst shipping clerk in New York. At twenty-four I suddenly thought, I don't know why, 'I'll go into advertising. Advertising will use my virtues and support my vices.'

"Only a few years ago I realized that what I had done was to run away to something I didn't think was significant. What advertising meant to me then was, simply, that I wasn't being a doctor. I could put my best into it because I didn't respect it. . . ."

Three, the head of a market research organization:
"My godparents sent me to the University of Michigan, I wanted

to be a biologist or a curator in a zoo. They didn't like the idea of either; they said it wasn't a good enough living. So I went into bacteriology with the thought that I'd go to medical school and be a doctor. In bacteriology I learned I was color blind. And my godparents weren't prepared to send me through medical school as well as college. I know I could have worked my way through, but I wasn't willing to do it.

"By that time I had lots of extracurricular interests, so I searched around for the easiest thing I could do in college, and that was sociology. One assignment in a course was to check a poll of public opinion. I found they'd done it all wrong, I had to do it over, and I got fascinated by public opinion research. I set up a student bureau just to do public opinion polls at Michigan. I'd get my data together and then beat it out all night long on the IBM machines in the statistical lab.

"I fooled around with question orders, how people answer questions. If you ask people what they think of the Trade Metallics Act, you'll find they all have an opinion, and there isn't any such act. Finally, I realized that the attitudes and opinions I was finding weren't new. They were traceable all the way back; they're an inherited body.

"We're dealing with a deep mechanism which was designed long before we were walking around. Finding out about this mechanism—and how it twists itself to fit something really new into the context of existing opinions—that's the fascination of this work."

1.

The only major New York street named after a President of the United States, Madison Avenue runs some six miles up the East Side of Manhattan, and a Madison Avenue address can mean anything at all. The low numbers are probably insurance companies, and the high numbers are homes in the misery of Spanish Harlem; between them the Avenue runs through an area of loft buildings and decent hotels, and through two of the best residential districts in the city. The stretch that has made the street famous takes up one-fifth its length, beginning at about 200 Madison and ending at about 650 Madison, slightly more than a mile of office buildings set side by side in parallel lines, forming what the vulgar call ad alley or ulcer gulch, what the more enlightened describe as the communications belt.

On Madison Avenue or within two or three blocks in either direction are the headquarters of the two largest radio and television networks and the offices of fifty "station reps" who sell advertising time on local stations; the central advertising sales office of almost every major magazine and the editorial offices of such periodicals as *Time* and *Life, Vogue, Look, McCall's* and *Redbook, Esquire* and *Coronet, The New Yorker, Mademoiselle,* and many, many others; the main offices of sixty "national reps" who sell white space in a thousand newspapers. Scattered in among them are the advertising agencies themselves, preparing and placing and billing their clients for nearly three billion dollars' worth of advertising in a year. Half of American industry's national advertising budget is spent by the agencies of Madison Avenue, and nearly half the remainder by branch offices controlled from New York.

Even before the war this was the home of the advertising business; but Madison Avenue as it appears today is impressively new. New York as a whole has had since the war an incredibly extensive building boom; the new office space added to the city in the past dozen years is greater than the total of all office space, new and old, in any other city in the world. The effects of this construction project are most immediately visible in the Madison Avenue area, where an explosively expanding industry has demanded space for advertising offices, space for communications offices, space for the headquarters staffs of manufacturing companies which live by advertising and need a location in the heartland. On Madison Avenue alone more than a dozen new office buildings, each more than twenty stories high, have been built since the war; a block away, Park Avenue below Sixtieth Street has been transformed from a boulevard of old brown apartments and hotels to a nest of green glass, brown glass, blue glass and chrome steel office skyscrapers. Including the new structures on Fifth, on Lexington and in Rockefeller Center, no fewer than forty large office buildings, with little less than twenty millon square feet of floor space, have been added to the half of a square mile compendiously covered by the name Madison Avenue.

On the outside, unfortunately, the new buildings are mostly very much alike; on the inside, it is every man for himself. Appearance (the pejorative word is "front") means a great deal in advertising. At the agencies, especially, décor is a means of expression; the agency tries to say something about itself by its use of space, color and design. At Young & Rubicam, for example, the spaces are large, the upholstery material is leather and the color is green—walls, carpets, chairs and couches are green, and the name plaques opposite the elevators on the twelve floors that Y & R occupies announce the agency by means of white letters against a green leather background. A visitor to the executive floor of Y & R could be pardoned the feeling that he was in a bank: a long, spacious, deeply carpeted hall broken by a few counter-height partitions to establish areas for the widely spaced secretaries, doors opening into obvious (and almost identical) distinction, the monochrome green enforcing an impression of solidity. McCann-Erickson, more strongly oriented toward sociological and psychological studies, uses a collection of correctly restful pastels in the halls and offices of its spanking-new fourteen-floor New York office, and a visitor to the executive floor of McCann could be pardoned the feeling that he had stumbled into a movie set: a vast center area almost as wide as a city street with secretarial desks of luxurious modern design, elaborately simple chairs and couches in black, red and yellow scattered for the ease of important people who have personal appointments but will have to wait.

Grey Advertising, of course, prefers gray in all its tones. At Sullivan, Stauffer, Colwell & Bayles the reception area is walled with dark walnut of a fine grain; the wood covers even the panels for the elevator buttons and the pointing arrowheads of the buttons themselves ("Most people," says a receptionist with some annoyance, "can't find

them"). A silvery wallpaper printed with a Chinese landscape hope-
fully suggests happy repose in the waiting room at Norman, Craig &
Kummel. Other agencies belligerently avoid even the suggestion of
chic: such giants as Batten, Barton, Durstine & Osborn, Benton &
Bowles, and Ted Bates & Company have snuggled into office settings
so nondescript or old shoe that a high-class accountant would scorn
them as insufficiently stylish. J. Walter Thompson, the largest of all
agencies, is here as elsewhere in a class by itself, following a house
rule that each of its hundred-odd private offices must be different,
and, if possible, personal, showing the visitor styles from Mies van der
Rohe (whose stark Barcelona chairs are in one reception room) to
Regency (a magnificent round gaming table with cups for chips is the
centerpiece in the office of a vice-chairman) to early New England
(the interior of a genuine colonial farmhouse has been reconstituted
for the executive dining suite) and back through the great periods of
European furniture making.

2.

People who can afford to indulge their tastes in furnishings can also
take their personal choice in food and drink and leisure surroundings.
To offer this choice, there has grown up in and around the half square
mile of Madison Avenue a neighborhood elegance of entertainment that
has no equal in America and few in Europe—and it can truthfully
be said that the great restaurants of New York are here quite simply
to serve lunch to men in the advertising and communications fields.
The list is headed by Brussels and Voisin, the peer of anything in
France; it includes such equally expensive and almost equally splendid
establishments as Pavillon, Chambord, "21," Laurent, Maud Chez
Elle; and it drops finally into the more bearable price brackets occupied
by Le Chanteclair, Swiss Pavilion, Mercurio, La Reine, San Marino,
and at least a dozen others.

All varieties of atmosphere are available: two kinds of Gallic grace
at Brussels and Voisin, the former a *fin de siècle* air of tapestries and

crimson velvet, the latter an earlier décor of white and blue, both with chandeliers; the dark intimacy of La Reine, one of the last remaining fine restaurants still crowded onto a single floor of an old brownstone house, long and narrow, rows of tables against the walls with an aisle in the middle for service; the rather hearty clubbiness of "21," its exterior collection of carved Negro jockeys reaching for the vanished horse and its interior collection of large, frill-free dining rooms which can handle among them some four or five hundred diners at a time. All are excellent; all are expensive: at the most reasonable of them a party of two at lunch can get away for eight dollars or so, including a drink for each and the tip; at the upper end, two drinks and two lunches can run twenty dollars. Not every party of two, of course, will be satisfied with two drinks.

But the company will pick up the tab. Salesmen have always had expense accounts (or vouchers—in the old days such blessings arrived singly rather than in tabular form), and advertising has been well defined as salesmanship magnified. Legitimately, men who represent newspapers, magazines and broadcasting stations pick up the check for men who buy space and time; agencies buy lunches for their clients and prospective clients; research firms and package designers entertain agency research directors and account executives. Out to lunch with the advertising man goes a fat satchel full of raw data and book-length marketing plans; for his boss, a sleek attaché case containing summaries and recommendations. Illegitimately, anybody in a contact job or a sales job, or on a high enough executive level, may buy a lunch on the company for anyone he likes. Again, the brief case comes along, making it hard for an observer to find out whether the lunch is a link or a break in the chain of the day's work. Surprisingly often, though, the business lunch really is for business purposes, part of a selling venture which may seem more certain of success after it is washed a few times in alcohol.

3.

Advertising men, in fact, rarely get much time away from their jobs. They work in a windy atmosphere of shifting preferences, where crisis is a normal state of affairs and (as an advertising manager puts it) "somebody is always hitting the panic button." No job is ever really completed except when catastrophe sweeps all the work away, and each individual is under constant pressure to produce more ideas, new ideas, better ideas. Every night the brief cases and attaché cases go home stuffed with work, because the advertising man is paid for his production, not his time, and the industry expects every man to do his duty whether he is in the office or eating lunch, on the commuter train or in the bosom of his family.

This is where advertising in real life departs most radically from the public image of the trade: the best people in advertising work terribly hard. There is literally no limit to the amount of information—about markets and products, people and their habits, the past and the future —which ought to be in the advertising man's head, ready to be pulled out for examination when questions are asked. The learning process is continuous, and the material to be digested is often difficult; and, once the advertising man has learned all there is to learn, he cannot sit back and admire his accomplishment. He is supposed to *do* something which will somehow change the situation. He gets paid for doing, not for learning.

Many of the most important men in advertising work from their rising in the morning to their falling down at night. At the agencies, especially, the hours are long to the point of brutishness. Clock watching is a vice with its humorous side elsewhere in industry; at an advertising agency it is a cardinal sin, a violation of the standard sales brag that the agency's people work harder and longer than anybody in the client organization, to serve the client's interests. The Robert W. Orr agency, now defunct, once ran an advertisement for itself, much admired in the trade, showing all the lights on in its offices at two in the morning. (The head of one of the few agencies which tries to get its people out on time claims that "this was the worst ad I ever saw. If I were a client looking at this ad, I'd think, 'I may want to call these people up about something at nine-thirty. There won't be anybody in the place fit to do business, they'll all be so groggy.' ") Leo Burnett, whose agency multiplied its billing tenfold between 1946 and 1957, to become one of the ten largest in the business, is reported by former employees to work "twenty hours a day, seven days a week, 365 days a year. He takes Christmas morning off." A man who used to work for J. Sterling Getchell, the blazing meteor of the advertising business in the 1930's, recalls that "you didn't dare have a telephone at home. You'd get back from the office at one o'clock, and just as you were dropping into bed the phone would ring, it would be Getch, he wanted to check something with you."

The human costs of such flagellation are easy to predict. Getchell died at forty-one. *Advertising Age* carries an obituary notice for every-one of any prominence in advertising itself or in allied fields, and every year publishes a statistical compilation of the results; in 1956 the average age of death for important figures in the business was 57.9, ten years under the national average of adult deaths. The prevalence of ulcers in advertising is a cliché, and men who stay the course of a full career often pick up some gastrointestinal or cardiac ailment of nervous origin. Those who remain healthy and active, moreover, may find advertising an unsatisfying trade in their later years, when they can no longer work harder than their juniors. "I sold my interest in Benton & Bowles when I was thirty-five," says former Senator William Benton, "and I'd been taking three or four hundred thousand dollars a year out of it. Any business where a kid can make that kind of money is no business for old men."

4.

The road ahead in advertising lies on a ridge line, with precipices on both sides and nasty curves to be negotiated. There are a few men in big positions who have arrived on the magic carpets of pull or social connection, and everybody seems to know someone in another agency who owes his executive vice-presidency to an uncanny knack for supplying ambiguous answers to hard questions. (In advertising as elsewhere it is sometimes better to be reliable than to be brilliant.) But the vast majority of the important men in advertising have come up from employee status either through a natural gift for mass persuasion or through a remarkable ability to analyze and judge the meaning of personal experience.

Such people can come from anywhere at all, and out of any background. The larger advertising firms try to maintain a geographical balance in their personnel, because product advertising is supposed to appeal to consumers all over the country; the smaller firms have found, quite by accident, that the most likely applicants for jobs often come from 'way out of town. There are more ministers' sons in advertising than simple probabilities would predict ("because," says one of them, "there were always books around the house, there was always a wrestling with words, and there was never enough money"), but the fact is an oddity rather than a pattern. Yale is the mother of advertising executives as Virginia was the mother of Presidents, but Yale's percentage of the total is statistically insignificant; in fact, all the Ivy League colleges together account for less than one-quarter of the major executives of the thirty largest agencies. Many important advertising men never went to college at all: the new president of J. Walter Thompson, for example, passed directly from high school to a job in the space-selling department of a Seattle, Washington, newspaper. Though the great majority of the young men presently coming into the field are college graduates, a boy without a degree probably has a better chance of getting a decent job in advertising than he has in the business offices of an industrial corporation.

Good looks are no hindrance, and personal charm is always a great asset to a man who is selling for a living, but many successful advertising men are neither good-looking nor charming. Personal neatness, however, is virtually required: among businessmen, advertising has a reputation for sloppiness, and nothing that furthers this notion can be tolerated around the shop. The standard of dress is high, for both men and women, and many men do seek to make an effect with their clothes—an effect that might be described as colorful conservatism. (The women want to look efficiently pretty, and, if single, *potentially* sexy.) Gray flannel was never really popular on Madison Avenue, and has scarcely been worn since the publication of Sloan Wilson's novel about the man who wore it (and he was in public relations rather than advertising, anyway); Brooks Brothers is on Madison Avenue, but its pink shirts are more likely to be seen in law offices than in the advertising business. Certainly there is no uniform, and the advertising man's habitual avoidance of clothing that might seem flamboyant denies him the role of a leader of fashion.

Above the clerical and assistant levels, most advertising people live in the Westchester suburbs and have lived there for some time: they were among the leaders of the great middle-class migration out of New York City. A few have moved even farther, to what A. C. Spectorsky has called the exurbs of Connecticut, forty miles and more from the desk—but only a tiny fraction of advertising men are exurbanites, and most of these are top executives who can also afford a small apartment, a *pied-à-terre,* in New York. Almost nobody drives to work, because the highways are packed tight with crawling cars and because Grand Central Station is right around the corner from the office. Around Grand Central are scattered a number of men's bars which are clubs for the business, places where executives on their way home can seize ten minutes to relax from the office tension. Some advertising men regard the railroad terminal itself as a kind of private preserve: they have found the unmarked doors which lead from the side streets off Park Avenue down flights of stairs directly to the loading platforms of the trains, and at the end of the day they vanish through these secret portals, to go home uncontaminated by the herd in the station concourse.

5.

Advertising is a tripartite business, composed of clients (the companies which make the branded products and pay to advertise them), agencies (which prepare and place the ads), and media (the newspapers, magazines, broadcasting stations—each an individual *medium* for advertising—which carry the message to the public). In each of its parts and as a whole, advertising is a salesman's business: all advertising work is essentially selling work. Within the client corporations, the advertising manager's primary job is to sell a budget to the sales manager or to some personage even more august; the agency must sell the value of its services to advertisers; the media must sell to both agencies and advertisers their potency and efficiency as message carriers. And the industry in its entirety exists solely for the purposes of selling goods and services to the consuming public.

The men who man the posts in the three divisions of the business are, by and large, interchangeable. Many advertising managers and media salesmen have had some agency experience, and the agencies are constantly drawing new talent from the media and from clients (other agencies' clients, of course). All research departments raid the same universities, sucking personnel away from chairs of sociology and psychology. Job hierarchies in the three branches are not easily comparable, which makes it difficult to compare the salaries paid for similar work; generally speaking, however, it is true that agencies pay more than media, and media pay more than clients. Which is fair enough, since people have to work much harder at the agencies than anywhere else in the business. Most agency account executives, who are in constant touch with the client offices, regard the advertising manager's job as a dream of ease: "You go to visit one of these guys in his office," says the head of a medium-sized agency, "and he's so grateful to see you, it's like visiting a man in a hospital; he doesn't have anything else to *do*. When you leave, his face falls, he's so disappointed." Media salesmen are not particularly fond of agency people, either, because the agency controls the spending of the client's money, and can give it or deny it to the media with a word—and often without supplying the reason behind the word.

The nagging itch of status in the industry aggravates the natural antagonism of its three parts and forces a man who has worked in all three to adopt the attitudes of the one which now employs him. "I always go to ARF meetings," says an officer of a research company, referring to the Advertising Research Foundation, which brings together representatives of clients, agencies and media for the purpose of judging research procedures and evaluating research reports. "We're not allowed to be members, but we're allowed to attend, and it's wonderful to watch. The media people come first, usually about ten minutes early. Then about the time the meeting is supposed to start, the agency people show up and start kicking the media people around. The advertisers come about fifteen minutes late and for the rest of the meeting they kick the agency people around. Then everybody goes out for a drink." It is a microcosm of the advertising world, seen through a glass, darkly: the advertisers ordering, the agencies suggesting, the media requesting, and the researchers observing (and, of course, interpreting their observations for the lay audience).

Such relationships are fairly common in commercial life. Superficially, the functions and attitudes of company, advertising agency and media are similar to those of manufacturer, purchasing agent and supplier in the normal course of business. One factor, however, makes the climate in the advertising world different from that anywhere else: agencies, acting as purchasers, are paid not by their clients but by the media, the suppliers from whom they buy. This method of agency compensation is known as the commission system, and commissions are standardized at 15 per cent of the list price (or "card rate") charged by the media. As a way of paying agents, this system is peculiar to advertising, and there are many advertisers and media owners who regard it as very peculiar indeed.

The idea that the media rather than the advertiser client should pay for the agency's work grew out of the origins of the business. Local advertising by local entrepreneurs has a long history: signs which could be nothing but advertising have been dug out of the ruins of

Pompeii. The printing of handbills for neighborhood proprietors followed closely on Gutenberg's invention of movable type. But advertising by manufacturers to support sales by dealers had to wait on centralized industrial production, the adoption of brand names, and the development of product distribution over a wide geographical area. These conditions were not met until the nineteenth century was some decades gone.

When the manufacturers were ready, however, the owners of advertising media were not. The United States swarmed with newspapers, but nobody knew what their circulations were (the owners certainly weren't telling) and few of them had established fixed rates for their space. The job of getting together a large list of newspapers to carry an. advertisement was immensely time-consuming and often more expensive than the cost of the space itself. Into this breach, in 1841, stepped a Mr. Volney B. Palmer, who opened an agency in Philadelphia to represent newspapers wishing to sell space to out-of-town entrepreneurs. For his services, Palmer charged the newspapers twenty-five per cent of their space rate, plus costs of postage and stationery. By 1849 he had offices in New York, Philadelphia, Boston and Baltimore. He also had competition.

In the early years, an agent's opportunities for graft and sharp practice were literally unlimited. The newspaper rates were what the agent said they were, and the advertiser ordinarily had no way of learning how much of the money he paid actually found its way back to the publisher. Many agents acted as wholesalers of newspaper space, bargaining down the publishers and then selling to advertisers for whatever the market would bear. Others developed interesting sidelines in paper and printing material supplies, which they would swap against newspaper space, picking up two profits for the risk of one. Those agents who refused to stoop to such jiggery-pokery were able to exert considerable pressure on their newspaper clients, and at one time in the 1880's the standard commission for their services had risen to 40 per cent.

George P. Rowell, who was later to found *Printer's Ink*, stabilized the agency business in 1869 by publishing the first open, accurate list of the nation's newspapers (he found 5,411 of them). Meanwhile, other agencies—notably Carlton & Smith (founded in 1864) and N. W. Ayer & Son (founded in 1868 and currently billing more than $100 million a year)—had become representatives for religious weeklies and farm journals, expanding the business. In 1878 Commodore J. Walter Thompson took over Carlton & Smith and began proselytizing for and among general magazines. By the 1890's Thompson controlled advertising in what he called his List of Thirty publications, most of them directed at the feminine market.

Meanwhile, however, N. W. Ayer & Son had changed all the rules. In 1875 Ayer began to offer advertisers an "open contract," which would give them access to the true rates charged by the newspapers and religious journals. In dealing with publishers, Ayer was to act at all times as the *advertiser's* agent. During the same year that Ayer wrote his first open contracts, L. H. Crall came out of the Middle West to New York to act exclusively as a national representative for newspapers, working always for publishers, never as agent or adviser to advertisers. With this inevitable split in functions, the organization of national advertising in newspapers achieved maturity.

The old methods of compensation persisted, however. In 1893 the American Newspaper Publishers' Association formally resolved to pay a commission to recognized independent advertising agencies and not to allow any discount whatever to direct advertisers; it was understood that in return for their commission the agencies would never attempt to break down the rates on behalf of their clients. Eight years later, in 1901, a letter from the Curtis Publishing Company to J. Walter Thompson established the same rules of order for magazine advertising. The numbers have changed since (Thompson was allowed only 10 per cent by Curtis), but the principles are still the same.

Once the lists of publications and their rates were public knowledge, the advertising agent could no longer justify a substantial commission simply on the basis of his purchasing skills and inside information. To hold his franchise he had to become an expert in advertising. From the beginning, agents had been willing to help an advertiser prepare his ads, but they had regarded such work as an unavoidable nuisance to be done only on urgent request. It was during the 1880's that agents first began using their knowledge of *how* to advertise as a business-producing argument, and in 1891 George Batten (whose name survives in Batten, Barton, Durstine & Osborn) established an agency to handle what he described as "service contracts." Under these contracts, in theory, it would no longer be necessary for companies to maintain their own advertising departments: Batten's people would do all the work, with no charge except the standard commission.

The service idea spread slowly. When Albert Lasker went to work for Lord & Thomas in 1898, at the age of eighteen, he found the agency staffed with one copywriter and one artist (they were paid $40 and $35 a week, respectively). Those advertisers who lived by the response to their ads, usually patent medicine men, hired their own advertising copywriters, and paid them a great deal more than the agencies did. Lasker saw immediately that the advertising agent could establish himself solidly with a client only by offering a high quality of creative service, and he used his contacts with newspapermen and other writers as the basis of his solicitations for new business. Lasker's success with this approach can be measured by the fact that in 1904, at the age of twenty-four, he was taking $52,000 a year out of Lord & Thomas, and he was made a partner in the firm. (He became sole owner eight years later, and retired in 1942, taking the agency name into retirement with him; the agency is now called Foote, Cone & Belding.) He had been a partner only a few months when he made the decision which he later described as the foundation of the modern agency business: he hired copywriter John E. Kennedy away from Dr. Shoop's Restorative at a salary of $16,000 a year, plus expenses. In 1907 Kennedy left, and Lasker replaced him with Claude Hopkins, whose genius for writing copy that sold goods made him the dominant figure on the advertising scene until he left Lord & Thomas, and the agency business, seventeen years later.

By then the work that agencies did for advertisers had well begun its expansion toward its present limits. The perfection of halftone engraving and the introduction of four-color printing made the artwork in advertising infinitely more expensive and put agencies in the business of supervising printing and production. The need to locate the prospective purchasers at whom advertising must be aimed made the agencies expert at market research. The growth of newspapers and magazines and the birth of new media, ranging from the immensities of network broadcasting to the minutiae of match covers for cigarette smokers, forced the agencies to begin the careful analysis of the different audiences that could be reached by different placement of the advertisements.

Each of these developments added to the cost of advertising as well as to its complexity, and the agencies obviously could not pick up the bills for such work out of the income received through media commissions. On most accounts, in fact, the agencies could not even afford to supervise the new work without some additional charge. For some of the jobs they supervise—photography, the preparation of printing plates, the production of programs for broadcast—the agencies usually add a commission (most often the same 15 per cent) onto the bill from the photographer, the printer or the program packager. On certain other work—the preparation of finished art for the engraver, the supervision of outside research jobs, the design of placards or displays for use in stores—the agencies tend to charge a flat fee, subject to negotiation.

Negotiated fees—and negotiated "commissions" on expenditures other than straight space or time—are far more common than the advertising business likes to admit they are. The argument about the commission system is a very old one; the Association of National Advertisers, which is spearheading the current, noisy drive to change compensation practices in advertising, was founded in 1912 primarily as a trade union with the avowed purpose of breaking agency commission rates; and it has returned to the attack every ten or fifteen years ever since. What has kept the ANA from success in its efforts is the fact that advertisers who feel strongly about these matters (only a few of them do) have always been able to start their own "house" agencies or to find agencies willing enough to cut their commissions or to do extra work without extra charge. Where commissions are in fact out of line with the quantity of work performed (as they may be, for example, when an agency charges 15 per cent of the $1,500,000 talent cost of a weekly half-hour network television show), few agencies will stand up for the letter of their rights. In 1957 the ANA released the results of a poll among members sponsoring television shows, indicating that about one-sixth of the advertisers paid no commissions on program costs; *Advertising Age* described the results as "startling." But James Webb Young, in 1932, had polled ninety-four advertisers sponsoring radio shows, and had found that one-third of them paid no commissions on programs. Nor is this rate cutting always confined to smaller, struggling agencies: of the sixteen agencies which reported "billings" of $40 million or more in the 1955 confidential survey of agency finances by the 4A's (the American Association of Advertising Agencies), two showed a high percentage of their income in commissions on broadcast space and time, and not a penny of income from commissions on broadcast production. (This blank statistic probably reflects accounting procedure rather than policy, but non-standard accounting procedures are always grounds for suspicion.) Most advertisers and agencies, however, feel that the compensation structure must be judged by total income and total work, rather than in bits and pieces. The question is whether the whole laborer is worthy of the whole hire, not how much work he did this morning.

Because of this complicated cross-structure of full commissions, split commissions and negotiated fees, the statisticians who measure the relative size of the different agencies always speak in terms of "billings"—that is, the total amount of its clients' money which the agency spends. Where fees are paid for professional consultation, rather than for work which is actually bought by the agency for the client, the statisticians will treat the fees as a 15 per cent commission on billing, and add to the agency's billings figure the amount that would be necessary to produce as much commission as the agency has received in fees. (Thus, a $15,000 fee for setting up a test market experiment gives the agency an additional $100,000 of "billings" in the statistical compilations.) On these terms, there are four agencies which show a billings figure of more than $200 million a year—J. Walter Thompson, McCann-Erickson, Young & Rubicam, and Batten, Barton, Durstine & Osborn (always BBDO; the customary & is a solecism). Another seven—Ayer; Benton & Bowles; Bates; Foote, Cone & Belding; Kenyon & Eckhardt; Grant Advertising; Leo Burnett—bill slightly more or slightly less than $100 million. The postwar growth of the business is indicated by the fact that it was not until 1947 that any agency billed as much as $100 million; as late as 1945 there were only two agencies—Thompson and Y & R—which billed as much as $50 million.

But the business has grown within its established frame. Albert Lasker's six-hour speech to his associates at Lord & Thomas in 1925 (printed in 1952-1953 by *Advertising Age* under the title *The Lasker Story*) covers most of the problems and arguments in the advertising business today. James Webb Young's book *Advertising Agency Compensation* (published by the University of Chicago Press in 1933) covers virtually all of them. Early in 1956, *Fortune* magazine sent a girl researcher up to see Jim Young at the Thompson company, where he works about twelve weeks a year as senior consultant and general supervisor of the agency's creative output. "She wanted to know about all the changes in the advertising business in the last twenty-five years," Young says. "When I told her there hadn't been any, she nearly fell off her chair. But it's true."

6.

Except that the importance of the business on the national scene, and the tensions within it, have grown enormously. It is possible but not very intelligent to dogmatize on the role of advertising in the American economy. Actually, nobody knows exactly how the production of farms and factories gets sold to the public for ultimate consumption; half a dozen of the nation's most able economists are still wrestling with the elementary mechanics of the problem. But there is no question about the trend: American business is rapidly eliminating the personal salesman at every stage of distribution, and advertising is rapidly becoming the primary tool in selling the output of our industrial machine.

Advertising today operates throughout the distributive system, stimulating wholesalers, loading dealers' shelves and showrooms, driving the obscure social processes that create product acceptance and product wants within the community, even extracting the requisite cash from consumer pockets. More than half the nation's grocery business and a quarter of the nation's purchases in drugs and toiletries are done in supermarkets, where the staff collects the money and looks out for thievery but never sells anybody anything. A growing percentage of the nation's output of electrical appliances is sold in discount houses, which cater exclusively to people who come into the store knowing what—usually exactly what—they want to buy. Even the automobile dealer today is pampered by advertising: the salesman who used to scour the neighborhoods for car prospects now sits in the showroom and waits for them to appear.

Only the very brave or the very ignorant (preferably both) can say exactly what it is that advertising does in the market place. The relative efficiency of advertising as a selling tool is arguable on the national scene and within specific industries. But advertising to the millions is unquestionably more efficient—less expensive per dollar of sales produced—than the old methods which saw individual salesmen working over individual customers. There can be no return to personal selling; capitalism is finally committed to the intensive use of advertising.

This commitment, however, has carried with it a certain amount of embarrassment for everyone concerned. Selling by means of a personal sales force is visibly profitable or unprofitable: each salesman sells so many units, and the profit on those units either does or does not cover the salesman's salary, commissions and expenses. In the usual course of events, however, it is impossible to discover how many sales have been made by advertising, or whether more or less profit would have come onto the books if the advertising budget had been greater or smaller. Most advertisers probably *do* make money by their advertising, but the standard business-school thesis that companies advertise to increase their profits represents the *excuse* at least as often as it represents the *reason* for advertising.

A quick glance at the community of advertisers will show the diversity of proximate causes for advertising:

Here is a man with a patent mousetrap, who is selling it by mail order: he advertises today to make cash next Thursday, and counts his coupon returns. (The Literary Guild's profits on new one-year memberships exceed its advertising costs.)

There is a man with a painkiller which will relieve pain more quickly in people susceptible to suggestion: he advertises to help his product work on its consumers. (Miles Laboratories spent some $9 million to advertise Alka-Seltzer in 1956.)

Over in the corner, reading the Federal Reserve Bulletin, is a man who makes children's clothing: he advertises so that his salesmen will have tearsheets to carry around in their portfolios, convincing themselves and their customers that these items are being presold to the public. ("All I want is the proofs," said a manufacturer in this line, referring to his $60,000 campaign in *Good Housekeeping*. "I don't care if the ads *never* get published.")

Downstairs talking with the bartender is a man who has invented an alcoholic beverage with an entirely different, tart taste: he advertises to tell people about it. (The Puerto Rican government puts $1 million a year into propagandizing Puerto Rican rums.)

In the temporary office upstairs is a member of the executive committee of a billion-dollar corporation which sells only to other manufacturers, never to the public: he advertises to make points before Congressional committees and the antitrust division, sometimes to convince the public that his organization is not a mere commercial enterprise but a beneficent institution. (Du Pont, by advertising, has changed itself from "Merchants of Death" to "Better Things for Better Living, Through Chemistry.")

Scattered around all the rooms, in various postures, are men who hope to make a decent living maufacturing and selling various goods and services: they advertise because the other companies in their business advertise. ("They don't really know about us," says an account executive wryly, "but they're damned sure their competitors are pretty smart fellows.")

Over in the game room one of the last great private entrepreneurs is watching his company's television program: he advertises because his wife has said to him that a man in his position ought to sponsor one of the big TV shows. ("I have this account," says a *Time* magazine salesman, "the guy buys twelve pages a year, he could get the thirteenth at half price, but he won't advertise in January; he says, 'I'm in Florida in January, playing polo. *Everybody's* in Florida, playing polo, in January.' ")

Most of all, however, companies advertise because advertising satisfies that overwhelming need for security which afflicts business *organizations* in a highly developed capitalist economy. Brand names have a social value, because they assert the manufacturer's responsibility for the goods he sells, but there is no business need for them. Many manufacturers do splendidly, selling unbranded products to food and variety chains, department stores, and even local liquor stores for these retailers to market under their own labels.

The major reason why many companies brand their products is the desire to free themselves from dependence on their jobbers and retail dealers, to build a "franchise" with the public at large. While no manufacturer ever escapes entirely from the personal element—even those who do no more than write letters to their dealers gain or lose sales by their phrasing of the letters—a business built around a brand name does not have to worry about its future when the popular sales manager, or the president with a genius for distribution, passes on to his final reward. Organizations, like individuals, have an instinct for self-preservation, though the instinct has developed in different degrees in different companies. The drive toward "committee management," toward the development of what William H. Whyte has called "the organization man," stems from this need for assurance that the business will survive the death or retirement of the men who have been running it. And the insistence on ever-larger advertising budgets grows at least in part from this irrational need rather than from a reasoned appreciation of the profits to be made by advertising.

Though the motives for advertising are often irrational, and advertising appropriations may be determined mostly by guess and by habit, the limits of an advertiser's expenditures are set by real economic factors, which determine profit *possibilities*. Heavy advertising can be profitable to a manufacturer only if one of three conditions is met:

1. The profit margin per unit of his product is very high, so that a high proportion of sales income can be put into advertising.

2. The number of units consumed by each customer is very large, so that each recipient of advertising who is persuaded to try the product may buy cases of the stuff in a reasonably short period of time.

3. Fixed, overhead costs of production are very high compared with the variable, operating cost incurred by making additional units, so that each added sale, once the break-even point has been passed, produces a higher and higher unit profit. The classic example is rail and air transportation: the railroad or airline must run its trips on a schedule and operate its equipment whether the seats are occupied or empty, so that each added ticket sale adds virtually nothing to costs. This requirement is equally fulfilled whenever retooling is a major expense item— as it certainly is with automobiles.

Virtually all the products advertised extensively on a national basis meet one or another of these conditions. The very largest advertisers, in fact, can be slotted into a handful of product groups. A statistical study of expenses by the nation's hundred largest national advertisers, performed for and copyrighted by *Advertising Age*, shows 73 companies which spent $10 million or more for advertising in calendar 1956. Of the 73, all but nine fit into one of six product categories— food and soft drink (17), automotive (15), soaps, drugs and toiletries

(14), beer and liquor (7), tobacco (6) and electrical appliances (5). The other nine are mostly companies (Du Pont, A T & T, Union Carbide, Sperry Rand) so big that they shake the floor of any house they enter.

According to the *Advertising Age* figures, the following companies (given with their many and often remarkable brand names) were the dozen largest advertisers in 1956:

1. General Motors (Chevrolet, Pontiac, Oldsmobile, Buick, Cadillac, Frigidaire, Delco, etc.): $162,499,248.

2. Procter & Gamble (Ivory, Tide, Cheer, Duz, Camay, Dash, Oxydol, Biz, Dreft, Cascade, Zest, Jip, Comet, Joy, Lava, Spic & Span soaps, detergents and cleansers; Lilt, Party Curl, Shasta, Velvet Blend, Prell and Drene shampoos; Crest and Gleem toothpastes; Crisco, Fluffo and Whirl shortening; Big Top peanut butter; Duncan Hines foods): $93,000,000.

3. Ford Motor Company (Ford, Mercury, Edsel, Lincoln): $88,650,-000.

4. General Foods (Jello; Post cereals; Maxwell House coffee; Sanka, Postum, Kool-Aid and Birely beverages; Good Seasons dressing; Log Cabin syrup; Baker cocoa and chocolate; Minute Tapioca; Birdseye frozen foods; Swans Down flour and mix; Gourmet Foods; La France, Satina and Go soap products): $77,000,000.

5. General Electric (GE and Hotpoint): $74,096,940.

6. Colgate-Palmolive (all Colgate and Palmolive brands; Ajax, Cashmere Bouquet, Fab, Octagon, AD, Vel, Super Suds, Kirkman soaps, detergents and cleansers; Brisk toothpaste; Lustre-Creme and Halo shampoos; Lustre-Net hair spray; Florient room deodorant; Veto people deodorant): $67,000,000.

7. Lever Brothers (Rinso, Lux, Surf, Breeze, Lifebuoy, Swan, Wisk, Hum, All, Silver Dust, Praise, Dove soaps, detergents and cleansers; Pepsodent, Chlorodent and Stripe toothpastes; Good Luck and Imperial margarine; Lucky Whip dessert; Spreez spread; Spry shortening): $60,100,000.

8. Chrysler Corporation (Plymouth, Dodge, DeSoto, Chrysler, Imperial, Airtemp): $60,093,000.

9. National Dairy Products (Kraft, Parkay, Miracle Whip, Sealtest, Sheffield, Breyer's, Hydrox, Breakstone, etc.): $37,470,000.

10. RCA (RCA, Victor, Victrola, NBC): $35,173,000.

11. Westinghouse: $32,000,000.

12. Distillers Corp.-Seagram's (all Seagram's brands, all Calvert brands, all Four Roses brands, Carstairs, White Horse, Chivas Regal, Hunter, Wilson, Paul Jones, Kessler, Pedigree, Wolfschmidt, Myers's Jamaica): $31,547,043.

Among them, these twelve companies used the services of some sixty-odd advertising agencies, and spent more than 15 per cent of all the money American manufacturers devoted to advertising in 1956.

7.

Association with such major corporate enterprise bolsters the advertising man's belief that what he does is important, and that he is needed. He requires this reassurance fairly often, because his work subjects him every day to the worst kind of commercial, social and psychological insecurity.

Commercially, advertising is a business in which there are no fixed relationships. The ties between advertiser and agency are personal and often insecure (some agencies still do not have written contracts with their clients, and most of the others rely on a single page which describes merely the bare bones of the relationship). Within the advertiser corporation the advertising manager is almost never on a policy-making level, and he rarely stands on footing any more solid than the pleasure or sufferance of the boss or the executive committee. Advertising is usually placed in publications or on the air one piece at a time, and any schedule of pages or programs can be canceled practically at will (though the television networks are currently flexing their considerable muscles in a campaign to secure firm 52-week commitments from their customers).

The advertising man, wherever he works, is always spending somebody else's money, which means that somebody else can always tell him

what to do. In the words of Ted Bates, whose agency billed more than
$100 million in 1957, the advertising man "has a great deal of the
responsibility and almost none of the authority." Maintaining a corporation's confidence in the people who handle its advertising is as
difficult a job as the advertising itself, and a single mistake in either
task can undermine a relationship that has been built up painfully
through a hundred meetings. Some agencies are especially vulnerable,
because they have stressed over the years their function of giving an
advertiser "an outside view." Once an agency has held an acount for a
certain length of time, it is familiar with every part of the client's
operation, and management begins to suspect that the agency can no
longer deliver "an outside view."

Death or departure of key people, mistakes in advertisements or in
client contact, changes in client policy or simply this desire to find
"a fresh approach" cost most advertising agencies several important
accounts every year. The agencies then go out and hook accounts
from their competitors to fill the hole, playing the ancient game of
musical chairs. Fifty to ninety major advertising accounts switch agencies every year, and the average tenure of a large account at a large
agency is four or seven or ten years, depending on which of three studies
you believe. The insecurities are not so great as the cliché about musical
chairs would suggest; the point of the parlor game is that there are
fewer chairs for the contestants every time around, while the beauty
of the advertising business has been the steady increase in the number
of large accounts. But few agencies are free of such worries.

Social insecurity is equally unavoidable. Advertising occupies today
in the public mind the social position hurriedly abandoned by stock
brokerage in 1929: it is glamorous, financially rewarding, and somehow
not quite honest. In the works of minor novelists, the advertising man
is either a flighty fellow of superficial brilliance, cracking cynical jokes
about regular people, or a nice boy in a bad trade, who will triumph
in the end by leaving it. More serious are the complaints of social
critics, who like to blame the advertising industry for most of what
displeases them in contemporary American society, for conformity,

materialism or false religiosity, the search after security or the rise in consumer credit. This double-barreled assault has its roots in a wild overestimate of the industry's effective power (as distinguished from its transient influence), and there are reasons both financial and personal which lead the business to agree, in public, that it *is* monstrously powerful. Acceptance of this false premise forces the advertising industry to conduct its defense by constant, slightly paranoiac reiterations of the plaint that nobody appreciates "all the good we do," a statement which inevitably intensifies public suspicion.

A more profound psychological insecurity is caused by a contrast between the objectives and the techniques of the business. The purpose of advertising is to sell goods and services. Salesmanship as it has developed historically relies largely on the personal presence and force of the salesman confronting an individual customer. Advertising, operating through mass media to reach millions of customers, must rely on adaptations of traditional art forms to put its message across. Only rarely is the industry lucky enough to find an individual who combines a strong selling instinct with a high order of talent in the arts. And where the two gifts exist together they are often at war with each other.

"Selling," says Victor Ratner of Benton & Bowles, "is a word which has bad connotations. It goes all the way back to Aristotle, that Greek, who had to write a special book called Rhetoric, something to be separated from Logic and Ethics." Nothing in their daily experience so disgusts the business executives of advertising as the realization that some of the most valued members of their creative staff are out of sympathy with the purposes of the business, and regard the ad itself as more important than the success of the advertised product. On the other side, the writers and artists struggle against their distaste for the businessmen who can measure the values of art only in terms of dollars paid and dollars received. More articulate than the businessmen, apparently more altruistic in their attitudes, the creative staffs have persuaded the public to share their concern about the alleged crassness and unscrupulousness of the advertising industry. Frederic Wakeman wrote *The Hucksters* only after some years of servitude in the copy department at Foote, Cone & Belding. It is the disgruntled advertising copywriter rather than the malign intellectual critic who has given the industry the unfortunate part of its reputation.

8.

To most men in the business, however, the sum of advertising's pleasures far outweighs the problems of brutal hours, uncertain social position, commercial and psychological insecurity. Some of the pleasures stem from the glamour of the business and others are the tangible rewards of a high-salaried occupation. What makes the men in the business love their work and spend themselves too quickly at it, though, is neither the glamour nor the money. Instead, it is the great game of advertising, and the satisfaction of making a personal score in the game.

Most people who speak of advertising as a game think of the game as something simple, like spin-the-bottle; actually, the game of advertising is a classic game, as complicated as chess. What the advertising man loves in his work is the constant testing of his efforts, the mysteriously changing numbers that measure, or seem to measure, his success or failure. The client's marketing problem is developed and analyzed, the advertisements prepared and presented. A few weeks later the Starch figures come in, reporting how many people saw the ad and read it and noted the product it advertised, and how the ad stacked up in these respects against other advertisements for similar products. Later, a client emissary delivers the thick reports from Gallup & Robinson, verbatim transcripts of what people who noticed the ad or the commercial had to say about it, what they thought the sales arguments were, and how important and believable the arguments seemed to them. Then the advertising man examines the new Nielsen index for his product, and sees how sales figures moved while the ads were running, the degree to which the product he advertised increased its share of market or lost ground to its competitors. Finally, the value of the effort as a whole is measured by the client with the one simple number that emerges from all the complexities: the size of next year's advertising appropriation.

The advertising man in the typical case needs the challenge and the thrill of the numbers game as much as he needs his salary. Advertising is selling, and the great satisfaction of selling is closing the sale. The advertising man never can close a sale; in fact, he can never be certain that it was his effort which made the sale possible. Worst of all, he works in black anonymity. Everybody in America may know his ad, but not one citizen in a thousand will know so much as the name of the agency which prepared the ad, and within the agency only a handful of people will know that this individual advertising man had anything to do with the ad. He is a cog in a little wheel that runs by faith inside a big wheel that runs by the grace of God; he puts his shoulder to the job, and watches eagerly for measurements of how fast the wheels are spinning.

Part II | A D V E R T I S E M E N T S
A N D   A G E N C I E S

CHAPTER 2

AND THIS IS HOW WE KNOW WE'RE RIGHT:

The Proposition

"What's new in Colgate Dental Cream that's MISSING—MISSING—MISSING in every other leading toothpaste?"

Advertisement by Ted Bates & Company

"Around our shop we like to use parables, and Bill Kearns, our president, tells one about a farmer who all his life wanted to buy a superior mule. He saved his money, and paid two thousand dollars for a mule, they tell me that's a good price for a mule, but he got a stubborn one. When he got it into the barn it wouldn't move. So he chained it to the tractor and dragged it ten miles down the road to a mule trainer.

"The mule trainer said he would train the mule, and the farmer asked him how much. 'Five dollars,' said the mule trainer.

" 'That's a reasonable price,' said the farmer. 'Go ahead.'

"The mule trainer dragged the mule into his barn, picked up a forty-five-pound sledgehammer and hit the mule right between the eyes. The mule went *oof*, like this.

" 'For God's sake,' cried the farmer, 'I hired you to train him, not to kill him!'

" 'Sure, I'll train him. But first,' said the mule trainer, 'first I've got to get his attention.' "

Rosser Reeves, chairman of the board,
Ted Bates & Company

"The Man in the Hathaway Shirt"
Advertisement by Ogilvy, Benson & Mather

"Every advertisement must be considered as a contribution to the complex symbol which is the brand image. . . . I am astonished to find how many manufacturers, even among the new generation, believe that women can be persuaded by *logic* and *argument* to buy one brand in preference to another—even when the two brands are technically identical. . . .

"The manufacturers who dedicate their advertising to building the most favorable image, the most sharply defined *personality* for their brands are the ones who will get the largest share of these markets at the highest profit—in the long run."

Speech by David Ogilvy

"I dreamed I was Cleopatra in my Maidenform Bra"
Advertisement by Norman, Craig & Kummel

"We call it empathy. The Halo ad is a great empathy ad, and we didn't write it—one of the greatest, most fantastic successes of all time. Listerine and halitosis. This is where empathy advertising started. We saw these ads and wondered what they had in common. Then, in 1952, we formalized it.

"A lot depends on the copywriter's intuition. Self-analysis. Ernest Jones says somewhere that Freud had this enormous ability to generalize from the particular. That's what we want in copywriters. Everybody dreams, many people dream of running around naked; but they can't talk about it. We *make* our copywriters talk about it. They've got to be bright.

"The theory of it is, the manufacturer is saying to the customer, 'I know all about you.' And the customer thinks, subconsciously, 'What a nice guy, he understands me; what a nice product. . . .' "

Norman B. Norman

1.

In 1923, when Claude Hopkins was president of Lord & Thomas, he wrote a remarkable piece of promotional literature for his agency—a 20,000-word book, published under the title *Scientific Advertising*. The book began with the words, "The time has come when advertising in some hands has reached the status of a science." In 1952, Hopkins' book was republished under the auspices of market researcher Alfred Politz, who was a physicist before he was a salesman and does not loosely throw around the word "scientific." Discussing Hopkins' contribution in a commentary which concludes the new edition, Politz wrote that "within the area he covered, his measurements were absolutely valid. To determine the value of advertising, he took as his standard of measurement, *sales*—the only accurate measuring rod."

The area Hopkins covered was mail-order advertising, the fundament on which the entire structure of the business had been raised. It was mail order which demonstrated to skeptical manufacturers that it really paid to advertise: you could see the results. You put your ad in the paper, telling people to clip the coupon and send it in with a dollar if they wanted the advertised product. Then you counted the arriving coupons and dollars, subtracted the costs of manufacturing, shipping and advertising, and banked your profit. Or put it into more advertising.

Mail order proved beyond any possibility of doubt the power of advertising as a selling force. Some of Hopkins' ads pulled returns totaling one-fifth the entire circulation of the magazine or newspaper in which the coupon appeared. In 1910 Hopkins put into the Sunday edition of every New York newspaper a one-page ad containing a coupon good for one ten-cent can of Van Camp's evaporated milk.

The ad ran exactly once in the one city; the coupon return was approximately 1,460,000.

Returns from mail-order ads could obviously be used to test the relative value of two different advertisements for the same product: if ad A drew 4,000 coupons and 4,000 dollars, while ad B drew 8,000 coupons and 8,000 dollars, then ad B was clearly the better selling message. Eventually this testing became refined to the point where only one element of the ad—the wording of the headline or the placement of the coupon or the size of the type—would be tested at a time. After all elements had been tested, a final advertisement would be prepared and run for as long as replies and dollars kept coming in. The advertisement "Wake Up Your Liver Bile!" was known as Old Number 9, because its headline was the ninth in a series tested for Carter's Little Liver Pills (the company now makes Miltown, too). The ad ran successfully for seventeen years.

Even further refinement was made possible by the development of the huge rotary presses which print newspapers and Sunday supplements (and certain magazines) two at a time, identical pages lying side by side on the wide sheets of paper. Except that the pages need not be exactly identical. Since two sets of plates are necessary to print the two sets of pages, an advertiser can place one version of an ad in one set, another version in the other. The cutting and folding machines at the end of the production process will deposit the two sets of papers in a single stack. Thus a newsdealer in the Bronx who orders a hundred copies of the Sunday *News* will receive fifty copies with ad A on page 17 and fifty copies with ad B on page 17 in the identical space. Among the few differences between the two ads will be a "key" letter or number on the coupon: one ad will call for a response to Dept. A and the other to Dept. B at the same address. At the end of this "split-run" test the advertiser simply counts the number of coupons and dollars arriving at the two departments, and he has an almost exact measure of the relative effectiveness of his two ads.

The use of "key" numbers, originally developed in the 1880's by Crall, Mack & McFadden, a firm of newspaper representatives, enables a mail-order advertiser to test his media as well as his ads, measuring the cost of space in each newspaper or magazine against actual returns. By placing different key numbers in different issues of the same magazine, he can also learn how rapidly he "uses up" the pulling power of this particular medium. A four-inch ad for a depilatory in a June issue of *Vogue* may pull 650 replies; in the July issue, 500; in the August issue, 400. By watching these figures slide, the advertiser can make a rational decision as to how frequently it will pay him to put this ad in *Vogue*. He can test color against black-and-white, large space against small space, capitals against upper-and-lower case type, photographs against illustrations. In every aspect of his advertising the mail-order man enjoys an efficient control of his expenditure and an observable relationship between advertising and sales. This control is what Claude Hopkins meant by Scientific Advertising, and practitioners in this limited area are still using Hopkins' measurements and arguments today.

For mail-order advertising is still very much with us—although, as Maxwell Sackheim says, "It has been killed, put to death, by many strong men. First it was the telephone: the farmer would be able to call the store, so he wouldn't send in coupons any more. Then it was the automobile and good roads: everybody could get to the store easily, so nobody would buy by mail. Well, the Sears Roebuck mail business is higher today than it ever was, though it isn't the same proportionately, they've opened all those stores. And the way the roads and the cities are crowded today, it's more convenient than ever to order by mail."

Sackheim, whose agency probably bills close to $10 million a year, all in mail order, has been writing mail-order ads since 1905. He is a short, round, lively man with a good tan and a remarkable quantity of brushed-down black hair, wearing a double-breasted suit. The author of what is considered the most successful mail-order ad ever written (Do You Make These Mistakes in English? which is still pulling students for the Sherwin Cody school after more than forty years), Sackheim has helped to launch such remarkable institutions as the Book-of-the-Month

Club, the Arthur Murray Dance Schools and, more recently, the Columbia Record Club.

"In the advertising business," Sackheim says, "you can't be an arbiter of what the public wants—you've got to test it. Arthur Murray came up from Aiken, South Carolina, came into the office, nobody paid any attention to him. He wanted to sell dancing lessons by mail. He came in to me, asked me if it could be done, I said, 'Why not?' It got to be a huge business.

"In 1919, Harry Scherman and I went out of Ruthrauff & Ryan, took some accounts—they gave them to us, we didn't take them—and set up as Sackheim & Scherman. We also had a book business, The Little Leather Library, copies of the classics in miniature size, bound in real leather, we were trying to sell them through stores at twenty-five cents each. It didn't work. So we cut the price to ten cents, bound the books in imitation leather, and began writing mail-order ads for them. We sold forty million little books by mail.

"Like a great many other mail-order businesses, the little books after a few years began to peter out, we tried to think of some other mail-order book business. In 1926, we started the Book-of-the-Month Club. I don't have anything to do with it any more, I sold out. Too soon."

From decades and decades of constant copy testing by coupon returns (because no ad is so good that you don't keep checking it against your new ideas), mail-order men have developed sets of rules and formulas to direct the writing of advertisements. John Caples' book *Tested Advertising Methods*, for example, lists "sixteen formulas for writing headlines"; the formulas include beginning the headline with the words "how to," "how," "new," "which," "at last," "this," "to" and "advice," talking about money, or using the words "free" or "amazing." Many of these rules have (obviously) been absorbed into the basic education of every advertising copywriter, but many of them are consciously violated every day by the authors of the broadcast commercials which fill the air and the "general" advertising which stuffs the magazines and newspapers. Whenever mail-order men see their most basic prescriptions ignored (for example, a failure to promise the reader some personal benefit from using the product) they cry out in horror at the waste of money. This attitude does not endear them as a group to other advertising men, who feel there is more to the business than coupon returns. But principles are principles.

"Now," says John Caples, "suppose I have to write an ad to sell a book by mail order. And then suppose I were writing an ad to get someone to go to Brentano's and buy the book. I'd use the same headline for both. With a few exceptions the same rules hold for both mail-order advertising and general advertising." Caples was only five years old in 1905, when Maxwell Sackheim began turning out mail-order copy, and he is a very different sort of person. An Annapolis graduate (Sackheim never went to college), Caples came out of the Bell System's engineering department in 1925 to write copy for Ruthrauff & Ryan; while he was still a raw cub he wrote the headline, "They Laughed When I Sat Down at the Piano but When I Started to Play . . . !" Since 1941, with four years off for renewed Navy service, he has been a vice-president of BBDO, an agency not notably oriented toward mail-order work. He is a slight, handsome, gray-haired man with a dry, modest manner, no nonsense about him at all, and he works in a small, square, plain room.

Aside from writing the *Wall Street Journal* ads (Men Who Get Ahead in Business Read . . .), Caples' main responsibility at BBDO is copy testing—or at least the testing of such copy as the powers in the upstairs print department wish to subject to his scrutiny. His main reliance is on split-runs in various newspapers, usually with the use of a "hidden offer." There is no coupon in either of the two tested ads; instead, the last paragraph offers a free or ten-cent sample of the product (or a free booklet about it) to anybody who will write in to Dept. Such-and-such. These ads are usually designed to test selling approach, headline or body copy, one at a time, rather than a finished advertising campaign. The sales pitch, headline and copy that come out highest in returns from a series of tests in four-inch space in newspapers will then be used as the foundation for full-page ads in *Life* and the *Saturday Evening Post* and *This Week* and *McCall's*, or in newspaper pages or even on radio and television. If an ad with a headline promising smooth skin draws more sample requests than an ad with a headline promising clear skin, the final display advertisement for the face cream will speak of smooth rather than clear skin. In this way, BBDO tried out dozens of approaches for a campaign to sell the Revised Standard Version of the Bible ("The Bible Jesus Would Have Loved," "How This Bible Can Bring You Closer to God," "A Bible for the Man Who Already Has a Bible"), and came out—as the copywriters had always suspected they would—with "Biggest Bible News in 346 Years."

Caples believes firmly in the values of split-run testing and feels that the technique is "very widely applicable. Since not everybody uses it, I can't say everybody agrees with me. You see, there's an increased demand for measures of the effectiveness of an ad. Advertisers have a lot of money. So some psychologists figure, if they can find a method, they can make a lot of money. The result is that there are a lot of methods, a lot of psychologists, and they don't all come up with the same answers."

2.

Mail-order advertising as Sackheim practices it is unswervingly "scientific"; it sells goods by mail, with measurable efficiency. The technique is relatively simple (though by no means easy to master): the headline singles out those readers of the publication who will be interested in the product; the copy, invariably long, tells them the complete selling story; and the coupon makes an immediate sale. No philosophy of advertising is necessary—in fact, strongly held opinions about the right selling argument are often a hindrance. "You can't be an arbiter of what the public wants," Sackheim says. "You've got to test it." So the mail-order man, using his proved technique, tries out all sorts of advertising appeals for his product, without prejudging any reasonable notion. Every time he tests he gets an absolute and unquestionably accurate answer in terms of coupons and dollars.

But only a small range of products can be efficiently sold via mail order. Large, bulky items like refrigerators are barred by the mails, while small, inexpensive items like toothpastes are barred by the costs of doing a mail-order business. Customarily, each mail-order advertisement should pay for itself in *one-time sales* to readers. A full-page ad in the *New York Times Magazine* will cost $3,000, and five thousand returns from it—at a cost of 60 cents per return—would be an extraordinary showing. Even when the postage rate is low and packing expense minimal, the costs of handling and mailing will run some 15 cents on each sale. So the profit margin on the product must be at least 75 cents per unit simply to bring the manufacturer to the break-even point. Finally, mail order simply cannot generate enough buying power to keep a business going when factories must be built and high output achieved to meet overhead expenses. In the end, the list of mail-order possibilities reduces down to the products which are today advertised by these methods: books and records, drugs, cosmetics, hobbies, household or garden gadgets, and exotic gifts. Even in these areas dealer distribution is often more profitable than mail-order selling.

Copy testing by mail-order ads, as performed by Caples (and others, including Ed Robinson, head of the largest creative group at J. Walter Thompson), is far less scientific. Mail-order advertising counts actual sales; mail-order testing merely counts the number of people who are sufficiently attracted by the ad to write in for a free sample or a piece of descriptive literature. It can reasonably be assumed that the ad which pulls more requests for samples is the better of two tested ads— reasonably, but not scientifically. As Caples himself points out, not everybody agrees with the assumption.

The reasons for disagreement are various and strongly expressed. To begin with, the two ads together in a typical Caples test will sometimes pull less than three hundred replies, which is not regarded as sufficient response to "prove" an argument on which $3 million may be spent. Then, mail-order returns come by definition only from those who clip coupons and mail them in. "My wife," says Richard Lessler of the Grey agency, "is immensely responsive to advertising, but she'd no more clip a coupon . . ." The general advertisement which will be produced

as the result of Caples' mail-order testing is supposed to influence the
entire community, not just the coupon mailers; and there is nothing
more than a strong guess behind the assumption that people who don't
write in for samples have the same reactions to advertising messages as
the people who do.

Even if mail-order copy testing could guarantee ads with immediate
sales results in the stores, there would still be a sizable school of thought
which would disdain it. Mail-order advertising in the typical case tries
to sell a product which is unique, nothing else like it, and which is
available—at this moment, at this price—only via the coupon on the ad.
General advertising tries to sell a branded product which is not in any
sense unique—in fact, it is usually indistinguishable from similar products carrying different brand names. Typically, again, mail-order ads are
supposed to pay out in one-time sales, delivering a profit on each advertisement. (Not always; the list of customer names may produce additional
profits later.) General advertising, except in the case of very high-ticket
items such as organs and automobiles, never pays out in one-time sales.
The back cover of *Life* costs anybody who can buy it about $45,000,
and the manufacturer's profit on cigarettes is something less than 2
cents a pack, so the ad can pay out only if it sells two million packs
of cigarettes. Obviously, no cigarette ad is going to make two million
readers of *Life* go out and buy your brand—but the ad might be the
final push that convinced four thousand people (less than $\frac{1}{15}$ of 1
per cent of the *Life* circulation) that your brand is worth trying. If these
four thousand people buy a carton a week, and remain on your side
for a year, they will buy two million packs of your product.

People buy mail-order items because the advertising sells them;
they buy branded products because they find the product itself satis-
factory. The purpose of general advertising is to make non-users try a
new brand, and to convince current users that Tide, say, is still the best
on the market. In the cliché of the business, mail-order advertising seeks
sales; general advertising seeks *customers*. As Sackheim himself points
out, most mail-order items begin to "peter out" after the first few years;
but brand names are built at vast expense to last a thousand years.

And it can be argued that what makes mail-order items "peter out" is the advertising which sells them so well. David Ogilvy has stated the case: "Mail-order advertising," he told a luncheon in Chicago in 1955, "is hit and run. In and out. Caveat emptor, and devil-take-the-hindmost. The less personality the more coupon returns. The smaller the illustration the more coupon returns. The fewer idiosyncrasies in the presentation the more coupon returns. The more buckeyed and boiler-plate the more coupon returns. . . . With what results? Well, in some cases perhaps, a temporary increase in sales. But in almost all cases this kind of sleazy advertising has given an incurable black eye to the brands which have used it over any period of time."

Though Ogilvy's position is extreme and his language strong (one must imagine it, of course, in an Oxford accent), his attitude is shared by the great majority of advertising agencies. The long texts, narrow margins and tiny illustrations of mail-order advertising have been judged inadequate if not positively dangerous as a way to sell branded mer-chandise via stores, dealers and supermarkets. But with the disappear-ance of the mail-order coupon and its accompanying dollar, the advertising agent has lost the definite proofs of his own worth. Once the coupon returns are gone, nobody can *prove* a direct casual relation between advertising and sales. Too many independent factors come between.

"You can run a bad advertising campaign," says Rosser Reeves, "and sales go up. You can run a brilliant campaign, and sales go down. Why?

"A) your product may not be right.

"B) your price may not be right.

"C) your distribution may not be right.

"D) your sales force may be bad.

"E) your competitor may be outspending you five to one.

"F) your competitor may be dealing you to death with one-cent sales and premiums and contests and special discounts to retailers."

"I once made a list," says Garrit Lydecker of the Thompson company, "of all the factors that can influence sales. I had forty-five of them written down before I got bored with it, I'm sure there are more. Ad-vertising was one of the factors."

A mail-order agency can literally demonstrate the value of its services.

Selling itself to prospective clients, it need speak only of techniques and its mastery of them. The general agency cannot prove anything, if a client wishes to apply rigorous standards of proof; the best it can hope to do is present a convincing argument. Out of the hole left by the disappearance of "scientific advertising" there grew a large crop of advertising philosophies, premises for convincing arguments.

CHAPTER 3

AND THIS IS HOW WE KNOW WE'RE RIGHT:

The Proposition (Continued)

1.

"What this agency has done which is different from any other agency," says Rosser Reeves, chairman of the board of Ted Bates & Company, "is to apply reason to advertising. We've grown from $2,900,000 in billings in 1940 to about $100,000,000 in 1957. Nearly $60,000,000 of what we do today comes from increases in client appropriations since they came to us—and in seventeen years we've never lost an account. [Bates has, however, lost individual *brands* from the accounts of large companies which make many branded products.] We're specialists—we handle products which are eaten or rubbed on or smoked. All our clients are package goods advertisers, sophisticated advertisers, they live by advertising. BBDO does advertising for U.S. Steel, that's fine, we call it 'Board of Directors' advertising. If U.S. Steel stopped advertising for a year they wouldn't sell one ton less steel. If Viceroy stopped advertising for a year you'd feel pain all over your body."

Reeves was all of thirty years old in 1940 when he followed Ted Bates out of Benton & Bowles to be a senior member of the small group that was starting a new agency; he had already been copy chief at Blackett, Sample & Hummert (now Dancer-Fitzgerald-Sample) and a copywriter at three other agencies. The son of a Virginia minister and a graduate of the University of Virginia, he was from the beginning (to quote a former employer) "a wild one," an experimenter in the arcane reaches of client contact, a brilliant creator of sales arguments and a theoretician of the business. Among the more personal and unpopular of his theories was one proclaiming that the sensible man worked at advertising not because of any deep dedication to the art but because of a desire to make money, which could then be spent at leisure. Aside from the usual woodworking and gardening (a generic term which can be extended to include the possession of whole herds of Aberdeen Angus cattle), the avocations of most advertising men are closely related to their work. Reeves, however, races a yacht in the International class, travels vastly and plays a serious game of chess (he was the captain of the American chess team that went to Moscow in 1955). In 1952 he dipped into politics (a subject that does not fascinate him as an ordinary matter) and organized and wrote the Eisenhower television spots.

Still youthful, Reeves has a serious, rather square face and wears a serious look from behind horn-rimmed glasses; but beneath the sobriety and the soft Southern speech is the wit of a top banana and a superb instinct for how well an oft-repeated story or sales pitch is going over. The calm manner also conceals a susceptibility to overwhelming enthusiasm which is at the heart of his great abilities as a salesman (and which is occasionally embarrassing to his more restrained associates at Bates). He has unlimited admiration for technical authority—the doctor who helps Bates develop sales arguments for drugs is "the man we believe to be the world's greatest pharmacologist"; the doctor who helped with a soap campaign is "conceded to be one of the three leading experts in the United States on dermatology"; the psychologists who tested the validity of motivational research on a special Bates grant were "three of the greatest academic psychologists, there are no better psychologists in the world." Like most enthusiasts, Reeves is also susceptible to hero-worship, especially of Ted Bates, a thin, quiet down-Easter who came to New York from Maine via Yale and who would far rather write copy than manage client relations or make speeches. Reeves says that Bates has "the most *unconfused* mind" (a more restrained admirer speaks of Bates's "great gift for simplification"), and he is particularly proud of the accounts—notably Wonder Bread—that have stayed under Bates's tutelage since he was a cub copywriter at BBDO some thirty years ago. "Any man who's ever dealt with Ted," Reeves says, "can't get rid of him—can't afford it." But it was Reeves himself who supplied and elaborated the Bates philosophy and boiled it down to the three initials by which it is known: USP.

"We can't sell a product," Reeves says, "unless it's a good product, and even then we can't sell it unless we can find the Unique Selling Proposition. There are three rules for a USP. First, you need a definite proposition: buy this product and you get this specific benefit. Pick up any textbook on advertising and that's on page one—but everybody ignores it. Then, second, it must be a unique proposition, one which the opposition *cannot* or *does not* offer. Third, the proposition must sell. Colgate was advertising 'ribbon dental cream—it comes out like a ribbon and lies flat on your brush.' Well, that was a proposition and it was unique, but it didn't sell. Bates gave them 'cleans your breath while it cleans your teeth.' Now, every dentifrice cleans your breath while it cleans your teeth—*but nobody had ever put a breath claim on a toothpaste before.* That USP is eighteen years old now. Using it, Colgate has had as much as fifty per cent of the whole toothpaste market; even today, against the toughest kind of competition, Colgate still has the largest share-of-market in the toothpaste business. And every time anybody else advertises that *his* toothpaste cleans your breath, he's really advertising Colgate even though he doesn't know it."

USP's grow out of analysis of the product and what it can perform for its users; the result of the analysis is a single specific claim which will be repeated over and over again—20,000 filters for Viceroy, better skin for Palmolive, deodorized laundry for Fab, more usable carbohydrates for Cream of Rice, high mineral content for Wonder Bread.

Ninety per cent of Bates's work is in food and drug products, so, Reeves says, "It all comes back to physiology. We have a staff of four doctors, headed by an M.D.-Ph.D., who act as liaison with consultants outside. Last time I counted, we were working with 198 independent specialists. We call them in, the copywriters and the doctors sit around in seminars and discuss the product. Out of the discussion grows an idea for a USP. Sometimes, if we don't know enough about the product to be sure that it will do what we want to say it will do, we'll recommend what we call 'open-end clinical research' to find out exactly what's in the product."

Bates's advertising, with its heavy emphasis on medical testimony, vastly irritates creative people at other agencies; the standard objection runs: "You can always tell a Bates ad by the white coat." And a high executive of one agency, showing deep distaste, described the Bates technique as "the philosophy of the uncheckable claim." Reeves does not deny the description. "Open your magazine," he says, "and you'll find ninety per cent of the food ads say, 'Ours tastes better.' Any housewife can verify a taste claim, and actually they all taste the same. We veer toward claims that are not self-demonstrable product puffery." When a specific benefit is to be asserted, however, Bates makes sure its claim can be checked—every USP must be, in Reeves's words, "FTC-able" (that is, it must be able to pass the scrutiny of the Federal Trade Commission, which is empowered to forbid fake advertising). Elaborate research projects, involving laboratory experiments and detailed clinical testing, lie behind many of Bates's most commonplace product claims. The doctors participate because the money is given to them on a hands-off basis, and the results of the work remain their own property. "The one thing we insist on," Reeves says, "is that the clinical work must be *duplicable*—no matter how much the government spends on research they'll come up with the same answer. When the scientists finish their tests they usually publish the results—and then comes the payoff."

Many of Bates's research projects have been designed to prove statements that everybody already knows—but that no advertiser had ever been able to use because the scientific proof was lacking. The

Federal Trade Commission will not allow *specific* claims unless the advertiser can demonstrate that people who use the product as directed will obtain the advertised benefits. To claim that Colgate's toothpaste would diminish the incidence of cavities if people brushed their teeth with it after every meal, Bates and Colgate spent some $300,000 through Northwestern University; to prove that washing the face thoroughly (for one full minute) with Palmolive soap would improve the skin, Bates's advisory staff set up an almost equally large clinical experiment. Once Bates's research had established the truth of such statements for Bates's brands, the manufacturers of and advertising agencies for other, similar brands were free to make the same claims— except that Bates's clients had already taken possession of the field and were driving the point home with their sledge hammer.

Sometimes these research projects can be set up only with great difficulty, because subjects for the experiment are as necessary as doctors to run it. Acting on a tip from a staff psychologist that virtually all constipation is psychosomatic (the result of bad toilet training in childhood or other, more profound emotional experiences), Bates once drew up an experimental design to prove that constipated people would flawlessly perform their natural functions if fed a course of Carter's Little Liver Pills. As a first step, Bates put an ad in the classified sections of the *Times* and *Herald Tribune,* asking for constipated people who wanted to be cured. "By some fantastic mistake," Reeves says, "I gave our office as the address. They descended on us like the Medes and the Persians. I came to work at nine o'clock and the halls were already full of them, we had every psychotic in New York. Some of them were carrying pigeons; one of them had a fried egg on his head. It cost a big piece of the research budget to sort them out." When the work had been done, however, Bates had proved that Carter's "Helps You Break the Laxative Habit." Incidentally, the study also verified a point which poets and philosophers had been making, unscientifically, for years: that the human animal does his intellectual tasks better (22 per cent better, according to Bates) when his bowels are in good order.

Once Bates has found a USP for a client, the agency will hang onto it like grim death until it is convinced that a better USP has been developed. "If an idea is a good one, and applies to the product," says Ted Bates himself, "it will be good for an indefinite length of time. You might quibble with this, but I'd say it *never* wears out; you might put a new dress on it, that's all." Bates is not alone in his belief in the value of repetition; one of the earliest slogans within the advertising business was N. W. Ayer's insistence that its clients "keep everlastingly at it," and few advertising men would argue with this principle, even today. The problem is that clients see and hear too much of their own ads—to them, the logotype of their brand name is by far the most important thing in a magazine, and a broadcast mention of their product seems a clarion call to the world.

The client has lived with the idea behind an ad for months before the public ever has the chance to meet it, and has seen the ad itself throughout its formative stages; so, very soon, he begins to feel that everybody knows all about his advertising campaign and is sick of it, and the time has come for a change. "I worked for a guy in Minneapolis," says Augy Becker, account supervisor on Pepsodent for Foote, Cone & Belding, "who had a trite little phrase—'When the client first begins to tire of an ad,' he'd say, 'you know it's beginning to catch on with the public.'" But agencies find it hard to hold off clients who want to change their campaigns. The client is always suspicious that the agency is making too much money on his account, and the sight of the same ad running over and over again—with 15 per cent commission to the agency for its every appearance—confirms him in his suspicions. When his agency fights to keep the old ad going, on the grounds that its effectiveness is actually increasing by repetition, he feels morally certain that he has wandered into a den of thieves. This is regarded as an unhealthy state of mind for a client to be in.

Nevertheless, over the years, Bates has had astonishing success in holding clients to their existing campaigns. (The agency has not been able to eliminate client supicions, of course. "I had a client down in the Caribbean with me on a boat," Reeves says, "and he said to me, more or less joking, you understand, 'You have seven hundred people in that office of yours, and you've been running the same ad for me for the last eleven years. What I want to know is, what are those seven hundred people supposed to be *doing?*' I told him, 'They're keeping your advertising department from changing your ad.'") One of the reasons for Bates's success is the nature of the clientele: Bates works mostly for very experienced advertisers, who have mastered the principles of the trade. Another is the fact that Bates is constantly at work to build new USP's, trying to improve on the existing campaign. But Reeves's salesmanship is probably the deciding factor: "Given identical products, identical budgets and identical sales forces," Reeves says in his sober way, "I will let you have a brilliant campaign every six months, provided you change it every six months—and I'll take a less-than-brilliant campaign and beat your tail off with it because I'll run it ten years." And what can the client say then?

This question of identical products lies at the heart of Bates's thinking about advertising. Reeves says, "Our problem is—a client comes into my office and throws two newly minted half-dollars onto my desk and says, 'Mine is the one on the left. You prove it's better.'"

Much of this, too, traces some years back, to Claude Hopkins. It was Hopkins who found that the executives of Van Camp's pork and beans couldn't tell their own product from its competitors, and promptly advertised the slogan "Try Our Rivals, Too." Hopkins, again, went for a tour of the Schlitz brewery, and nodded politely at the wonders of the malt and hops; and then came to life when he saw the steam bath that washed the bottles before they were filled with the beer. His hosts assured him that every brewery did the same, it was the standard procedure of the industry. Hopkins patiently explained to them that the vital fact was not what the industry *did* but what the individual brewers *advertised* they did, and the steam bath had never been advertised. He went back to his office and wrote an overpowering campaign around the slogan "Washed with Live Steam."

"That's right," said Reeves. "I'm a great admirer of Hopkins. What we want to do for our clients is to say that their bottles are washed in live steam."

2.

These arguments seem suicidally shortsighted to David Ogilvy, of Ogilvy, Benson & Mather, apostle of the "brand image," creator of "The Man in the Hathaway Shirt," popularizer of "The Man from Schweppes," poet of the charms of Puerto Rico. "I know all about such stuff," Ogilvy says in his pleasant British voice, "I was practicing it practically in my cradle. In selling Dove soap, I employ exactly the procedures Bates uses. But we've got some other clubs in our bag."

Few disagreements in any business have been so thoroughly thrashed out as the conflict in viewpoint between Ogilvy and Reeves. They have been brothers-in-law, and over the years have seen a good deal of each other socially. Each regards the other as a great personal salesman; each shakes his head over the way the other wastes his clients' money on bad advertising. When they talk about each other, however, it must be understood that they are playing a private game, the rules of which are known to them alone. Competitive with each other both personally and professionally, they conduct their competition within the framework of a mutual admiration society.

"Most brands that need help today," Ogilvy says, "were given sleazy, bargain-basement brand images in the thirties, when money was scarce and it was a great help to seem cheap. They've suffered from it. When I first came to this country Packard was one of the great quality cars. Then they began getting tough, going after the middle-priced market. What do you think they would give today to get back their old image?

"I don't think we advertisers should run campaigns that we'd rather not have our children see. People will say, 'That sort of thing is unmeasurable, it's all a lot of airy-fairy nonsense.' Well, is it? Look at the top firms in this country. They're not run by sleazy bums. Advertising is a place where the selfish interest of the manufacturer coincides with the interests of society."

Two years younger than Reeves, Ogilvy was an assistant chef in the Hotel Majestic in Paris, cooking dinner for the Président de la

République (he died the next week), when Reeves was a copy group head under Frank Hummert. A product of Edinburgh private schools and Oxford, Ogilvy had gone to Paris because jobs were unobtainable in depression-ridden Britain; and he made use of his hotel chef experience by selling stoves from door to door in Scotland when he returned to his native island. As the biggest stove seller in the company, he was brought to headquarters by top management to write a sales manual; and from there it was merely a short step to the advertising business. His first job was with Mather & Crowther, who thought so highly of him that when he decided to open up his own advertising shop in New York in 1948 they joined S. H. Benson, Ltd., in putting up the initial capital. (The two British agencies still own a considerable piece of the business, as the firm name indicates; Ogilvy has been slowly but steadily buying them out.) Ogilvy's first visit to the United States was in 1937, as a remittance man from Mather & Crowther; in 1939 he returned on his own and became the head of George Gallup's Audience Research Institute. He moved directly from Gallup's office to his own agency, stopping briefly along the way to try his hand at tobacco growing in Pennsylvania.

Ogilvy is still British enough to be slightly exotic on Madison Avenue, where his donnish appearance—middling height and weight, slightly stooped, dark blond hair and very pale skin, black-rimmed glasses—achieves that rarest and most valuable of personal impressions: youthful solidity. He is a charmer and a very appealing personality, one of the few men in advertising who has a good word to say for almost everybody else in the business (even Reeves: "He taught me more about advertising than anybody I've ever known; the pity of it is that I couldn't teach him anything." Scenting battle, Reeves replies, "If we ever get out of packaged goods and into luxury items, I'll be glad to go sit at David's feet and listen"). Having worked for a research organization which operates all over the field, he knows literally hundreds of major agency executives, with the result that he has literally hundreds of friends in advertising. He, too, is a close student of the business—"I've always been interested in it, I know more about it

than most people; the job I really want is to suceeed Neil Borden"
(as professor of advertising at the Harvard Business School). Unlike
most people anywhere, he talks openly, honestly and ruefully about
his own mistakes and the accounts his agency has lost. "The remarkable thing is," he says, "that in spite of all my mistakes and all our
misfortunes we are the biggest agency founded since 1948." (Not
quite: Ogilvy bills about $17 million a year, and Doyle Dane Bern-
bach, founded a year later, bills three or four million more. But
Bernbach and his associates started with a decent list of accounts
which they had brought with them from Grey Advertising, while
Ogilvy started from scratch, just himself and a secretary and no
business until the little Wedgwood account walked in the door.

Ogilvy's offices are dramatically modern, with heavy use of brilliant
upholstery colors, especially red, yellow and black. In the reception
room and in his own large office (which seems even larger because it
is so sparsely furnished, a couch beside the door and a desk before
the window, with a great expanse of carpet between; a door behind
the desk, almost always open, leads to a private terrace), the main
decorations are printers' proofs of the agency's advertisements set in
shadow boxes and treated as transparencies, a glow of light coming
through them from the rear. "We're not a very big agency really,"
Ogilvy says, prowling about his office, hopping up to sit on the desk
or a radiator cover, kicking his tweed-covered legs, "we're only the
fiftieth largest or something like that. But have you noticed that we're
the most talked-about agency in town?"

This conversational eminence results, of course, from the wonderful brand image, the air of intellectual luxe, Ogilvy has given his
agency. Brand images can be of all sorts: over the years, Young &
Rubicam has made Jello the happy family dessert, Thompson has given
Pond's cold cream a feeling of society elegance, MacManus, John &
Adams has made Cadillac the symbol of arrival in an income bracket.
Recently, Leo Burnett has made the possession of a pack of Marlboros
a mark of masculine confidence, and BBDO has built Betty Crocker
as the understanding friend of the lonely housewife. Ogilvy's most

successful work has come in the field of social acceptability: his ads give a brand prestige value. As he puts it in an indoctrination booklet he gives to new employees, "It pays to give your brand a *first-class ticket* through life. People don't like to be seen consuming products which their friends regard as third-class." This view of brand image provokes a certain amount of dissent. "Let's face it," says an admirer of Ogilvy's work (who happens, however, to run a rival agency), "David's a snob. He patronizes waiters. Everybody does best what he really believes in, so David gives his products snob appeal." Even if the stricture is valid, however, the Ogilvy approach is obviously a useful one, both for selling goods (the desire for social position is a very strong drive) and for selling the services of the agency (every advertiser wants prestige for himself and his company).

Occasionally Ogilvy has tried to improve a brand's social position by direct means—the World's *Three* Great Whiskies campaign for Calvert, the diplomat who sent his son to Groton on the money he saved by driving an Austin, or the succession of Twombleys for Puerto Rico and Puerto Rican Rum. Usually, however, he looks for a model whose person reflects beyond argument the desired elegance: Baron George Wrangel of the Russian nobility for Hathaway, a kilted Highland Scotsman for Thom McAn shoes, Commander Edward Whitehead for Schweppes, tea taster Albert Dimes (not elegant but very English) for Tetley's Tea. The ads in which Ogilvy takes the greatest pride come out of his campaign for the Commonwealth of Puerto Rico, which has the double purpose of luring tourists and enticing new industry. "We want people to think of Puerto Rico," he said in a speech, "as a country in renaissance, a country of beautiful mountains and romantic beaches, inhabited by brave and friendly people who are equally proud of their Spanish traditions and their American citizenship." This is a large order, as Ogilvy well knows: he works from a study made to his order by Elmo Roper, to determine the existing image of Puerto Rico in the minds of the American people. "But that's what makes it so exciting!" he says. "Nobody before has ever tried to change the image of a whole country. *And we're doing it!*"

To prove the success of the Puerto Rico campaign, Ogilvy points to the fact that new industrial projects on the island went from twenty-two the year before he took over the advertising to a hundred eight the year after. Ordinarily, however, he does not base his case on immediate sales results. "We have twenty-two clients," he says, "and all twenty-two of them have had increases in sales since they came to us. I always start my new business presentation that way. Then I tell people that any twenty-two businesses in the United States, chosen virtually at random, would show sales increases over the last half dozen years." Ogilvy's essential argument centers on the long run; his agency hopes to "build the kind of indestructible image which is the only thing that can make your brand part of the fabric of American life. . . .

"Let us remember," he once said at the end of a speech to a luncheon meeting of the American Association of Advertising Agencies, "that it is almost always the total *personality* of a brand rather than any *trivial product difference* which decides its ultimate position in the market."

3.

Ogilvy's brand-image advertising, like Bates's reason-why advertising, works essentially on the consumer's conscious mind in an effort to convince him that brand A, technically identical with brand B, is somehow a better product. All advertising, of course, edges its way below the conscious level in driving home its point, because consumers at the moment of purchase do not stop to analyze why they regard brand A as safer or better for them, more reputable or more dependable. And the loyalties established by brand images can be psychologically interesting. Every year tens of thousands of women write their personal problems to friendly Betty Crocker, the leading General Mills brand name, and it cannot be argued that these women are motivated by any logical process (indeed, it is reasonable to assume that they are incapable of logical processes). Nevertheless, somewhere inside their skulls they know they have been told *by an ad* that Betty is an understanding person. Though the final effect occurs on a semiconscious level, it originates in a perfectly conscious suggestion.

To Norman B. Norman of Norman, Craig & Kummel such conscious suggestions are usually a waste of the advertiser's time and money; what is meaningful to Norman is the unconscious suggestion. "Why does a man use a cologne? To be sexy, of course. Sportsman toiletries came to us, they were using fishing rods in their ads to show they appealed to the outdoor type. What good is that? That girl we gave them has been one of the highest rating ads since it first appeared. Take Veto deodorant. *Of course* it should stop perspiration, people *expect* a deodorant to stop perspiration, the way they expect bread to be fresh. Why advertise what everybody expects? We gave them a slogan with empathy—'Because You Are the Very Air He Breathes.' That gets at the heart of the matter."

A high-voltage salesman ("the perfect huckster," says the head of an unfriendly rival agency), Norman is a very tall man with high cheekbones and deep-set brown eyes under thick brown hair. He speaks with a deep, loud voice which on dry days may be audible in the apse of St. Patrick's Cathedral, across the street twenty-one stories down from his office window. A social psychologist by academic training, he entered advertising on the research end with the Milton Biow Company in 1934, and moved on to William Weintraub as an account executive. He was senior vice-president of the agency, responsible for the Revlon, Maidenform and Ronson accounts, when he and Eugene Kummel and David Kaplan bought out Weintraub in the fall of 1954. One of their first steps was to lure Walter Craig, a broadcasting expert, away from his job as advertising manager of Pharmaceuticals, Inc. (Serutan, Geritol), and into a titular position in the agency, which now bills about $30 million a year. Weintraub continues as chairman of the board although he is no longer a principal owner of the agency.

Shortly after Norman took over, the agency found the word for its approach to the problems of advertising: "Empathy." Norman hopes that his agency's ads will involve customers with the advertised products at the deepest levels of their beings, by expressing the *real* reasons why people buy these products. Since his orientation is Freudian, and a large part of his agency's business has been in cosmetics and lingerie, these real reasons are often sexual, which means that the ads can do no more than suggest them—although the photographs for Veto deodorant, with the girl stretched on the leopard-skin rug and the man's shoulder intruding, are as close to the literal as the law allows. In one of the great new-business coups of 1957, Norman's partner Gene Kummel won the Pabst account ($7 million worth) with a "motivationally researched" campaign ("Pabst Makes It Perfect"), stressing what the motivational researchers like to call the leisure-time significance of beer drinking.

The Maidenform Brassière ads are, of course, the classic example of the philosophy. Late in 1956 the Leo Burnett agency threw a few thousand dollars into what it called "wastebasket research" to find out which ads housewives *liked*, and the Maidenform ad ran third in a group of three fashion advertisements. " 'It goes too far,' the ladies kept saying," Burnett's A. F. H. Armstrong reported to a 4A's meeting. " 'It combines dress and undress. She would be decenter if she were entirely in her underwear.' " Kay Daly, a svelte, nervous, immaculately turned out blonde who is Norman's fashion director and one of the agency's two copy chiefs, was delighted with the results of the Burnett tests. "Housewives," she said, "*should* think those ads are shocking. That's the point."

In this approach to advertising, the choice of photographers and models for the ads is vital, and Kay Daly spends much of her time scouting the photographic scene. Norman, Craig & Kummel was the first agency to use photographer Richard Avedon, whose pictures were causing ga-ga among the readers of *Harper's Bazaar* (his career has since been celebrated in the movie *Funny Face*, which also made liberal use of the word "empathy"; he does many Maidenform ads). When the basic idea of the Sportsman campaign had been set, Daly went to Dan Wynn, who is basically a magazine rather than an advertising photographer, and the two of them found the fresh face (and legs) that the campaign required in the person of a model who had never appeared in a national ad before. When the agency decided to make a separate appeal to the teen-age audience for Chanel No. 5 (abandoning in this market the classic-bottle ad which still runs elsewhere), Kay Daly searched for weeks for "a noncommercial photographer," and came up with Todd Webb, who had never taken a fashion photograph in his life. Usually, forty to fifty photographs are taken for each ad, and then Norman and Kay Daly sit around a table and argue with each other about which one should be used. "He wins about half the time," Miss Daly says amiably. "She's soft-soaping me," Norman says. "I haven't won yet."

Though Norman was the first to systematize it as an agency philosophy, there is nothing particularly new in the use of direct or hidden emotional symbols to advertise a wide range of products. Norman's new ad for Veto deodorant is merely a short step forward from "Within the Curve of a Woman's Arm," which James Webb Young of the Thompson company wrote for Odorono in 1919. The famous Lucky Strike campaign, "So Round, So Firm, So Fully Packed," was calculated to arouse the need for oral satisfaction, a need which, according to theory, begins at the breast in infancy and stops only with death. When David Ogilvy had a salt account, research director Michael Helfgott urged the use of virility themes in the copy, on the grounds that "salt is a semen symbol." Ruth Waldo of the Thompson company, a wiry lady who has been with Thompson for more than forty years, recently explained to a young copywriter, from the depth of her experience, why his wife wanted to buy a preposterously expensive new cold cream: "Well, the advertising says there's turtle oil in it, and the royal jelly of the queen bee. Turtles live forever. And the royal jelly is what the queen bee has that makes her that very special and *highly delightful* kind of bee." The Norman campaign for Ronson lighters was built on findings by Ernest Dichter (Ph.D.), that flame is a sexual symbol and that flame-producing implements in anthropologically significant communities were shaped to show it.

"Empathy is more difficult when it's a man," Norman says. "Let's face it. It's easy to make a girl sexy, but a man—the only way is roughness. Men have to fight, that's how they win dames, it's fundamental. But it's ugly in print. What you want is the Park Avenue guy who's walking with a girl, and some thug comes up and makes an indecent remark, the Park Avenue guy beats hell out of him because he was champion intercollegiate boxer at Princeton. That's Walter Mitty, it's every man's dream world. Leo Burnett did it for Marlboro, he lucked into it with that tattoo—the guy is rich, but he's been in the Navy, see, that's where he got his tattoo. He's rich and rough at the same time."

Despite the solid Freudian base, Norman's "empathy" approach is not restricted to the search for sexual significance. His greatest triumph— the first year of *The $64,000 Question,* in which his agency's Walter Craig was as important as Lou Cowan's Entertainment Productions —used "empathy" in the simple dictionary definition, as an establishment of personal identification. It was the only time in the history of broadcasting that an agency bought a program with its own money (using a $130,000 loan from the Manufacturers Trust Company for the purpose) before it had sold the show to a client. "I suppose I was so enthusiastic," Norman says, "because I'd been at the Biow Company in the days of *The $64 Question* on radio, I knew how that program moved Eversharps. But even I was surprised at what we had. There never was a show that sold goods the way *The $64,000 Question* did while we had it. That show puddled the water, roiled people up, bared their nerve ends. The first couple of weeks, the rating was just average, fourteen or fifteen, but Revlon sold out its stock—they sent up here to get a couple of dozen lipsticks we were using to build a display piece, so they could send them out to dealers. Then we lost the account, BBDO got it, and the show went downhill. The important thing when we had it was the poor slobs we put on—people could identify with them. BBDO began using prominent figures. Randolph Churchill, for Christ sake! You lose all the empathy."

4.

In the early years of this century the central problem of advertising was simply to achieve recognition for the brand names which were rapidly replacing unlabeled bins of yellow soap and white flour in the grocery stores. The necessities were a name easily remembered for associations (Dutch Cleanser), descriptive qualities (Cream of Wheat), or some humorous touch (Uneeda Biscuit). Later came names that could be tied to a bad joke or a slogan (Squirt beverage, "It's In the Public Eye"; Broken Drum vegetables, "Can't Be Beat"). Eventually, a simple sales argument, usually in rhyme, was attached to the brand name and often achieved complete identification with it. The words "Spotless Town" were synonymous with Sapolio soap; the "Route of Phoebe Snow" conjured up the Lackawanna Railroad (Phoebe Snow kept clean while traveling because there was no dirty bituminous soot in the Lackawanna cars: "My gloves are white/ As when last night/ We took The Road of Anthracite"). At the time the most successful such campaign was a bit of light verse for Force breakfast food:

> Jim Dumps was a most unfriendly man
> Who lived his life on the hermit plan.
> He'd never stop for a friendly smile
> But trudged along in his moody style.
> Till "Force" one day was served to him.
> Since then they call him Sunny Jim.

The signature was " 'Force'—The Ready-to-Serve Cereal—A Better Builder than a Vacation." Constipation runs through the history of American advertising like a bright black thread.

Such advertising must be pleasing to make its point, and these early car cards and newspaper quarter pages were always pleasantly laid out, with more or less attractive drawings, considerable white space, and large type. In advertising which is intended merely to make a brand name memorable in itself, execution is at least as important as the sales argument employed. If a strong product claim is made, it must be masked behind a charming, happy presentation.

Albert Lasker of Lord & Thomas, aided in the creative end by copywriters John Kennedy and Claude Hopkins, wrecked this school of advertising before 1920. Hopkins, as usual, put the case most forcefully: "Money comes slowly and by sacrifice," he wrote in his autobiography *My Life in Advertising*. "Few people have enough. The average person is constantly choosing between one way to spend and another. Appeal for money in a lightsome way and you will never get it. 'Sunny Jim' proved that, so did 'Spotless Town.' So did many others which are long forgotten. Nobody can cite a permanent success built on frivolity. People do not buy from clowns." Radio, with its wonderful opportunities for what *Fortune* once described as "the drip-drip-drip of Chinese-water-torture methods of endless repetition," brought brief revivals of advertising designed primarily to make a brand name seen important. But from Lasker's day to the foundation of Doyle Dane Bernbach in 1949 no agency was willing to place memorability and originality over sales argument as the correct ad criteria.

The general view is expressed by David Ogilvy in his indoctrination booklet for new employees. Rule 2 for copywriters runs: "*Content* is more important than form. *What* you say in advertising is more important than *how* you say it." To this argument Bill Bernbach answers that "execution can *become* content, it can be just as important as what you say." Drawing on Romain Rolland's *Jean Cristophe*, he likes to say that "a sick guy can utter some words and nothing happens; a healthy, vital guy says them and they rock the world." For Schenley's Ancient Age bourbon, Bernbach built a campaign around a slogan which the company had been using for some time—and won mentions in *Advertising Age* and *Advertising Agency* magazines for the originality of the ads. Some of Bernbach's ads have contained no sales argument at all, most notably the campaigns for Levy's Bread, a local New York brand which nobody had ever heard about before Bernbach took over their advertising. He used subway posters which showed a full slice of rye bread, then a slice with several nibbles out of it, finally a slice with only the crust remaining, the three drawings against a red background, with a slogan superimposed: "NEW YORK/ IS EATING/ IT UP." His broadcast commercials featured a horrid child asking his mother for "Wevy's Cimmanon Waisin Bwead" and getting his pronunciation corrected. And without urging a single product claim he made Levy's one of the best known brands in town.

Bernbach does not talk about himself or his background, but if he wished he could claim to be one of the few completely rounded advertising men, with experience in every branch of the business. He first swam into the national advertising ken in 1939, as research director for the New York World's Fair. In 1943 he was director of public relations for Weintraub, and in 1945 he moved to Grey Advertising as a creative group head. Two years later Grey made him vice-president in charge of all creative work, and in another year he was gone, the boss of his own agency. Identified over the years neither with copy nor with art, he is immensely capable in both; he regards himself as "an ad-maker." He also has the basic gift of agency management, the ability to spot talent: the two top creative people in his shop, art director Bob Gage and copy supervisor Phyllis Robinson, are both young and were both minor employees at Grey when Bernbach found them and pushed them into prominence.

Unlike most heads of agencies, Bernbach is not a salesman. "People walk in here," he says, waving at his dignified but not very impressive office (the ashtrays were made by his kids), "and they're disappointed in me, I know it. I'm not the pompous or important guy or the huckster they expect to find as the president of an agency." Rather short, with a widow's peak of graying hair and very light blue eyes, Bernbach is handsome in a way lots of independent businessmen are handsome: he lacks the advertising thrust, he wears rather colorless suits and unimportant ties. An Olivetti portable typewriter sits unobtrusively on a shelf, with Webster's New World Dictionary beside it; a swivel of his chair, and Bernbach is practicing his trade, making ads, away from the usual executive's round of personnel problems, client contact, personal appearances.

The closest Bernbach has come to stating an agency philosophy was in a 4A's regional convention in 1956, when he gave his speech the title, "How to Do It Different." "Why," he said, "should anyone look at your ad? The reader doesn't buy his magazine or tune in his radio and TV to see and hear what you have to say. . . . What is the use of saying all the right things in the world if nobody is going to read them? And, believe me, nobody is going to read them if they are not said with freshness, originality and imagination . . . if they are not, if you will, said 'different.' " ("Certainly," said Leo Burnett, reacting in some horror to the idea that the Marlboro tattoo was a clever novelty, "we were not merely trying to be 'different.' ") Bernbach is by no means oblivious to the importance of a strong sales argument, and if his client has one he will push it for all it is worth. "Memorability and originality," he says, "should be based on something worth saying." He has rung literally dozens of changes on the Polaroid camera selling theme, the fact that a Polaroid gives you finished pictures a few seconds after you push the button; and he has found a hundred ways to argue that at Ohrbach's you can buy things more cheaply without sacrificing *chic*. But to Bernbach the setting is most important, and the setting is a visual image which stops the reader (or wins the attention of the television viewer), and stops him by telling him a story.

"We try to boil everything down into one idea," says Bob Gage, head of the art department, "and we want it to be the strongest idea the client can get over. We try to economize a lot in our thinking. We want realism in our ads, and not decoration. And we don't want anything at all in the ad that doesn't *work*—we want everything to be lean." For Ohrbach's, for Chemstrand and for Cole bathing suits Bernbach and Gage have used photographs as cartoons—cartoons composed at the height of contemporary taste in design—setting real people in unreal situations to illustrate an idea. The agency believes strongly in the humorous approach ("Humorous copy," says Ogilvy's Rule 13, "does not sell"), on the grounds that humor puts potential customers in the right frame of mind. "But it has to be a sophisticated form of humor," Gage says, "and it has to be right. If there's too much of it in an ad, people don't get it. People can get only so much at a time." A particularly spectacular example of this approach was an ad for Max Factor lipstick—a montage of the Colosseum, a Roman senator's bust with alive and staring eyes, and the head of a glamorous girl, all to illustrate Bernbach's headline, "Any Man Will Come to Life When You Wear Roman Pink."

Bernbach does not believe in rules of advertising, whether they apply to content or to technique. The final Bernbach ad emerges from constant interchange between copywriter and art director, operating on an equal organizational level within the agency. "A copywriter might have a good line," Gage says, "and I think how I can visualize it. I do a visual, and he looks at it, and that might give him still another idea for a line." When both copywriter and art director are pleased with the ad, it goes up to the account executive, who cannot simply turn it down; he has to have a reason, and a good one.

So does the client. "When we initiate relations with a client," says Joe Daly, Bernbach's account executive on Polaroid and Chemstrand, "they accept us on that basis. We say, 'We think we know how to make ads and you must agree or you wouldn't want us to do your ads.' Factual error and a violation of corporate policy are the only reasons we'll accept for correction." Bernbach himself puts the matter simply: "I feel that if the agency makes an ad and the client doesn't like it, the client ought to run it anyway." Ned Doyle, who runs the agency's account service department, believes that many clients at first accept this approach "with tongue in cheek. I'm sure every agency tells clients, 'We're experts in advertising, and you'll have to take our advice.' But we really mean it."

Bernbach deliberately rejects most of the tenets of modern agency operation. His account executives do not draw up "marketing plans," which are solemnly prepared at almost every other agency of any size. "I always tell clients," Bernbach says, "not to be taken in by a plan. The best plan in the world isn't going to make an ad that sells merchandise. Besides, what does the client want—somebody who knows *his* business or somebody who knows the advertising business?"

Most shocking of all, Bernbach has little use for research—that is, he thinks it has a role, but not a major role, in advertising. "Research can tell you what people want, and you can give it back to them," he says. "It's a nice, safe way to do business, but who the hell wants to be safe? Small companies these days can't afford to run just competent advertising—the big guys have competent advertising, too, and a hundred pages to your one. Anyway, advertising isn't a science, it's persuasion. And persuasion is an art."

5.

Other large agencies do not espouse a single philosophy of advertising. Most of them argue that each client presents a different problem, and that the agency must be free to select from all schools the technique that seems most promising as a way to solve the problem in hand. A few say simply that their personnel consists of individuals with individual approaches to advertising, and that a good man does his best work when he is allowed to go his own way. "When I first came to Young & Rubicam," says George Gribbin, now senior vice-president and head of the agency's copy department, "I was put to work on the Packard account, and the supervisor told me to write the ads the way Jack Rosebrook had been doing it. I got lost in the minutiae of phrasing, imitating Rosebrook. In six weeks they took me off the Packard ads. I said to myself, 'Well, maybe I can't write the Packard account, I don't know. But what I do know is that I can't write like Rosebrook. I've got to write like Gribbin.' Over the years I've learned that if we have a writer and we tell him, 'Do it in this particular style,' we'll get less good advertising. One of the great assets of this agency is that a man here feels he can express himself as a writer."

The general statement of the Thompson company's position is Stanley Resor's famous line: "What is it that makes this product the white pea in the pod?" Over the years Thompson has shown some orientation toward brand image, asserted simply by the use of testimonials from movie stars (Lux), Countesses (Pond's) or simply famous people (U.S. Lines, International Silver). But the agency can do, and does, any kind of advertising in the world. Its general position, as expressed by a senior officer, is that "we apply the personal and corporate experience of the agency to the problems of our clients."

At McCann-Erickson the orientation is toward "motivational" advertising, built on the "real" reasons why people use this kind of product. "We are eclectic," says Dr. Herta Herzog of the agency's research department. "We use clinical psychologists of all schools." But McCann has done far more work than any other agency in Adlerian analysis, with its heavy emphasis on power drives. (Another interesting example of the dictum that "everybody does best what he really believes in.") And McCann does not consider the making of advertisements to be the most important part of its work: McCann likes to think that it deals in the problems of "total marketing," of which "total communications" is a single aspect; and advertising (though, of course, it should be total, too) is merely an aspect of communications.

Elsewhere the concentration may be on marketing tactics rather than marketing strategy, with advertising again only a part of the agency's job. Grey Advertising, the fastest growing of the medium-large agencies (about $45 million in billings), has in the words of a client "come up Seventh Avenue," and Grey likes to stay close to the sale. Board Chairman Lawrence Valenstein enjoys pointing out that in 1937 his agency's house organ, *Grey Matter*, was already urging companies to regard their advertising as "part and parcel of a complete marketing program." *Grey Matter* has been published every month for more than twenty-two years, and one recent issue pulled requests for 16,000 reprints (at a quarter each) from 243 companies. The bulletin—it runs only four pages—is always full of practical detail on current selling problems. Fifteen years ago such an approach would have meant concentrating on one-cent sales and premiums. (These gimmicks took on in the 1930's the stature of an advertising philosophy. Duane Jones, probably the most accomplished practitioner of the school, called himself "The Boxtop King"; a man who worked under him recalls that Jones once planned a one-cent sale on personal loans for the Household

Finance Company.) Today, however, the world is a much more complicated place, and Grey's sales promotion department does more than three thousand jobs a year—everything from salesmen's kits to leaflets that dealers can stick in shopping bags—for the agency's sixty clients.

The Leo Burnett agency works on the assumption "that every product has inherent drama. It is often hard to find, but it is always there, and once found it is the most interesting and believable of all advertising appeals." Foote, Cone & Belding is particularly proud of the pleasant external symbols it has tied to its clients' products (Little Lulu for Kleenex). Compton Advertising, built primarily to service Procter & Gamble, operates from the most meticulous imaginable research preparation (such as analyses of newspaper circulations in the Ohio Valley in terms of grain hardness of water). And almost any agency will borrow almost any idea which is currently wowing the customers. As an officer of BBDO put it, mostly as a gag, "You can always tell an Ogilvy ad or a Bates ad, but you can't spot a BBDO ad, because we'll steal from everybody." Verifying the likelihood of the quote, BBDO's Jean Rindlaub said, "We're proud of the fact that there's no BBDO style; we think it proves we take each client's problem seriously."

CHAPTER 4

HOW TO RUN A GREAT BIG AGENCY:

Mostly J. Walter Thompson

"It's never been proved that even the biggest accounts must be handled by a very big agency. And it has been proved over and over again that medium-sized accounts get far better attention from a medium-sized agency."

Advertisement by Roy S. Durstine, Inc.

"No agency is small by choice."

Statement by Roy S. Durstine, when president of Batten, Barton, Durstine & Osborn

----

"All our progress to date has been by the division of labor."

Stanley Resor, chairman of the board, the J. Walter Thompson Company

"You cannot begin to understand the J. Walter Thompson Company until you realize that it is basically an extension of Mr. and Mrs. Resor's living room."

Former officer, J. Walter Thompson Company

1.

In 1957 the J. Walter Thompson Company billed nearly $300 million, roughly three-quarters of it in North America, the rest on the other four inhabited continents. The agency has thirty-four offices in nineteen countries, and it is important in all of them. It belongs, in effect, to one man—Stanley Resor, chairman of the board and majority stockholder, who in 1957 celebrated his seventy-eighth birthday and his fortieth year as an owner of J. Walter Thompson.

Stanley Resor is a large old man with square shoulders bent slightly forward below a large, squared head with a strong jaw. His white hair, once a mane, is now considerably thinned, and his step has been slowed by years. In 1955 he stepped up from the presidency of the agency to its chairmanship. ("I remain, however," he says, "the chief executive officer of this agency.") He is not and never has been a fast talker; he likes to think before he says anything, to study the situation and the people in the audience with a clear, blue gaze, and preferably to find a document which will be useful in the discussion. He spends most of his working time listening, and he likes to feel that the people to whom he must listen can back what they say with logical arguments; he dislikes airy nonsense for its own sake. This deep feeling for solidity has given many observers what is probably a wrong view of the man: Eric Hodgins wrote in *Fortune* in 1947 that "Stanley Resor has an abiding distrust of the word 'brilliant' or of any individual or any process that can be so described." Walter O'Meara, who for more than a decade shared with Jim Young the general supervision of Thompson's creative output, read the Hodgins article when it appeared and was vastly annoyed with it. "At bottom," O'Meara says, "brilliance is about the only thing Resor does have any respect for."

Born in Cincinnati, Resor was the son of substantial people in a highly substantive community: his father owned a factory that manufactured coal stoves. He majored in Classics at Yale and is still a good

Latinist (one finds little bad grammar in Thompson copy). It is said that he contemplated an academic career, but that a decline in the family fortunes kept him from continuing his studies after he received his A.B. in 1901. Whatever the circumstances, he was already earning money during his Yale vacations, selling Bibles door to door. (No better experience for an advertising man could be imagined, because the people who buy Bibles already own Bibles; to sell them another one is an exercise in pure salesmanship.) He worked in an office for the Central Trust & Safe Deposit Bank, on the road for a machine-tool manufacturer and "for a soap company," which can be none other than Procter & Gamble. (Since Thompson's soap affiliation is Lever, the name would not be mentioned.) In 1904 he went officially into advertising with Procter & Collier, then the "house agency" for the giant soap manufacturer. (P & G, as it is known in the trade, was one of the earliest of the big advertisers. Julian Watkins, in his book *The 100 Greatest Advertisements,* traced the key Ivory Soap slogans—"It Floats" and "99-44/100% Pure"—back to an ad which appeared in 1882.) In 1908 Commodore J. Walter Thompson hired Resor to start a Cincinnati office, and in 1912 he moved on to headquarters, in New York. In 1916 young Resor and an older associate, with help from friends, bought out the Commodore; a year later, Resor was in personal possession of the agency, which was then billing $3 million a year.

By then, however, all possessions were jointly held: in 1917 Resor married Helen Lansdowne, a coworker who had been with him in every one of his offices for more than ten years, since the Procter & Collier days. Those who have studied the history of the Thompson agency believe that Helen Resor's contribution to its growth has been in every way as great as her husband's. David Ogilvy has called her "the greatest copy-writer of her generation." Thanks to her influence, Thompson was the first advertising agency to hire women into major positions, and one of the first to elect a lady a vice-president (the lady was Ruth Waldo, still general supervisor of feminine copy, rather than Mrs. Resor herself, who has always stayed much in the background). The Resors have three children, none of them in J. Walter Thompson (nor would they be accepted if they applied: Resor has established a policy of refusing to hire any relative of anyone on his staff or in an advertising capacity at a client corporation).

It has never been possible to pinpoint Stanley Resor's contribution to the Thompson company. He has written copy once in a while, but rarely; he has corrected copy with a pencil even more rarely (he prefers to have things read aloud to him, and to make his contributions viva voce). He has participated in meetings with clients and in solicitations for new business, but most often as a benign and dignified presence rather than as a salesman. His influence makes itself felt in a few questions at a conference, and in private discussion with a key member of the group after the conference is over, rather than by dramatic assertions before an audience. But there is nothing that goes on in the Thompson company that does not interest him; he has a habit of looking at details. The people who work at Thompson feel a now-pleasing, now-disturbing consciousness that the man up top knows what they are doing. "Well . . ." Resor says, "my role in these matters is greatly exaggerated."

In the cliché of the trade, "an advertising agency is nothing but people," and there is no talent more important to the head of an agency than the ability to convince top-quality personnel that they ought to work for him. Claude Hopkins, explaining how Albert Lasker had hired him into Lord & Thomas when he didn't want the job, put his finger on the secret of Lasker's success with the words, "So far as I know, no ordinary human being has ever resisted Albert Lasker." Resor, too, has an extraordinary ability to seduce people over to J. Walter Thompson, away from jobs where they appear to be happy enough. Early in 1957 Resor hired Donald Longman, then director of marketing for Atlantic Refining, previously director of research for Dun & Bradstreet to run the Thompson research operation. Longman's recollection of the event is: "They came around and said, 'Longman, we want you,' and I said, 'No.' That's how I'm here." Resor smiled at the story and said, "We pointed out to him that at Atlantic Refining he was becoming more and more an *administrator*, and less and less a *researcher*."

Similarly, Resor has been able to rehire people who once left Thompson for other jobs (most agencies hate to do it: they have sold themselves too thoroughly on the idea of loyalty, and regard anyone who leaves as a pariah). Among those at Thompson who have returned to the fold are such key figures as Jim Young (who retired in 1928 to teach at the University of Chicago, run his New Mexico ranch and sell hand-loomed ties and home-grown apples by mail order), Richardson Wood (returned after a career as managing editor of *Fortune* and independent consultant to businesses, municipalities and foreign governments), and Robert Colwell (back from ten years with his own agency, Sullivan, Stauffer, Colwell & Bayles, now billing upwards of $40 million and by far the largest founded since the war. Colwell did not need very much persuading to return to the relative calm of an established organization. "While I was president of SSC&B," he says, "I was in the hospital four times, I had a heart attack, they took out my stomach, I almost lost my eyesight. My doctor said to me, 'Bob, I don't think this place agrees with you.' ")

Resor's original and continuing contribution to his agency and to the advertising industry as a whole has been his conviction that advertising is neither a circus sideshow nor a business, but an independent *force* in the community—and a profession which should have a status comparable to that of law or medicine. Because he feels that advertising is a force, he has been unwilling to use it on behalf of products which he does not believe should be forcefully promoted—most notably, hard liquor; Thompson in his administration has never had a hard liquor account. Conversely, Resor believes strongly in the use of advertising to promote charitable and social causes (of an essentially conservative nature, of course); he was among those instrumental in founding Blue Cross and Blue Shield, and not even the ads for Ford receive more attention from Resor than the agency's little campaigns for Blue Cross.

Resor's efforts to have advertising accepted as a profession fall into two parts: the attempt to establish recognized canons of ethics and the work toward a generally accepted body of techniques which would constitute a professional discipline. Thompson has never made a "speculative presentation" to a prospective client—that is, it has never sug-

gested to an advertiser that he switch his account to Thompson on
the basis of a campaign which the agency has worked up for him
without charge, as a sample. Speculative presentations obviously require
the diversion of the agency's people from work for existing clients to
work for the prospect, which is shabby practice; and they also assume
that good advertising can be created without that fund of intimate
knowledge which an agency secures only by close association with its
client, an assumption which Thompson vigorously rejects. In the early
1940's, Thompson could have had the giant Camel cigarette account
if Resor had been willing to give Reynolds Tobacco as little as an idea
for a slogan; Resor told Reynolds that if he submitted such a slogan, he
"would be prostituting my profession."

The body of knowledge which Resor hopes will someday give advertising a professional discipline is being built up in a series of monographs, thirty-four in all, submitting the techniques of the trade to
rigorous logical analysis. Nine of the monographs are finished, and are
available to employees of the agency; the other twenty-five are still in
outline form. Eventually, all of them will be published, for the use of
anyone who will take the time to master the material. "We have no
illusions," Resor says, "about the percentage of people who will sit
down and read a treatise." He is unwilling to indulge in profitless
argument about the validity of the rules Thompson is setting down
in its monographs. "It has taken us forty years," he says, "to get
captions under illustrations and get them in the right place. We're still
working to make people illustrate comparisons on a plane, reading
from left to right. People will say, 'How can there be laws when you
can't prove them?' Well, there's no way on earth you can get the maximum out of a comparison except reading from left to right.

"If you start with the belief that the universe runs by law, it's just
fascinating to try gradually to find out what these laws are. That's what
we're doing at Thompson."

2.

As a rough rule, advertising agencies require ten to twelve employees to service each million dollars of billings. Thompson, with something like $225,000,000 of domestic billings, has about twenty-five hundred people working for it in the United States, half of them in the "World office" in New York. This relatively small staff represents a vast range of human enterprise and talent: there are writers and artists for print and drama, salesmen, sociologists, psychologists, economists, typographers, statisticians, public relations flacks, stage and dress designers, electronic technicians, financial experts, space and time buyers (a fine, futuristic occupation, this), dietitians, accountants, lawyers, photographers, engravers, geniuses, secretaries, stenographers, file clerks, comptometer operators, switchboard girls, and executives. They are all strapped together into a single organization which operates, as president Sigurd Larmon of Young & Rubicam says about his similar organization, "for one purpose—to help sell goods and services for our clients."

Exactly how this strapping together is accomplished is one of the mysteries of advertising—especially at Thompson. Thompson has no "table of organization," no set of "flow charts," no fixed system of work. Every once in a while the agency becomes disturbed about its organizational fluidity and wonders what its clients—most of whom have elaborate charts with lines and boxes—must think of it. At these times somebody is sent off to make still another attempt to draw a chart. All such attempts run into Resor's deeply felt suspicion of "military systems" which inhibit creative effort. Only once has he looked with pleasure on an organizational chart drawn up for his inspection. This one, he said, was almost right; it needed only one simple change, which he proceeded to effect. He picked up an eraser and neatly removed all the lines that connected all the boxes. Incidents like these lend weight to copywriter Dick Neff's remark that "working for the Thompson company is like being in business for yourself."

Thompson's principle of organization is the "group system," with a separate group for each account. (An account at Thompson is a brand, not a client; there are separate groups for Lever's Lux and Lever's Rinso, Ford cars and Ford trucks.) Each tribe of Indians has two chiefs, a "group head" and an "account representative," and many tribes are gathered into a clan with an account supervisor as grand sachem. (The Thompson word for account supervisor is, for some reason, "backstop," but nobody except Resor himself uses it without embarrassment. "I hate that word," says one backstop, "because it implies that somebody is always dropping the ball, which isn't true.") There are about a dozen account supervisors for the eighty-odd major accounts serviced by the New York office.

The key man in each account group is the account representative (or account "executive," in non-Thompson teminology). All information from the client comes to him, and he presents to the client the agency's suggestions and the advertising campaigns prepared by the creative staff. In theory, at least, he is ultimately reponsible for the quality of the work which Thompson does for the client and for Thompson's thorough understanding of what the client needs and wants from his advertising agency—keeping in mind, as a Thompson account supervisor puts it, "that what the client needs may be something different from what he wants." Basically, the account representative's specialty is personal relations, his ability to get along with the client's advertising people and with the people inside the agency who work on this account. There are account representatives who have no other talent whatever, at all agencies, and they get along. But the best representatives, the ones who become account supervisors, are also thoroughly trained advertising men (often with a background in copywriting, media or research) or shrewd businessmen who have been persuaded to try advertising. Stanley Resor, in a memorandum, put the nature of the job in its simplest terms: the account representative, he wrote, "will know what constitutes the best advertising for the product in question."

Resor defined the task of the group head with equal simplicity in the same memorandum; group heads, he wrote, "must organize and stimulate the writers and artists with whom they work to obtain the most effective advertising that can be prepared in conformity with the standards of good taste." The group head is almost invariably a promoted copywriter, though it is not impossible for an artist to make the grade (Wally Elton, head of the Ford Car account group, the largest in the agency, came out of the art department). In most cases, he sees the client only rarely, when the representative feels that his presence at the conference table would help to sell the client an agency product or when he needs a piece of specialized information which the representative feels he could best get on his own. Representative and group head are coequal within the group, and, obviously, their reponsibilities overlap: one must "know . . . the best advertising," the other must "obtain the most effective advertising." Disagreements arise, usually, says group head Ed Robinson, "because somebody has insufficient information. Not always. In case of dissension, the squabble is settled by the backstop."

Keeping the account group all in one harness is the central job of the account supervisor; his central responsibility, says one of them grimly, is "holding the account." The supervisor at Thompson is usually, though not always, an older man; he can come out of almost any background at all. Garrit Lydecker, who supervises the work for Scott Paper (an important account, since Resor sits on Scott's board of directors), comes out of research and copy at Young & Rubicam and client contact at the Leo Burnett agency. Charles Rheinstrom, supervisor on Eastman Kodak, New York Central, Northeast Airlines, and Douglas Aircraft, was operations manager for American Airlines before he went into advertising. Kennett Hinks, who supervises all work for Lever Brothers, entered the Thompson company in 1921 as a copywriter, worked in the Chicago research department, managed Thompson's offices on the West Coast and then in Central Europe before he entered the client contact end of the business. The account supervisor maintains his own liaison with the client, usually at the level above that reached by the account representative. If the representative is working with a brand manager, the supervisor will talk with the vice-president in charge of advertising;

he usually keeps on good terms with the client's sales manager, and at Thompson he often knows the people who own the business.

In one way, each account supervisor has his own separate advertising agency working under him. Each account group contains a permanent representative from the media, research and television programming departments (if television is used) and is serviced by regularly assigned engraving experts from the production department and clerical help from traffic control, accounting and billing. And it is the supervisor who, like the principal owner of a smaller agency, must make the decision about what goes to the client. But he has assets a small agency cannot command. He can call on specialized departments (a legal staff, a medical expert, a woman who does nothing but gather testimonials, an economist) whenever he feels the need for a specialist's opinion. If his own staff becomes overwhelmed with work, he can borrow junior assistants from elsewhere in the agency (checking first with the "traffic control" department) or call on top-priced creative talent, often men who are group heads on other accounts, to show his people the way out of a rut (checking first with Howard Kohl, Resor's personal assistant, who runs a traffic control system on senior personnel). And he never has the full authority of an agency head, because the work done by his groups is examined periodically by an *ad hoc* Review Board of senior men, most of them outside his authority. The Review Board has no powers of compulsion, and the account supervisor (especially if he knows the client is on his side) may disregard the board's advice; but, obviously, there is no future in doing so.

At other agencies the account supervisor has far less power. Though there is always a relatively stable account group, final responsibility for the work of the members of the group resides with department heads rather than with the account supervisor. At Young & Rubicam, for example, no major piece of creative work will be allowed to go to a client until it has been passed by George Gribbin, head of the copy department, and Fred Sergenian, head of the art department. If there is an argument between the account supervisor and the copywriter about a piece of copy, the arbiter is Gribbin. "It's ingrained in us," Gribbin says, "that a copy man knows more about copy than a contact man." A permanent Y & R Plans Board formed by the department heads (plus a few senior men without departmental or client responsibilities, who devote much of their time to review assignments) looks over the work on each account on an annual or semiannual basis. But the Plans Board exists, in the words of senior vice-president Harry Harding, head of the account service department, "to make sure the group has really walked all around the problem." It will rarely reject work that has already been blessed by the department heads, acting individually.

In smaller agencies, certainly in those which bill less than $10 million and perhaps even in those which bill up to $20 million, the final say on what goes to the client belongs to the man who owns the agency. David Ogilvy actually writes a high proportion of the headlines on Ogilvy, Benson & Mather ads, and even in a shop as big as Ted Bates the top three men look over every print layout and every television "story board." At McCann-Erickson, a conscientious attempt has been made to centralize control of a vast agency's output, through the device of multiple review boards. A Marketing Plans Board okays or revises the basic campaign ideas, a Creative Plans Board checks over the ads themselves, and at the end of the process (but still before the client sees the work) a Plans Review Board looks over the whole Gestalt. Everything is reduced to written form—the presentations to the boards and the boards' opinions of what they have examined. McCann likes to feel that, in the words of Anthony Hyde, vice-president in charge of planning and development, "we know and apply the principles of advanced management." The agency swims in paper, a different kind of binding for each sort of report, a different color edging on the paper for reports made by different departments. Up top, the Plans Review Board forms what chairman Terence Clyne calls, "a Supreme Court. We may affirm completely or negate, or send back for further hearings." And this judgment, too, is solemnly written out. What finally emerges in the line of advertising work can truly be said to represent the agency as a monolith, rather than the work of persons. McCann has had great success in selling this system to prospective clients, somewhat less success in selling it to middle- and lower-echelon employees (who are deprived of certain personal satisfactions in their work; copy chiefs at other agencies have noted that there is always a rash of applications from people at McCann when new top executives are hired into the agency and begin handing down dicta).

Thompson relies on its conception of advertising as a profession to establish equality in the client-agency relationship; Y & R and McCann go a step further, placing the full prestige of their organizations on the scale whenever a serious recommendation is made. One purpose of the Y & R Plans Board, Harry Harding says, is to give the contact man the feeling that "the weight of the agency is behind him." Y & R especially will fight for its views as long as there seems any chance that the client can be converted, and this willingness to do battle for its employees' work has made Y & R by far the best *liked* agency in the business, by agency people. ("If I were a client," says the head of a considerable rival agency, "I wouldn't give my business to us; I'd give it to Y & R." George Gribbin of Y & R feels that this popularity is one of the agency's great assets: "We're always described to clients as the second best agency, right after the agency that's making the pitch for itself.") Y & R advertises its services extensively (the media list includes the *Detroit Athletic Club News*), and one of its best-known ads showed an anatomical drawing of a human spine with the copy: "This is a backbone. You can't run a good advertising agency without it. . . . It means giving service instead of servility." There is a story in the agency about Charles L. (Roy) Whittier soliciting a new account from a difficult advertising manager, who asked him what Y & R would do if his company flatly rejected a proposed campaign. "If you reject our best idea," Whittier said smoothly, "we'll present our second-best idea." The advertising manager was unsatisfied, and asked what would happen if the company didn't like any of Y & R's ideas and insisted on having the campaign done its own way. "Then we'll do it your way," Whittier said, "because you might as well waste your money with us as with somebody else."

Creative people at Thompson have less contact with the client than their opposite numbers at other agencies. On the whole, Thompson feels that the information a copywriter needs is best funneled to him through the account representative rather than given directly by the client. "If copywriters see too much of the client," says group head Ruth Waldo, general supervisor of women copywriters, "they get too many ideas of what *can't* be done. They begin thinking about Mr. X as the client rather than about the people who buy the product." Ned Doyle of Doyle Dane Bernbach believes that no copywriter can do so good a job as an account executive in *defending* a piece of creative work, because the copywriter will always feel personally involved with the criticism. Other agencies recognize this danger that a copywriter working closely with a client will, as president Rolland Taylor of Foote, Cone put it, "begin to play customer's golf." But they feel that the advantages he derives from gathering his material firsthand outweigh the threat to his integrity as an advertising man who writes to the public. In fact, the copy group head at Foote, Cone presents the agency's advertising to the client for approval, while the account executive looks on. At BBDO, where each account group forms itself around its strongest member rather than around a titular position, the creative group heads are often more closely in touch with the client than the account executive is, though he will see the client's people more frequently.

In most cases, of course, the decision rests largely with the client himself. At one point, Lever Brothers decided that the creative people working on Lever accounts at the agencies should keep on the closest possible terms with the company's advertising department. David Ogilvy is usually credited with inspiring this decision (if credited is the right word), and he pleads no defense. "They called me over," Ogilvy recalls, "and offered me Rinso, provided I would handle the account myself. They said they wanted the copywriters to service their accounts at all their agencies, and would I go along with that? I said, 'It's like asking the Archbishop of Canterbury whether he believes in the Anglican faith. I *am* the Archbishop of Canterbury—I sold this idea to *you.*' Well," Ogilvy adds ruefully (partly because he lost the

Rinso account a year later and feels that he deserved to lose it), "I was wrong." The difficulty with Lever's approach was not so much that the copywriters gave too much weight to Lever's supposed prejudices in preparing their campaigns (at this time Lever had a policy of never rejecting an ad), but that they had no time to write the ad—they were always on the phone with the client or attending client conferences. Presently, Lever returned to the standard procedure.

CHAPTER 5

HOW TO RUN A GREAT BIG AGENCY:

The Extras— Still Thompson

1.

After taking out the rent, essential salaries and necessary overhead, most agencies have about 10 per cent of their income to put into the miscellaneous expenses of advertising—travel and entertainment, research for the agency's own use, new business preparations and special services for big clients. In an agency that bills $10 million, this 10 per cent reduces to $150,000 a year—a sum easily eaten up by what might be called the inevitable miscellaneous. At giant agencies like the big four, however, the 10 per cent produces a supplementary budget of $3 million to $4 million, which will buy a lot of miscellanies—among them, extras and luxuries for the agency and its clients.

Some of the money goes into incidentals pure and simple—to test kitchens for food accounts, to paying the salaries of McCann-Erickson executives who have been sent to the Harvard Business School to sit at the feet of Neil Borden, or to the maintenance of Young & Rubicam's private theater ticket and travel bureau. Some of it goes into client services that might otherwise be performed, for a fat fee, by an outside organization—Foote, Cone sets up the Miss Rheingold contest for Liebmann Breweries and stages a show at the Waldorf to get it off the ground. But most of the money, these days, goes into elaborate television departments and extra research work.

Thompson, as the biggest agency, probably buys the greatest range of extras. The agency has twenty-three "field representatives," whose local bureaus supplement the basic New York, Chicago, Detroit, Coral Gables, Los Angeles and San Francisco offices; when local information is needed or local help desired, the field representative is on the spot. Thompson actually produces weekly television programs (the agency's *Kraft Theater* goes back to 1947, and is the oldest continuing feature on television), but the television staff is far larger than would be necessary simply for the production of Thompson's shows. On every program which a Thompson client buys, regardless of who actually is paid to produce it, the television department "proceeds," department administrator Jack Devine says, "as a full partner in the production." (This situation is standard: As Grey's Alfred Hollender put it, "There is no great difference in the amount of work between an agency-produced show and a show produced independently with agency supervision.")

Thompson maintains a permanent TV workshop with its own studio, recently expanded by the addition of a special color television laboratory, and films rough versions of commercials so that clients will be able to see more exactly what they are going to get. (McCann owns a subsidiary company which actually produces final films for some of the agency's clients; Thompson always contracts for the final version on the outside.) In addition, Thompson maintains a flying squad of seven production experts, headed by a director, which "travels all around the country," Jack Devine says, "to make local programming as good as network programming." If Shell Oil wants to buy the local news and weather programs, Thompson's travelers will go to the town, pick the right announcer, build a special set for him, set the right props in place, buy the right time period, and produce the first show. Then they come back every once in a while to see how the show is going. Among the functions which a national sales representative performs for a local television station is to tip it off in advance when Thompson's flying squad is nearing.

Two of the larger agencies, Y & R and McCann-Erickson, maintain their own research organizations, each with more than twenty-five hundred full-time or part-time interviewers, and use these organizations partly for their own experimental work. Y & R under George Gallup pioneered in "reading and noting" research to test the effectiveness of advertising; McCann was probably the first agency to take "motivational research" seriously (and remains the only agency which really believes that clinical psychiatric techniques can be successfully extended to marketing problems). Y & R runs a continuing "test market" in Providence, Rhode Island, auditing inventories in some seventy-five stores at regular intervals to check on changes in purchasing patterns and to measure the success of new products.

At Thompson, the agency's own research has always been concentrated on the basic problems behind temporary marketing situations. Surveys of market and industry trends are performed especially for Thompson under the direction of senior economist Arno Johnson (economists are rare at advertising agencies; advertising men, like other businessmen, usually think they know all they need to know about economics); one of these surveys produced the "interurbia" concept much noised about in the business community these days. Every decade Thompson publishes a tome on *Population and Its Distribution* in the United States, defining the size and nature of the market in every city and town in the nation, and giving data about the number of grocery stores and shoe stores and such. The first edition of the book was published in 1912, and since 1944 its preparation has been in the hands of Dr. Vergil Reed, a short, peppery and perhaps bloodthirsty man (behind a glass door on a wall of his office is an astonishing collection of deadly weapons, including his own dress sword from World War I, a medieval French halbard, a 31-caliber Texas gun, a Chinese torture feather, a Nazi dagger, a Brazilian Indian throwing spear, and a Ghurka kukri), who was acting director of the federal Census before he went into advertising.

As business demanded it, Thompson has extended the basic population and markets research work to Western Europe and Latin America, publishing books on both, and Reed has gone abroad to supervise the work. (He also travels for the government, taking leaves of absence from Thompson to set up U.S. exhibits at international fairs.) A good deal of the needed information can be gathered in New York, of course, via the United Nations or the consulates of the countries involved. Seeking population data on the British Isles, for example, Reed put his questionnaire through the British trade mission in New York. Some months later he received a file of data from the mission; he looked at the title page and was amused to note that the British government had got its information on this subject from J. Walter Thompson, Ltd., of London. "It wasn't that surprising when you thought about it," Reed says, holding his pipe just out of his mouth. "We've got a 136-man marketing research division in London."

Another branch of Thompson's fundamental research deals with consumer habits on a nation-wide basis, and is conducted via the J. Walter Thompson Consumer Purchase Panel. The panel, first formed in 1939, is a sample of some 5,500 households, chosen to be representative of the nation as a whole. These households, in effect, are on the Thompson payroll: Thompson pays them (by means of "points" good for merchandise in a special catalogue) to report monthly on their purchases of grocery products, certain toiletries and items of clothing, and other commodities in which Thompson maintains a continuing interest. Special questionnaires on special subjects—baked goods, mixes and bakery ingredients, or purchases of gasoline and automobile supplies and accessories, or television viewing habits—go out periodically to sketch in the full picture that Thompson wants to have. For filling out all the questionnaires and sending them in on time, each household on the panel receives roughly $50 worth of merchandise a year (at a cost to Thompson of only $30, because Thompson pays wholesale prices).

As far as the people who answer the questionnaires are concerned, the panel is run by a woman named Emily Rogers, who also sends

Christmas cards and notes of congratulation when a baby is born. In the flesh, Emily Rogers is a young man named Wallace Flynn, Longman's assistant in market research. There is no attempt to conceal from the members of the panel the fact that they are working for J. Walter Thompson, but they are never told which of the brands listed in the questionnaire are Thompson clients. The agency does not believe they are curious about it, anyway. "Obviously," Longman says, "most housewives don't have the vaguest notion of what the Thompson company is."

2.

To the client who does a considerable export business Thompson can offer a massive international network of agencies, all of them wholly owned subsidiaries of the American company. In all, Thompson operates in eighteen countries and colonies outside the United States. Only two other agencies—McCann-Erickson and Grant, which specializes in such work and has half its billings abroad—can offer a comparable foreign service. "We open an office in an area," says vice-chairman Sam Meek, who runs Thompson's "World" operation, "when there's enough volume of our clients' business to justify it, to justify a large enough staff to provide a standard of service. And we've found that if you do the job well enough with your own client you inevitably attract important local clients, so our business everywhere turns out to be fifty-fifty, half from companies outside the country, half local." Thompson will handle a client from any of its offices in all the others (unless there is a serious client conflict in another country); it advertises Pond's cold cream (American) in Great Britain, and Rowntree Chocolates (Britain) in South Africa, Canada, Australia and Holland. The agency believes firmly in free trade.

There was a London office when Resor took over, but he promptly closed it during his first consolidation campaign (which also involved the lopping off of some 160 accounts, all of them too small to justify the kind of service Resor wished to give). London was reopened in

1923, and in 1925 Sam Meek went over to take charge of the London and Western European operation. Though he has given most of his attention to world trade for more than three decades, Meek remains the closest of Thompson's top executives to the old-fashioned literary stereotype of the American. He wanders around his office, hands in pockets, with true American restlessness; thinks on his feet, repeating the last half of the previous sentence to consolidate his thoughts before proceeding; wears aggressively striped shirts, aggressively exposed by the fact that he buttons only the bottom button of a single-breasted suit jacket. And he refers back constantly to the importance of new inventions, speed, progress. He feels it is important as a sign for the future that Pan American presented Danny Kaye's film about the world's children on the same day in every one of the world's capitals which has commercial television. "When you get off the plane at Hong Kong," Meek says enthusiastically, "you find on the newsstands the same magazines that were on the newsstands in New York."

The essential unity of the world-wide organization is maintained by close supervision from New York, and by full use of modern means of communication. Thompson has been careful to build its own offices abroad. "You might go to Nairobi," Meek says, "find the best agency and buy it—it wouldn't be too difficult, you could prove you'd bring in new business—but then you'd have a purely *local* service. We want to give a *Thompson* service, with local people. In this office right now there are six guys from all over the world, studying how we do things, and when they go others will come." Thompson's four offices in India are staffed with two or three Englishmen and two Americans, plus 250 Indians. Often the top man in the office is local, and when the manager has been imported he is not necessarily American. "Why," Meek says, "we've had an *Englishman* managing our office in *France*."

Usually, Thompson and other agencies which work abroad prefer to use the same basic advertising appeals for their client in all countries. The Hollywood movie stars who bathe with Lux are effective almost everywhere—though in India the agency will use Indian movie stars. "People are very much alike the world over," Meek says. "You try to take something away from them, they resist. They all want some security. They're all a little lazy. And there isn't a housewife anywhere who doesn't want to look presentable—or who wants to hear the truth about how she really looks." Lou Wasey, who started in the advertising business at Lord & Thomas in 1904 and later built a considerable international branch for his own agency, told the illustrative story in an interview in *Advertising Age*. "There was a man in those days named Harry Kramer," Wasey said, "who started Cascarets and made an international business out of it. I asked him one day if there was constipation in other countries, the same as in America. He said, 'Mr. Wasey, the whole world is constipated.'"

3.

The advantages of bigness do not lie entirely in such large areas as basic research and foreign trade; there are little things, too. Thus, Thompson has a one-woman, walking medical library, Mrs. Mary Beaty, whose job is to read all the medical books and periodicals and keep in touch with all medical developments which might influence sales arguments for consumer products. Mrs. Beaty, a tall, lean lady with somewhat undisciplined gray hair and the manner of a born enthusiast, came to Thompson originally as a secretary, with her eye on copywriting. "Then there was an illness in the family," she recalls, "and I found I wanted to do my own research before I would accept a medical man's opinion." A hobby in medicine turned into a full-time job when account groups found that they could save themselves much time and the expense of medical consultations by checking first with Mrs. Beaty. "I don't consider myself a final authority on anything," she says, "but I can help them a lot, even if it's only a question of picking the right laboratory for a research job." Mrs. Beaty's walls are decorated with electron-microscope photographs of various viruses and funguses, which the art connoisseurs of the office often regard as remarkably beautiful on their first visit, before they know what is portrayed. She always thinks they are beautiful. "Look at that one," she says, "that was for Absorbine, Jr., it's athlete's foot. But look at the beautiful shade of pink on the mold growth."

In the trade, the best known of Thompson's specialists in the more remote aspects of advertising is Lucile Platt, who runs what Thompson calls its personality department. Miss Platt (the name is a *nom du travail*; her real name is nobody's business) gathers testimonials for the products Thompson advertises, mostly from society leaders and British aristocracy, but also from blue-ribbon bakers at state fairs (for Fleischmann's Yeast), from the men who climbed Everest (for Aquascutum), from race horses (for Absorbine, Jr.) and from many others. "But," she says, "the word 'testimonial' is a misnomer. This department has to do with people in relation to advertising, and they don't have to say, 'This is the best so-and-so I ever tasted.'" Miss Platt is a small, round, gray-haired lady with a pleasantly businesslike manner and a brusque voice; she has been gathering endorsements for the agency since 1928.

"The testimonial per se at J. Walter Thompson," she says, "seems to stem from our Pond's campaign, the idea of using really important society people who had never given a testimonial before. But it wasn't so difficult, Pond's is a good cold cream, we weren't asking anybody to say anything she couldn't sincerely say. We still don't. I'm an old nanny about that—copywriters go all out for a product, but I believe people should say things the way they naturally say them. Even when you don't have to do it that way—and sometimes you do. Ernest Hemingway gave us a testimonial for Pan American, and of course you wouldn't want to change a word of it—but you couldn't, even if you wanted to."

Miss Platt's methods of securing endorsements are her own, but almost every approach involves some flattering of the prospect and the payment of hard, taxable cash. ("Some agencies," she says scornfully, "will give people Cadillacs or pearls—but at Thompson we won't give a can of peas without reporting it to the government.") Photographers for the testimonial ads are chosen with particular care, both for their social standing and for their talent (the first Pond's photographs were taken by no less then Edward Steichen, and during the war Thompson brought Cecil Beaton over on a convoy to continue the series). And Miss Platt tries to start each campaign on the highest possible note. When Thompson planned a testimonial series for the S.S. United States, Miss Platt went over on the first crossing, and while on ship gathered an endorsement of the U.S. Lines from fellow passenger Mrs. Vincent Astor. "I always go after the best," she says, "and if I can get the best it becomes a kind of club. Today, there's never a sailing of the United States but we get calls from all sorts of people, they want to be pictured in the ads." Since Miss Platt works under an assumed name, and most of her friends do not know what she does at Thompson, she quickly finds out how considerable a cachet the ads carry. "Why," she says, "I've sat at dinner parties and had a woman tell me she was offered five thousand dollars for a Pond's advertisement—and she wasn't even considered for the list!"

4.

All this activity must be visualized in the context of Thompson's elaborate New York offices, which occupy the tenth, eleventh, twelfth and half of the fourteenth floors of the enormous Graybar Building, beside Grand Central Station on Lexington Avenue. Each floor represents something more than an acre of space, broken by the shape of the building into three separate blocks joined at the receptionist's lobby. On each floor the visitor to Thompson is likely to go the same way, up a long hall interrupted by a small open "square" of offices, into an open rectangle the length of the building, with offices on all four sides. The visitor, as he heads toward his own appointment, will see the people at work in their offices, because Thompson has an unspoken rule that doors are to be kept open—and prevents violations of the rule by providing nothing more substantial than a wrought-iron grillwork, or a set of vertical wood louvres, to break the private offices apart from the wide corridor. The theory is that everybody should be available for consultation at any time.

Executive headquarters are along the rectangle on the eleventh floor. Beyond the receptionist, on the way to the sancta, stucco walls and rows of wrought-iron gates and apertures, iron peacocks ornamenting the twisted bars, give the corridors a baronial aspect. At the entrance to the main rectangle, a wide, open interior staircase connects with the twelfth floor, a slightly less expensive replica of the eleventh; and with the tenth floor, where the creative staff labors in more modern surroundings, with wood louvres and lightly clouded glass where executive headquarters has wrought iron and stucco. A two-story lecture hall and screening theater, originally designed by Norman Bel Geddes in the 1920's, cuts a swath out of both the tenth and the eleventh floors.

On all three floors the private offices are elegant; there is no other word for it. Probably no other organization in the world has *done* so many offices in so many different styles. Wherever possible, the designers (working under the general direction of Mrs. Resor herself) have attempted to express in the furniture the personality of the room's occupant or of his job. Though the basic orientation is suitably conservative, club Victorian and eighteenth century, there is no prejudice against any furniture style: as far back as 1931 Thompson had an office decorated in the new Swedish manner, with imported Swedish furniture to put in it. Ladies' offices may be decorated as outdoor patios with banks of plants in the middle. There are extraordinary pieces that are to be seen nowhere else—like the predecessor of the swivel chair, a heavy antique with a circular seat and a back that moves along a track on the seat's circumference, and can be swung to face any direction. Where the occupant of the room seems to have talent in this direction, he is encouraged to do his own decorating, at Thompson's expense. Thus, when Wally Elton was promoted into his tenth-floor corner office, he was urged to design his own desk and easel, conference table and wall cabinets.

This individual attitude toward employees' furnishings is symbolic of the firm's personnel policy, which is a case study in enlightened and highly personal paternalism. Until the entire office was air-conditioned, for example, Resor would not allow an air-conditioning unit to be placed in his room, though other executives might have them. In addition to their salaries, Thompson's people benefit from a group life insurance policy, Blue Cross and Blue Shield (of course), and since 1957 a special major-medical-expense plan. Ownership of the agency's stock, all of which is held by people who work at Thompson, is spread all through the executive level, though Resor retains control. On all levels employees participate in the agency's profits up to 15 per cent of their annual salaries. Such plans are common in the agency business, but Thompson's is probably the most generous, since the employee participates from the day of his arrival and can never forefeit more than the company's first-year contribution, even if he quits after only a few years; after five years, the entire fund is irrevocably his. At BBDO, by contrast, an employee does not participate in the profit-sharing plan until his fourth year of employment and those above the clerical and junior level cannot take all the money with them for fourteen years. The most elaborate such profit-sharing plan at any agency is Compton Advertising's Pension Trust, which gives no benefits whatever to anyone who quits or is fired in his first ten years at Compton, but provides for retirement at age sixty at a yearly income of 32½ per cent of the employee's highest previous annual salary.

Every organization likes to say that it fills vacancies by promoting up, but Thompson genuinely makes the effort. Junior personnel are encouraged (but not required) to take courses in advertising technique given within the agency, and those who show promise begin moving up; most of Thompson's junior copywriters started off as stock boys, mail boys, secretaries and file clerks. All such reckonings are somewhat artificial, since the stock boys, etc., were mostly recruited from the colleges; but Thompson is also full of high executives, including president Norman Strouse and senior copywriter Ed Robinson, who started off on a very low level and rose without help from college degrees or family connections. Promotions from junior rank in creative work flow from weekly meetings of half a dozen or so from the ranks of copy and art supervisors, at which work problems and personnel achievements are talked over in an informal way, with Stanley Resor himself occasionally in attendance, just listening. Outside the creative area,

Resor feels, it is easier to spot the outstanding man. "The thing rubs off," he says. "People are being reached for. You don't have to break anybody's head open to find out Jones is doing a wonderful job—instead, it's always, 'Why can't we get Jones in on this?' "

A similar informality characterizes promotion procedures at most other agencies, with the inevitable result that advertising people who want to better themselves go looking for new jobs which will do it. McCann-Erickson, however, has a training program worthy of the largest industrial organization, and each major Y & R department runs its own "indoctrination and training" program, though the people in the program may have been hired through personnel rather than by the department itself. Research director Peter Langhoff has set up an executive training program for business-school graduates; he started it, he says, "because I was tired of being at the mercy of whoever hired people for the mail room." Kenyon & Eckhardt, alone among larger advertising agencies, gives prospective employees a battery of personality tests—apparently, however, the tests have not helped with the turnover rate.

At every agency a substantial proportion of middle- and upper-echelon openings are filled from outside—from other agencies, from advertisers and other businesses, from government and universities. Sometimes what started off as a single hiring becomes a full-fledged raid, because the new executives want to bring their old associates over with them. In less than two years, for example, Thompson hired six men who had worked for Leo Burnett. Garrit Lydecker, who was one of them, explains the process in terms of his handsome attaché case. "I had seven men working under me," he recalls, "and when I came back to my office after lunch on my last day they were all gathered around my desk, and they gave me the briefcase. I started to say, 'Gee, boys, you shouldn't have,' and one of them said, 'Shut up and open it.' " Lydecker opened the attaché case and found, stamped in gold on the black leather of the inside of the cover, the legend "KEEP US IN MIND." "Best investment the little rascals ever made," Lydecker says. "I've got three of them here, working for me now."

CHAPTER 6

HOW TO RUN A GREAT BIG AGENCY:

Marketing, Merging, Worrying

1.

Most agencies of any size—over $15 million in annual billings, say— have a department which Thompson does not have: a marketing, or merchandising, department. (The words are supposed to have different meanings, but there is great disagreement between people who say that marketing is merely a subsection of merchandising and people who say that merchandising is merely a subsection of marketing. Taking the industry as a whole, the words are interchangeable.) In its broadest terms, the marketing department works with the advertiser in those aspects of his selling effort which do not directly involve advertising. Grown to fully finished state, as it is at Grey Advertising and at McCann-Erickson, the marketing department will advise clients about sales organization, salesmen's compensation, dealer discounts, premium deals, and all the other aspects of getting the product to the consumer. Or, as at Ted Bates, the marketing department may exist strictly to keep the agency itself informed of what the clients are up to, so that advertising recommendations can be kept realistic in terms of the client's sales system. Or, finally, groups may be set up within departments to handle certain special markets, as in BBDO's separate Negro marketing department.

McCann-Erickson works partly through marketing experts employed at the agency itself, partly through its wholly-owned subsidiary company, Market Planning Corporation. "The target basically for a manufacturer today," says Marion Harper, president of McCann, "is to do a total marketing job, to achieve *control* of his market from the laboratory to the ultimate distribution. To service our clients, we at McCann have developed a marketing concept. We deal with the whole chain of distribution, from board chairman to retailer. We are not a marketing organization, because we don't have the responsibility. Are we an advertising agency? I don't know what you'd call it."

George Park, who runs Market Planning Corporation, has an equally ambitious view of the marketing function. "Here we are now," he says in a voice that rolls like thunder, "with the great challenge that all business faces: to become consumer-oriented, and to concentrate all our efforts on marketing. Production, inventory, warehousing— historically they were responsibilities of manufacturing. But they are not. They can't be. They must be the responsibilities of marketing." Park, a big, strong, bronzed man who used to be an appliance salesman ("I loved it—I sat on electric stoves to prove that people wouldn't get electrocuted. I stood nickels on their end on a washing machine to prove it didn't vibrate—and that took some doing"), came to McCann-Erickson from a post as assistant to the vice-president in charge of marketing at General Electric, he is, in the sense that William H. Whyte has popularized, an Organization Man. But behind his awesome rhetoric is the shrewd intelligence of a top salesman who feels certain he knows the market better than management does.

Park believes that the future belongs to the advertising agency which, like McCann, accepts marketing as the key element in its work. "We are coming into a time," he says, "when there will be more and more top-level attention paid to advertising. Soaps and cigarettes show it already. In the durable goods industries, however, the top officers still come from finance, production, engineering. It is from them that one hears the three most dangerous words in advertising: 'My . . . wife . . . thinks.' The advertising agency has a great and golden opportunity to change all that crap—but it demands day-to-day contact at the very top level. You cannot get into that level if you arrive carrying proofs of advertisements. You must give a marketing counsel."

This chance to get in on a higher level than the client's advertising department is also one of the reasons for Young & Rubicam's "merchandising" department, a group of some fifty senior men who come from what department head Sam Cherr calls "the sales managerial field. In their previous jobs, they were all responsible for the planning of sales, the managing of sales, and the managing of money." (Cherr himself came out of the newspaper business in 1925, leaving a secure job as assistant publisher of the New York *American* to join Y & R, then only one year old; at the start of 1958, he retired from his departmental responsibilities.) A merchandising man is assigned to each account group, and his primary responsibility is to keep himself and the group informed of what is going on in the market and in the client company's sales organization. He maintains his own liaison with the client, almost always in the sales manager's office, and he spends about one-third of his time in the field, checking up on sales, dealers and consumers. All projected Y & R advertising will be shown to him for his comments, and merchandising men sit on the Plans Board, but the department has no special authority, outside its own field. "If they can't persuade their associates that they know what they're talking about," Sam Cherr says, "they don't belong here."

Y & R's merchandising men write "marketing plans" for clients and make suggestions for improved sales effort, based on their observations in the field and on the agency's research work—but, unlike their confreres at other agencies, they do not strain to project sales quotas for the client. ("You don't need experts for that, you need clerks," says Sam Cherr. "All these sales quotas are just guesses, projections of past trends. If they don't come out, nobody bleeds.") And they never interfere with the client's own sales organization—

"That gets into a sphere of management that seems none of our business, and we pretend to no expertise in it." By and large, Y & R's merchandising men perform specialized work which the account representatives and their staffs try to do at other agencies, with the result that Y & R has a relatively small contact group. "Well, naturally," says Sam Cherr, glaring out from below gray eyebrows through half horn-rimmed glasses, "you can't afford this sort of thing if you have a lot of men carrying bundles."

Elsewhere, at agencies which cannot afford large marketing departments or which dislike the idea of them, executives like to ask what such departments can do that a good account representative can't do. Norman B. Norman, who says that his account representatives are all former businessmen from the sales department of corporations, refers scornfully to "merchandising men who sit around all day, until somebody says, 'Let's put a coupon on it,' and everybody goes home." Stanley Resor has grave doubts that an advertising agency can afford such great distraction from its central task. Thompson has been establishing a marketing consultant group within the agency, as a service to the account groups, and Resor feels it is important to avoid interference by marketing people in the advertising work. "It's hard enough to get this *feel* of a product all through one department," Resor says. "And the profile of a product is such an intangible thing, you can lose it so easily."

The fullest and most direct attack on the idea of marketing as an agency function comes from Thompson's Garrit Lydecker. "What most agencies fail to realize," he says, "is that there are at least as many facets to marketing as there are to advertising. They'll hire one man who worked for a client or he's the son of a client—this happens more often than you might think—and he's supposed to be an expert on all phases of marketing.

"Well, maybe he can analyze hell out of Nielsen figures and that's all he can do. Or he can hang pretty point-of-sale stuff from the chandeliers—or he's a whiz on salesmen and incentives and compensation—and that's all he can do. But he's supposed to be a *marketing* expert. Or you have the man who comes in and says, 'Keep your eye on the Southwest.' How the hell do you keep your eye on the Southwest? I had a guy come in here, the greatest sales promotion man I ever saw. If you sent him up to New England to find out what was wrong, he'd never find it—but if you *told* him what was wrong he could work up a promotion to fix it. He was supposed to be a marketing expert, too."

2.

The proliferation of added agency services has made life hard indeed for medium-large agencies, whose larger accounts are always being wooed by big agencies with extras to give. "We have a choice," says David Ogilvy sadly, "of underservicing accounts and losing them, or overservicing them and going broke." Small agencies, whose clients could not expect red-carpet treatment from the big boys, can make do with sporadic free-lance assistance from outside the agency, to impress clients or even do a bit of work. Martin L. Smith, for example, whose agency billed something less than $2 million a year but in 1957 won a major client (Emerson Radio-Television) from a major agency, keeps a file of names of people at big agencies—research experts, marketing men, sales promotion authorities—whose personal situation is such that they are always glad to pick up an extra hundred dollars or so by doing a job for Smith. Agencies like Ogilvy's, however, are expected to provide a continuing expert service, and on the whole they cannot afford it. The 4A's confidential survey of agency finances shows that no agency in the $10 million to $20 million group has a profit ratio as good as the *average* of agencies billing more than $20 million.

Obviously, the pressure is to merge (as Martin Smith did after winning Emerson), with a bigger agency or a smaller agency, to build up the billings somehow until the cost of the extra services can be taken as a thin slice from a big sausage of commissions. The pressure is felt even on higher levels: the economies to be secured by consolidation of their nonadvertising work was given as the major reason for the merger in 1957 of Erwin, Wasey & Company with Ruthrauff & Ryan— both of them agencies billing around $40 million a year.

But no agency is free from insecurities and worries. Benton &

Bowles, with billings of $100 million, has made an executive decision that it is too small and must go to $150 million before the agency can consider itself "safe." Fairfax Cone, stepping happily through the construction work on the sixth floor of Foote, Cone's handsome Chicago office building, commented: "We have a nice business, I wouldn't really want to be any bigger. But, of course, you can't plan to stay where you are." And even the very biggest of agencies, the four giants, do not feel themselves safely established in the way that great industrial corporations are firmly based.

At Thompson, obviously, the concern is over what will happen when Stanley Resor's hand leaves the controls—though Resor himself feels that the new president, Norman Strouse, has already demonstrated his ability to hold in harness even an agency as disparate in its members as J. Walter Thompson. At Y & R a similar concern is felt, because president Sigurd Larmon is nearing retirement age and the agency is divided between those who would like to see control return to the creative departments (Raymond Rubicam was a copywriter) and those who would feel more secure under the direction of a businessman like Larmon (preferably more so, since Larmon has tried as much as possible to follow Rubicam's policies).

BBDO has already switched to new leadership. Always a fantastically disorganized shop ("which is fine," says a vice-president; "there's something about a fantastically disorganized shop which *compels* individual responsibility"), BBDO was run for years as a kind of constitutional monarchy, with Bruce Barton and Alex Osborn and president Ben Duffy occupying the chairs of the mighty only by the consent of their own employees. Out of the agency's two thousand employees, some two hundred fifty are stockholders, and the governing triumvirate among them held less than 20 per cent of the stock. The fragility of this arrangement was always obvious—every year Bruce Barton told the stockholders at their annual meeting that they could throw him out any time they wished—but until the 1950's there was never any serious thought of trying it.

What set the scene for new management at BBDO was president

Duffy's skill at garnering new business for the agency. Before the war BBDO was, in the words of a vice-president and director, "an advertising agency for people who didn't need advertising"; it had few package goods accounts and virtually nothing in the line of soaps, drugs and toiletries. The attitude of the agency in those days is perhaps best expressed by one of the agency's senior copywriters: "I hired Ted Bates, you know, gave him his first agency job, and he did well here; but he was never really our sort of person. He always wanted to take those fifty-nine-cent items and move them off the shelf, and that wasn't our kind of thing at all." In the late 1940's and early 1950's Ben Duffy began pulling in accounts which literally required high-quality advertising and high-pressure work: American Tobacco, General Mills, Campbell's Soup, Revlon cosmetics, Bristol-Myers and others. An easygoing shop which could give its employees rewards in terms other than money (people who moved on from BBDO used to say that "it's a wonderful club, but the dues are too high") was shoved by unexpected success into the jetstream existence of the modern, competitive agency. The few people who were carrying the new work load, the copy group heads and the more live-wire account representatives, began to take over the agency without even knowing it.

In 1957, it became obvious that Duffy, a desperately ill man, would no longer be able to exercise authority as head of the agency. Barton and Osborn had a candidate for a new "general manager" to run BBDO, and it turned out that their candidate was not the man the younger directors had in mind. After a brief wrangle, the board elected creative head Charles Brower to the job; at the end of the year Brower became president and chairman of the executive committee (replacing Osborn). Brower has not publicly announced his goals; but change is in the air at BBDO.

Even McCann-Erickson, by far the fastest growing agency in the business, cannot look into the future without nervousness. McCann, which had never billed as much as $100 million before 1953, crossed the $200 million mark in 1956 and has definitely set its sights on Thompson's number-one position. Acceleration under forced draft,

however, will strain the resources of any organization; and at McCann
the stresses caused by a flood of new personnel and by the use of
insufficient old facilities (or overexpanded new facilities, bought to
provide for future growth) have been multiplied by the introduction
of management procedures previously unknown in the agency business.
"We would like to be the leaders in this business," says president Marion
Harper, "and after studying the examples of others we felt we would
be better off if we made a few examples of our own."

McCann's new organization is obviously patterned after the decen-
tralized systems pioneered by General Electric and General Motors
(though McCann's clients are Westinghouse and Chrysler). The
agency maintains a separate corporate headquarters (called "Fifty
Rock" because it is at 50 Rockefeller Plaza) in addition to its New
York home office and has spun off from itself or purchased on the
outside half a dozen subsidiary corporations—Market Planning, Communications Counselors (for public relations), Sales Communications
(for sales promotion), film production organizations, and even a smaller
advertising agency, Marschalk and Pratt, which has retained its
identity as an independent division of McCann. All these separate
organizations have been required, Harper says, to extend the efficiency
of McCann's service to its clients—even Marschalk and Pratt. "There
are some advertisers," Harper says, keeping his eyes in the middle
distance and his face straight, "who elect to work with a smaller agency
rather than a large one—which is their privilege. We put a smaller
agency in our organization simply to be of service to them."

Decentralization at McCann has not meant that any part of the
agency's operation is far removed from the direct, personal control of
Marion Harper. An Oklahoma boy but a Yale graduate, Harper is a
round-faced man in his early forties, wearing strong glasses and unusually well-tailored clothes, displaying an apparently unceasing drive
to success. He has worked at McCann since his graduation from
college (he has caused it to be noted in Who's Who that he started
as an office boy), and he came up to the presidency of the agency
through the research department. From the beginning of his presidency

it has been his avowed intention to make McCann the largest agency in the world; and, unlike Stanley Resor (who believes in the diversity of individuals) or Raymond Rubicam (who once told Harry Harding, head of Y & R's contact department, that "you can't staff a department just with your kind of guy; you need every kind of guy"), Harper has always felt that a monolithic organization is the quickest and most secure path to the top. He has surrounded himself with people who believe, as he does, in certain theories of business management and of human psychology; everyone at McCann talks the same language. The effectiveness of this language with businessmen has been enormous, and McCann has used it resourcefully in its elaborate speculative presentations for new business.

Constant raids on other agencies' clients and personnel have made McCann immensely unpopular in the advertising business; the usual line of attack is to say that the agency does not have enough real talent in its ranks to give a high quality of advertising service to its long list of clients. ("They don't have anything at all over there," said Milton Biow, whose own $50 million agency went suddenly out of business in 1956, "except clients.") The agency's mild rebuttal points out that two-thirds of its growth between 1952 and 1957 came from increases in the billings of its present clients. Nevertheless, many advertising men feel that McCann's growth has been that of a bubble rather than of a solid structure and that the bubble will eventually be pricked. "I think Marion *will* make his agency the biggest in the world," said John Orr Young, cofounder of Young & Rubicam, now partially retired to a role as elder statesman and consultant. After a suitable pause, Young added, "For about ten minutes."

CHAPTER 7

ADVERTISING
CAMPAIGNS:

1.

"So far as I was concerned," says Fairfax Cone, then president and now chairman of the executive committee at Foote, Cone & Belding, "it all started on August 15, 1955, when we were fired from Frigidaire. I was called down to Dayton, Ohio, and this sentence was said to me by the general sales manager of Frigidaire:

" 'I should have gone to your office to tell you this, but I have an appointment here in Dayton and I had to ask you to come here to tell you that we are going to change agencies.'

"I said, 'May I ask why?'

"He said, 'Please don't ask me.'

"The next morning, I returned to my desk and I got a message from a friend to call a man named J. C. Doyle at Special Products Division, Ford Motor Company. I didn't even know what Special Products Division was. I called Doyle on the 17th, and I said, 'Mr. Doyle, I understand you want to talk to me.' Doyle said, 'No, I don't *think* so.' I didn't have much to say after that. I called back my contact and asked him where he had got his information, what was going on here? My friend said he couldn't understand it, and would check.

"A while later my friend called back and said, 'They're going to bring out a new automobile. They wouldn't actually go after anyone who's working for GM—but if you approach them, it will be different.'

"I told my friend, 'That's very interesting, because we don't work for General Motors any more. Frigidaire just fired us.' Then I called Doyle and I said *I* wanted to talk to *him*. He said he'd be delighted."

2.

It would not be too much to say that from this moment, Fax Cone, as head of his agency's creative department and its chief copywriter, was thinking about the advertising for Ford's new car—though the name Edsel had not yet been chosen (in fact, it had been considered and rejected, and some six thousand other names were to be sifted before Edsel won out) and six anxious months were still to pass before Foote, Cone had actually been assigned the account. In the interim, Special Products Division heard presentations in Detroit from nineteen agencies besides Foote, Cone and thought highly enough of six other agencies to visit their home offices and look them over on the spot.

None of these presentations was "speculative" in the agency sense of the term—that is, nobody offered advertising ideas for Ford's new car as the reason why he should be awarded the account. (A Ford lawyer was present at all the presentations, probably, Fax Cone believes, to head off any suggestion of specific ideas. This problem of how to handle unsolicited ideas dogs all agencies and advertisers, because people who believe their notions have been appropriated may sue for damages. But nobody in his right mind could have tried to work up a full speculative campaign for Ford's new car, because Ford had revealed no information about the car to any of the competing agencies.) Instead, each agency presented its facilities and its people, particularly the people who would head up the work on the account. Foote, Cone's first presentation (carefully rehearsed beforehand in a suite at Detroit's Sheraton-Cadillac

Hotel) took five hours to get through and required the participation of seven agency executives—among them Cone himself, who promised to head up the creative group on the account, and Charles Winston, a big young man with a firm jaw, whom Cone pledged to assign as over-all supervisor for the account if his agency won the nod. Winston, who had been an account executive on Hiram Walker (liquors), account manager on Frigidaire, and account supervisor on S. C. Johnson (wax) products, could offer one unique qualification for the job: until a few months before, he had been two-thirds owner and over-all director of an automobile dealership. He knew about selling cars.

At this distance in time, Cone is not sure why he was so nervous about his agency's chance of winning the Edsel assignment. Foote, Cone, with some $76 million of 1955 billings, was the country's largest agency without an automobile account (no agency already servicing an automobile company would have been eligible: it is traditional in the advertising business that an agency does not handle competing products). Cone knew that Ford had asked its three existing agencies to recommend someone for the new car, and he had good reason to believe that at least two of them (Thompson and Y & R) had plumped hard for his bunch. He had the necessary service offices scattered through the country (New York, Chicago, Houston, Los Angeles, San Francisco) and enough funds to open a Detroit office to maintain direct contact with Ford's new division. Moreover, the circumstances of his dismissal from Frigidaire (which was then, as it had been throughout the years that Foote, Cone and its predecessor Lord & Thomas handled the advertising, the largest-selling icebox in the world) had left Cone "anxious," as he puts it, "to kick the be-jesus out of a General Motors automobile if we could."

All of these factors had to weigh on Foote, Cone's side in the Ford decision—and would be augmented by the agency's stability in personnel (with twenty-five employees of more than thirty years' service), record of handling large accounts (Foote, Cone's average client spends more than $2 million a year through the agency), and history of introducing successful new products (among them Armour's Dial soap, Toni Home Permanents, Sea & Ski, various Johnson's wax and International

Cellucotton—Kleenex and Kotex—products). As the months went by without the appointment of an agency for Ford's new car, Cone received soothing messages from friends of his who were also friends of Richard Krafve, general manager of Special Products Division; once, after three weeks had passed without any communication of any kind from Ford, Cone received a telephone call from Doyle himself, who said, "I don't know why I'm calling you exactly, but relax."

Nevertheless, Cone worried; he is a worrier by nature, and though he is still some time short of sixty his hair had been graying for years. A Californian originally, and a graduate of the University of California at Berkeley, he suffered acute attacks of nervous exhaustion from the day of his introduction to New York and big-time advertising—until Albert Lasker, who had early fixed his eye on this promising young copywriter, told him what was causing the trouble and insisted that he ease off. Today Cone maintains an abiding calm around the office, looking around through outsize horn-rimmed glasses, speaking softly and in a matter-of-fact way. He did not let his associates see how troubled he was by the hanging Ford question, and went about his daily work. In fact, he was in a client conference at Paper Mate (pens) on February 8, 1956, when the final call came in from Larry Doyle. As reported in *Fortune*, the ulitmate conversation went this way:

"Are you busy, Fax?"

"Who . . . me?"

"We would like to meet you and your people tomorrow in Detroit. Also, bring your lawyer."

3.

To the ordinary American, no purchase except the house he lives in is as important as the car he drives. "The automobile is the only thing you can get in and it becomes part of you; you're in it, you're part of *it*," said David Wallace, head of Edsel's marketing research department, two months before the first Edsels hit the road. "You get satisfaction out of the maker, the maker's name. With the Edsel, the

imagery of the car is entirely within our control. We start off un-
burdened. The only thing people are going to know about this car is
what we tell them."

This unique situation offered Foote, Cone and the Edsel advertising
department what both often defined as a challenge and an opportunity.
"The role of advertising with us will be different from what it ordinarily
is with a car," said sales manager J. C. (Larry) Doyle. (J. C. Doyle
became Larry Doyle about forty years ago, when the teen-age J. C. was
playing second base for a Ford team, and an older, unrelated Larry was
playing second base for the New York Giants.) "I don't like to talk
about advertising alone. We like to say advertising does this and that, but
it doesn't—unless it's supported by sales promotion, public relations
and solid sales effort. Right after the war, the ad people thought they
were responsible for all those sales, the promotion people the same, the
selling people thought they did it. Then competition set in, the ads
didn't go, the promotion didn't work, the salesmen couldn't sell. Everybody stopped waving his own flag. At the beginning here, though, advertising will have a special importance. It will have to establish the
image of the car, a state of mind, a receptivity to it."

The simple originality of the whole procedure made it difficult to
establish criteria: Edsel was the first new car to be introduced since 1938,
when Ford launched Mercury, and the first ever to be thrown on the
market in an entire range of models—four different series, eighteen different cars in all. "The Edsel is going to be the only really new car many
legitimate prospects have ever seen," said assistant sales manager Bob
Copeland. "This is sort of an Adam-and-Eve deal: every salesman is
going to have to sell his first Edsel to a man who will be Mr. Adam and
a lady who will be Miss Eve. We don't have to worry about what our
dealers think of the advertising; they can't say it's no good because
they've tried it and it won't work—this is a new car, they don't know
it won't work."

At the same time, the fact that the car was brand new and that
people would be drawing their first impressions of it from the advertising
put a certain limit on what the selling angle could be. "Buick can run

any kind of advertising they want," Fax Cone said, "without changing the public idea of a Buick, and we can't do that. Here in Chicago, Buick has been running full-page newspaper ads, screaming that you can buy a Buick for no more than you'd pay for the low-priced three. If we do something like that, people won't think much of the Edsel."

Before Foote, Cone could prepare advertising for Edsel, all those concerned with the account had to learn as much as possible about the car itself, the automobile market, and—since it was Ford's car—Ford views on both. Shortly after the formal contract with the agency was signed, Ford's Special Products Division organized a "Product Information Committee" to indoctrinate people from the agency. At least every other week, and sometimes more frequently, a delegation headed by Cone took a day in Detroit to sit in on private seminars which added up to a thorough course in the automobile business. "We wanted to expose them," Doyle says, "to stylists, engineers, product planners, everybody, so they could determine in their own minds the relative importance and value in advertising of certain features and facets of the product. Advertising people have a nose for news that other people don't necessarily have. We could stumble over something of great importance for advertising and forget about it, because it was of little importance in building the car. The engineers always want you to talk about their engines—'If you knew the trouble we've gone through,' that sort of thing—but there are features of comfort and convenience that mean a lot more to people. Anyway, we exposed them, then let them ask their own questions."

The man who answered the greatest number of advertising questions was Edsel's market research director David Wallace, a lean, brisk sociologist who started in advertising research in 1939, with *Time* magazine, and served at Ford International and in David Ogilvy's agency before coming to Edsel. Starting early in 1956, Wallace began assigning research contracts to Columbia University's Bureau of Applied Social Research, which accepted the assignments on the condition that it have the right to publish the results. (Wallace also allowed *The New Yorker* to publish his correspondence with Marianne Moore about a name for the Edsel.) Two theses and a dissertation have been done on aspects of Wallace's initial project, which he calculates at only one-fifth the job Columbia will do for Edsel before 1960.

"To begin with, it was almost pure sociology," Wallace said. "Status symbols. The automobile is a very powerful status symbol. Then, the obvious question one was, How do people perceive existing makes of cars? What are the gaps? The misfits? We dabbled, threw in the kitchen sink, a dragnet operation to see what came up. We dragged up a lot of images." Generally speaking, the Columbia people dragged up much the same images that others—notably the Chicago *Tribune* research department—had been finding for the past few years; this unanimity of result is one of the few things that makes this sort of research plausible. They found that Pontiac and Dodge, for example, were generally regarded as "workingmen's" cars, dependable but in no way exciting; that Chevrolet was regarded as an older man's solid vehicle and Ford as the brash young man's choice, a fast but hard-riding car (the words "Tin Lizzie" continue to hurt Ford at a time when the majority of car customers no longer know which vehicle the phrase affectionately described). And they found that Oldsmobile had an almost ideal image: it was the choice of the adventurous man in early middle age, an exciting car, an experimental car. ("When you ask people which car will be the first to have a big new advance, they'll almost all say Oldsmobile," Wallace said. "It's because Oldsmobile had the first hydramatic.")

To supplement the image studies, Wallace's group did analyses of automobile registrations, especially in Michigan, where a man who buys a car must list on his license application the make of the car he traded in when he bought the new one. The figures showed that less than 30 per cent of the people who traded in a Ford to buy a more expensive new car were going to Mercury and Lincoln. More than that percentage was going to Buick alone. "We pulled together our package," Wallace says, "a coherent whole for the agency so they could start working. This package provided a blueprint of operations: you could put your finger on a spot and say, 'We want to be here.' "

Wallace put the idea which was to underlie the advertising campaign into a single sentence: "The Edsel is the car for the young executive on his way up." To get this message across (since the slogan itself is not the sort of thing one can use in consumer advertising), Wallace proposed a program. "Our theme," he said, "is elegance. We're classy. The other cars are all fixed in a hierarchy of status, but with the Edsel, nobody knows who snoots whom. Fine. We're going to stress what this car will do for its owner. We'll have a powerful car, but we won't stress that. We won't skip the mechanical features by a darn sight, but our message, what we're really talking about, is what this car does for the individual, in terms of status."

To get these ideas beyond the position of a research man's palaver, Wallace had to sell them first to Emmet Judge, Edsel's director of merchandise and product planning, to assistant sales manager Bob Copeland and sales manager Larry Doyle, and to Fax Cone. On the whole, he did splendidly: Judge was enthusiastic from the first presentation, and even Doyle finally came around—although Doyle said, "as sales manager I'm very concerned that we don't do anything that will tend to exclude. Our first desire would be to have the car for *all* people." But Doyle had agreed that the function of the advertising would be to build an image, a state of mind—and, provided that what he called "snob appeal" was avoided, he was willing to go along with the central conception.

In Chicago, Foote, Cone's people were delighted. "Our research staff," said Fax Cone, "thought this was the best research they had ever seen." And Cone accepted what he called "Wallace's prescription," changing only a single element: in his terms, the Edsel was to be the car for the "middle-class family" rather than the "young executive" on the way up. In Detroit, where the contact men were closer to Doyle's influence, there was some reluctance to buy the idea that the product features should be secondary in the advertising. "We've heard so much about 'image' in connection with the Edsel," said Charles Winston, over-all supervisor on the account, "that we're all a little gun-shy." But the creative job was essentially Cone's responsibility, and Cone was the head of the agency.

When the arguing was done, Cone and artist Fred Ludekens, executive vice-president of Foote, Cone and one of the few artists ever to rise so high on the advertising ladder (another is chairman John Cunningham of Cunningham & Walsh), sat down to map out three separate campaigns for the Edsel. One of them was standard automotive advertising, showing the car against country-club, opera-house and stock-exchange settings, with headlines heavy on superlative adjectives and much loud talk about allegedly unique product features. ("Very stud-horsy," said Bob Copeland.) The second, a compromise between the Wallace position and industry habit, was to be built around headlines quoted from actual newspaper comment on the car. (Cone was sure that Ford public relations director Gayle Warnock, who had kept the Edsel in the public prints for some eighteen months before the car went on sale, could plant whatever statements he needed.) The third campaign closely followed the Wallace line, and it was by far Cone's favorite of the three.

The headline for the campaign—("This Is the Edsel")—was the most restrained imaginable, avoiding even the word "new." Subheadlines were actual quotes of statements made by prospective Edsel dealers and awed copywriters at their first sight of the car, kept as simple (even as banal) as they could be—such as "The Edsel Looks Expensive but It Isn't." The body copy was almost entirely declarative, with very few adjectives, giving the bald facts about Ford's new car and allowing the reader to draw his own conclusions about the importance of the various product features (the new and radically simplified motor, the self-adjusting brakes, the push-button transmission on the steering shaft, the trunk that could be unlocked from the front seat).

To match this approach, Ludekens gave the ads a simple basic layout of three incomplete horizontal bars—the top bar for the headline, the middle for the car, the bottom for the body copy—with occasional accents in the form of other, smaller drawings of the car. Throughout the opening campaign, the car was to stand alone in an island of white space, with no setting; "since no one will have seen the automobile before the ads," said John Cook, Foote, Cone's Detroit copy chief, "backgrounds would just confuse them about the lines of the car." The only nonautomotive touch was people, standing around or sitting in the car, "to scale the car," Cone said, "physically, and economically." This very quiet approach, Cone hoped, would stay the same throughout the first model year: a college-educated salesman telling a college-educated customer, in a reasonable way, why he should buy this car and why he would be pleased to be seen riding around in it. "After the first year," as Copeland said and Cone admitted, "we'll be screaming, too. But we hope we won't have to get hysterical." (Disappointing initial sales, however, forced Edsel to raise its voice after only four months.)

In January, 1957, Foote, Cone photographers "shot the clock" around a "mock-up" of the first Edsel, and the photographs were hurried back to Chicago for the artists. (Automobile ads rarely use photographs of the car, if it can be avoided. "When you take a photograph," Cone says, "you do something to an automobile which makes it look different from the way it looks when you look at it." Some special feelings about a car which most enthuse people—as the Foote, Cone staff was excited about the look of the Edsel hood from behind the driving wheel, "long and low, like a Jaguar"—simply vanish when a camera looks out on the same angle). In Chicago the artists worked under the strictest security precautions, behind locked doors, preparing from Ludekens' sketches the "comprehensives," the virtually finished advertisements which would be shown to Edsel and by Edsel to Ford's central staff. All three campaigns were fully prepared in this way—the type was set for several of the ads in each—despite Cone's feeling that only one of them was just right. Though the agency knew that the Edsel staff was in agreement with its recommended approach, Cone had to be prepared for what Winston later called "the very real chance that Henry Ford and Ernest Breech would come down on the other side." In the early spring Cone made a full presentation of all three campaigns to the Edsel people (who already knew what he was going to say), and then they carried the material up to "central staff." Ford and Breech bought Cone's recommendations—though, Copeland says, "they wanted some things pointed up here and there, quite rightly"—and advertising began to roll out to the photoengravers.

4.

"We think it would be awful," said Fax Cone, "for the advertising to compete with the car." So the copy was quiet, asserting the smallest number of claims for the car, and the illustrations were planned to make the Edsel look its natural self, rather than some long, low impossibility. But the impression which advertising gives is not merely a matter of what is in the ads: there is also the question of volume, of insistence, of omnipresence. Working on a new car, which had a reservoir of public interest to draw upon, Foote, Cone faced the problem of how large a splash should be made at the very beginning, how far the faucet should be turned.

It would not have been particularly difficult to make the first days of the new car "Edsel Week" all over the country, and on several occasions the agency was tempted to try it. At one point the account group considered the idea of a magnificent color television spectacular, to appear on all three networks at once (or at least on NBC and CBS), at the very moment the car went on sale. According to this plan, no pictures of the car would be released to newspapers or magazines, and the new Edsel showrooms would be draped until the evening of the television show. In each showroom a color television set would be installed. As the show went on, the dealers' doors would be flung open for the first time, and the American public—at home by its television sets or crowded by the doors of the new showrooms—would have the glory of the Edsel revealed to them in a single sunburst. This plan went far enough so that John Simpson, head of Foote, Cone's Chicago television department, sounded out the networks on "availabilities," the time periods that could be made available for such a show. When all the figures were in, however, it appeared that the TV show (time and talent, plus penalties to be paid to the regular sponsors at this hour) would run well over $700,000; and the plan as a whole would involve more than a million dollars—out of the $8 million set aside for the entire first four months. It was too much money—and, moreover, the brilliance of such an announcement might well blind people to the car itself, going against the grain of the entire campaign.

There was another way to start the car off with an explosion: a "teaser" campaign, a series of ads which would announce that the car was coming, coming, almost here . . . without revealing anything much about it. N. W. Ayer had done such a campaign for Ford's Model A, nearly thirty years before; and, while the public excitement attendant on the first Edsel was nowhere near so great as that awaiting the Model A, a comparable fever might have been attained by lighting a few matches under the thermometer. Here, again, Foote, Cone was hard put to make a recommendation, and the Edsel Division had difficulty with its decision. A large-scale nation-wide teaser campaign would cost, again, well over a million dollars, money which might be much better spent on selling the car later on. Moreover, building expectation was at least partly the job of Edsel's public relations staff; and public relations chief Gayle Warnock had worked out an imposing list of magazine articles and news stories for the week just before E-day. Warnock's news breaks might tease the public far enough, without the expenditure of advertising money. The final decision, by the agency and the division, was to go halfway with a teaser campaign, to run a series of four preannouncement ads in *Life, Look* and the *Saturday Evening Post,* to broadcast a crescendo of radio spots in the weeks directly before the car went on sale, and to run one big teaser ad (showing only the Edsel's steering wheel, with the electric shift buttons on the center post, as a symbol for the entire car) in some twelve hundred newspapers the weekend before the showrooms opened.

In the event, this plan, too, collapsed: Ford central staff decided to eliminate the teaser campaign entirely (saving only the four preannouncement magazine ads, which were run only in *Life* and concentrated on the idea that this car, though new, had been on the testing grounds for years) and to put the money into special institutional advertising for the Ford Company itself, keyed to the introduction of the Edsel. Neither the division nor Foote, Cone was at all happy with this arrangement (which also cost Foote, Cone about a million dollars of

billing on the account, since Kenyon & Eckhardt does all Ford institutional advertising). But Ford had put up some $250 million to start
the Edsel, and if central staff felt that a million dollars should be spent
to publicize this fact rather than to tout Edsels, there was nobody at the
agency or the division who could quarrel. "We counseled with them
about it," said Larry Doyle dryly.

The end result was a staggered rather than an instantaneous introduction. Photographs of the car were released to newspapers and magazines
for publication August 27. Edsel billboards blossomed on the Labor Day
weekend, starting August 31. The first newspaper ads ran the evening of
September 3, heralding the public opening of the showrooms the next
day; the first three magazine ads were on the stands—in *Life*, *The New
Yorker*, *Time*—on September 5. Other magazine ads were scattered
through the month. Ads were placed in one set of Sunday newspaper
supplements for September 8, in another for September 15. There was
no radio or television advertising whatever during the early weeks, except
for the Ford institutional campaign. Edsel's first use of television did not
come until October 13, when the division sponsored Bing Crosby's first
television appearance, with Frank Sinatra as co-star, in the time slot
usually occupied by the Ed Sullivan hour. By that time, of course, most
of the news value had worn off the Edsel: partly by accident but
mostly by design, the car had slipped into the American consciousness
so gradually that it might have been there all along.

The strategy and tactics of the Edsel launching will be subjects of
argument in the automobile and advertising business for years to
come—especially attractive subjects since nobody will ever be able to
prove that Doyle and Cone and Wallace were right or wrong, that
more or fewer Edsels would have been sold if the introduction had
come with a bang. If Edsel in 1960 sells 400,000 cars, few people
at Ford or Foote, Cone will regard the argument as very interesting—
even though not everybody who buys an Edsel happens to be "a young
executive on his way up."

CHAPTER 8

ADVERTISING
CAMPAIGNS:

*Idea and
Execution—
Every Day*

"It is far easier to write ten passably effective sonnets, good enough to take in the not too inquiring critic, than one effective advertisement that will take in a few thousand of the uncritical buying public."

Aldous Huxley

"My children know I'm in advertising, but it doesn't interest them much. They don't ask me about it. The other day, though, we were all sitting watching television, and one of these cartoon commercials came on. It showed two big wrestlers coming into a ring, one with the label PAIN on his robe, and the other with the label ORDINARY PAINKILLER. Something like that. Anyway, PAIN threw ORDINARY PAINKILLER right out of the ring, and stomped around afterward. Then another wrestler came on, with this brand name stenciled on his robe, and he threw PAIN out of the ring, knocked him out completely, you see.

"I didn't think much of it, one way or the other, but my younger boy called me aside, out of the room. He said, 'Dad, am I to understand that a bunch of grown men sat around and thought up that thing? And another bunch of grown men sat around and said it was a good idea? And another bunch of grown men went to all the work to make a movie of it?'

"What could I say? I told him that was just what had happened. He walked away, shaking his head."

Ed Zern, vice-president,
Geyer Advertising

1.

Nothing could be more atypical of normal advertising procedure, of course, than the introduction of a new automobile. The workaday copywriter spends the great bulk of his time writing new words to fit old themes for products which have been around some time. Every agency will turn out a certain number of new campaigns every year— but the need for something fresh and different is still rare enough so that it causes great agitation in an agency, a vast flap of overtime work and nervous indigestion, every time the demand is made.

The basic creative job is the discovery of what is variously called the "sales" or "purchase" proposition, the "platform," or the "campaign theme," and there are a dozen different ways of handling it. At Foote, Cone the primary responsibility lies with the creative group, whose members start work with a general meeting at which the copy chief outlines the nature of the problem and the factual frame within which a solution must be found. Members of the group then go off and think about it, and a second meeting develops one or more campaign themes which look promising. Ads are prepared in rough form (a good art director can turn out in fifteen minutes a rough illustration which suggests everything that will be found in the finished advertisement, down to the sweat on the glasses which hold the cold drinks), and a week later the group meets again to look over what sort of advertising the suggested themes have produced. "We go down the line," says Melcon Tashian, head of Foote, Cone's New York art department, "picking all the ads apart—is this headline right? should we have two children here, or a mother and one child? After we've talked over all the rough ads, we'll usually find a single *direction* we want to proceed in." As an ordinary matter, the account representative does not participate in these meetings of the creative group; only after the group has decided on the direction, and made some advertising to demonstrate where the direction leads, does the copy chief call him in, to "show him the philosophy," Tashian says, not intolerantly, "and sell him what we've done."

At Ted Bates & Company the development of the Unique Selling Proposition is the responsibility of the copywriters alone, though they may call in help from the world of medical research if they feel the need for it; since virtually all the heads of the agency are still working copywriters, responsibility lies mainly in their hands. In David Ogilvy's agency, similarly, the individual copywriter, sitting alone at his desk, is the man in charge. "Planning a campaign," says David McCall, the very young second-in-command of Ogilvy's copy department, "I sit down with all the facts I can get on the product, soak all that up, absorb it—except maybe the very technical stuff that you can't use with the public. Then I get old *U.S. Cameras,* because I find looking at pictures a great stimulus to ideas; and I get the Watkins book and the *Printer's Ink* book on the Hundred Greatest Advertisements, because I'm a great cribber. You've got to know the precedents—it's just like the law, in a way. So you sit leafing through with no ideas, but with your head full of information about the product, and something's bound to hit. At least you hope it will. Then, before giving the idea to the art director, or writing the copy, you might take it to the account executive or you might not, depending." It can be even more simple than that; Norman, Craig & Kummel's Kay Daly, for example, gets all the facts and then "forgets them. Instead, I think, if I were a woman—which I am—what would make me want to buy this product?"

At McCann-Erickson, on the other hand, the emphasis is on the marketing experts and the research department. A product group chaired by the account supervisor and containing six to eight senior men (of whom two will come from the creative department) sifts through the factual material and arrives at a "purchase proposition" which is written down in full detail, with explanations, as a "start-work report." This report is the agency's plan of attack on the client's overall problem, and though it is built around the campaign theme, it will contain much more than that. "Normally," says Larry Deane, head of McCann's management service department, "it takes twenty weeks to prepare a plan." The full report then goes up to a "marketing plans board," on which there are two representatives of the creative department, which accepts the plan or revises it. By and large, McCann copywriters do not come into the job until after the purchase proposition has been approved by the client; they are, as Anthony Hyde puts it, "left free to develop the proper 'audience strategy,' which is the *real* creative problem." In other words, they make the ads rather than think up the ideas. (Or so, at any rate, flows the chart; in fact, McCann's creative procedures are not greatly different from those at other agencies. As creative director Jack Tinker puts it, "When David McCall sits down with all the facts he can get, he is doing just what our people do when they sit down with the 'start-work report.'")

The Thompson company, inevitably, occupies a middle ground. Discussion of the "sales proposition" begins at a meeting of account supervisor, account representative and creative group head. According to group head Ed Robinson, the account supervisor opens the meeting with the words, "We have X amount of advertising to do next year for this client, and these are the problems." Long discussion by the three men produces one or more sales propositions, which the group head relays down to his copywriters and artists, who may or may not like the proposed ideas. Comments from the creative staff are carried by the group head to a second meeting of the three top men, and a single sales proposition is agreed upon—subject to further discussion after one of Thompson's *ad hoc* Review Boards has examined the idea, and after Jim Young, who comes in for two weeks every two months to act as "senior consultant" and look over all the agency's major advertising campaigns, has given the account group the benefit of his forty-two years' experience as a working copywriter. Final decision, as always at Thompson, rests in the hands of the account supervisor, a power which is allowed to him, in the true Thompson tradition, on condition that he does not get ornery about it.

The original source of the basic selling idea may be outside the agency; these days, it is no surprise if the campaign theme is something which has been worked up by a research firm. Those researchers who are in business to discover what "motivates" consumers will automatically, as part of the service, suggest campaign themes to their clients. Thus, Ernest Dichter found that most women refused to bake cakes because of "fear of failure," and bought cake mixes to eliminate mischance rather than to save time; he recommended to General Mills and BBDO the campaign built around Betty Crocker's "I Guarantee," and featuring illustrations of very simple cakes which a housewife might see herself producing. (Actually, BBDO was doing its own research, leading to the same results, at the same time.) Alfred Politz will compare "issue values" for his clients to find one best advertising theme; Politz told Coca-Cola and McCann-Erickson that Coke's great asset was its omnipresence, the fact that everybody and every place served it, it was irrefutably part of the American scene and the advertising should stress its comparability to apple pie as the primary American gastronomic phenomenon. And not infrequently, of course, the client knows just which sales argument for his product he wants to have the agency push, and he is not going to be talked out of it. Once Leo Burnett had made Marlboro a big seller with his masculine image campaign, the Philip Morris Company demanded similar advertising for its Parliament and Philip Morris brands—and could not be dissuaded.

2.

"Once you've found a Unique Selling Proposition," says Rosser Reeves of Ted Bates, "any good copywriter can write a good ad. The rest is just wordsmithing. Not that wordsmithing isn't important—we pay a fortune for copywriting talent. But five top copywriters might turn out five entirely different ads, all good, from a single USP—while all the wordsmithing in the world won't move the product off the shelf if the claim isn't right."

Most copy people would take a different tack; admitting the primacy of the sales pitch when there is a significantly new claim to be made, they would argue that in most fields where advertising is heavy everybody is making pretty much the same pitch, and it is the creative man's ability to present the claim most effectively which pulls his client into the lead. The decision about the basic sales argument may have been taken out of the copywriter's hands by an executive committee, but the copywriter's talent for ways and means is still, in this view, the determining factor in a campaign's success or failure. It was easy enough for Foote, Cone to decide that Colgate had pre-empted the bad-breath business and Gleem the cavities business, so Pepsodent should stick to cleaning the teeth; but without copywriter and jazz hobbyist Don Williams to write "You'll Wonder Where the Yellow Went" the Pepsodent claim would never have drawn much public attention. Similarly, Young & Rubicam, like every other agency, knew that beer drinking was a way to let your hair down; but it took a creative man's intuition to come up with Bert and Harry Piel.

Basically, the advertising copywriter and the advertising artist work to make the product claim believable, in terms of the product itself and in terms of the people who will use it. Agencies (mindful, perhaps, of Claude Hopkins' "Washed With Live Steam") make sure that every copywriter who works on an account has had a thorough tour of the client's factory; these excursions rarely produce a new claim, but they almost always give the copywriter an added command of detail, which adds conviction to his writing. (They also give him some respect for the client, which he does not always have before he sees how complicated the client's business is.) For the same reason, the copywriter is also expected to master most of the technical literature in the product field; "working on toothpastes," says Thompson's Dick Neff, "I've read a shelf of dentistry books as long as my arms."

Sometimes these one-man research jobs, done by people with a copywriter's intuition, lead to changes in the product itself, because the creative department feels the sales pitch will be more believable if these changes are made. Thus, Thompson urged the J. B. Williams Company to make its shaving cream yellow, which would "demonstrate" the lanolin content. When new products are in question, many agencies like to sit in on the planning from the laboratory stage, hoping to build in a feature which will make a claim more believable. Norman, Craig & Kummel suggested to Revlon the idea of silicon in a hand lotion, and the name Silicare, to make a medical sales argument more convincing. Sometimes, in browsing around a product field, the copywriters will find a completely new idea for a product feature, which they think can be sold. Random investigations in toothpaste brought Thompson's creative staff to a man who had invented a tube nozzle which colored the sides of the emerging ribbon of toothpaste. Without even telling Lever Brothers what they were up to, the copywriters and artists picked a name (Stripe), designed a box, and laid out in rough form an advertising campaign on the slogan "Looks Like Fun, Cleans Like Crazy." Then they took the package to Lever Brothers, which most unexpectedly found itself with a new product.

Most of the time the shrewd copywriter works on the technical end of a product not to explore its manufacture but to find additional use values for it—to suggest, for example, that Q-tips are good, clean substitutes for fingers in children's finger painting. A man who worked intimately for some years with Jim Young on the Thompson Review Board recalls that Young's first question on a food account was always, "Can you think of some new *way* to eat it?" BBDO's Jean Rindlaub applied exactly this approach to the Campbell's Soup account. "We didn't have any share-of-market problem," she says. "What we had to do was increase the consumption of soup. We went out into the market and talked about soup—everybody had already heard about soup. The motivational research wasn't much help; it just said soup was warm and comforting. So we began having fun with it, myself, all the girls in the office. We had soup in mugs, soup for breakfast, soup on the rocks, soup shakes, scrambled eggs with soup, chilled tomato soup from a pitcher. We had more damn fun," Mrs. Rindlaub says, making her black eyes dance in the house-motherly manner she cultivates as a personnel technique with her girl copywriters, "and it worked."

Usually, of course, as almost every advertising man will admit, the client knows more about his product and its uses than the agency is ever going to learn (the head of merchandising at Lennen & Newell claims that he wouldn't have anybody working for him who didn't know more about the client's product than any single person in the client company; but this attitude is uncommon). What the copywriter usually contributes to the client is not so much his understanding of the product itself as his intuitive knowledge of public attitudes. His job is not to make the campaign theme logically watertight in terms of the product and its features, but to convince his readers, with whatever logic or illogic best buttresses the claim, that they want what he is selling.

Technically, the task falls into two parts: catching the readers' attention and then winning their belief. Both halves of the job require, however, much the same insight into the workings of the public mind. Every agency has rules to guide copywriters and artists in their efforts to "stop" the reader or television watcher. (David Ogilvy's codex contains the bald prescription, "to attract women, show babies or women; to attract men, show men"), but nobody contends that these rules can pull an ad any higher than the standard level of mediocrity. Research of the various kinds can help the copywriter find the arguments the public wishes to believe, but research, like rules, can do nothing to make an ad extraordinary. Only the copywriter's talent, working on the research reports as though they were part of the copywriter's own experience, can give an ad unusual effectiveness. Outside the few agencies which are strongly research-minded, like McCann-Erickson, most advertising men would rather have a copywriter ignore the research reports if the material they contain does not convince him. "Too many copywriters," says Ogilvy, "are using research as a drunken man uses a lamppost—for support, rather than illumination."

Almost every copy chief believes that the people under him spend too little time going into the market place and talking to customers. "They don't do enough investigating of what the product is like where it's being sold," says George Gribbin of Y & R, who started his advertising career with the May Company department store in Cleveland.

"Department store training is inadequate for agency advertising, because department store advertising is *news,* and it's read as news. But it has one advantage. In a store, the copywriter has to be his own reporter, his own contact man with the buyers. He doesn't have a research department to feed him information, a merchandising department to feed him information. He has to go down where the customers are to get his information by himself."

Talking with customer, dealers, and people at the client company will often give a copywriter the necessary verisimilitudinous headline for his ad; sometimes it will even provide a slogan for an entire campaign. All the Foote, Cone headlines for the first Edsel campaign came out of eavesdropping while visitors and prospective dealers discussed the car with the Edsel sales department. "I'd Walk a Mile for a Camel" was, if legend may be believed, said to a billboard painter by a man who had just bummed a cigarette from him. "Ask the Man Who Owns One" appeared in a letter from the president of the Packard Company to a correspondent who had inquired about Packard's car. One of the best-remembered of all advertisements carried as its headline the astonished remark of the co-owner of a mail-order fruit business when the head of his advertising agency showed him the proposed media schedule for the next season: "Imagine Harry and Me Advertising Our Pears in *Fortune!*"

Special problems for the copywriter may be posed by the medium in which the ad will appear. "All women want to be beautiful," says Howard Connell of Foote, Cone, "and that's always the basic theme for a cosmetic. But you'd use a different appeal for a sixteen-year-old girl and a thirty-five-year-old woman; you wouldn't run the same ad in *Seventeen* and in *Vogue.*" Again, the advertisement may have to be tailored to the talents or the prejudices of a television entertainer: thus Grey Advertising, putting a commercial for Lilt on *I Love Lucy,* worked long and hard to write something which Lucille Ball and Desi Arnaz would feel was "our kind of thing," and thereby eligible for delivery by the stars of the show themselves. Or the special interests of the audience may dictate a particular approach: Ed Zern's ads for Nash in *Field & Stream* are about hunting and fishing almost as much as they are about Nash, though they keep the same selling points that Nash uses in more general media.

Every once in a while the copywriter's feeling for believability will force an odd change in a client's marketing pattern. Foote, Cone, for example, worked up what it considered to be a particularly persuasive campaign on the excellence of Johnson's car polish and what it could do for the finish of an automobile. But the creative staff felt that nobody would believe it of a wax selling for 69 cents a jar and that people would be wary about applying a cheap wax to the paint job of their expensive automobile. Tests were run at different prices, and the higher-priced cans sold better. Johnson added some new and expensive ingredients to the polish, upped the advertising budget, and priced the product at $1.69.

3.

The copywriter's talent is merely one of the many that go into the production of a finished advertisement, in print or in broadcast; but it is generally true to say that the art director, the television director, the photographer or artist, the cameraman or photoengraver, must all fit their work within the frame of the copywriter's presentation of the established campaign theme. A few individual art directors have shown themselves to be first-class salesmen, and the copywriters who work with them listen carefully to what they say—but articulate artists usually move up to be copywriters, or factota in the over all creative department, where the pay is better. A few agencies—most notably Doyle Dane Bernbach—work on the principle that the copywriter and the artist are equal, and that an art director's inability to find a powerful visual image for a copywriter's idea is quite possibly the copywriter's fault and not the artist's. "There was a time," says Bernbach's Bob Gage, "when copy people would write copy and make little sketches; they'd send in a typed sheet and some bad little drawings, and tell the art director to make layouts. But it was hollow. Here, in this shop, every art director has to be an idea man. He has to know how to think and he has to want to sell."

As an ordinary matter, however, the approach Gage regards as dead and gone persists as normal operating procedure at other agencies, and the art director who wishes to exert influence in the final advertising can do so only by consistently and quietly making the copywriter look better than he is. Decisions about the kind of illustration to use— photographs, paintings, line drawings, cartoons—are worked out by the copywriter and the art director together, the art director proposing and the copywriter disposing (subject to further approval higher up). Usually, the art director chooses the artist or the photographer and models who will do the actual art work (except at small agencies, which live partly by extra fees for finished art, agency art directors do not paint the pictures; they do layouts, and rough sketches to guide an outside artist or a subordinate employee). But a new photographer or artist on an account must be approved by the copywriter and the account executive before the art director can give out the assignment. And at some agencies the choice of photographer or artist is in the hands of the copy chief, with the art director merely cheering from the sidelines. Kay Daly of Norman, Craig & Kummel chooses photographers and models for the ads she supervises, and goes to the photographer's studio to make sure he gets the mood she wants.

Backgrounds, clothing and accessories in the final illustration are almost as carefully watched as the sales argument itself. Most large agencies have "styling departments," which are responsible (under the art director and, probably, the copywriter) for setting the right scene in the ad. Thus, for example, art director Harry Olsen of BBDO tells his styling department to be sure that the bowl in which the Campbell's soup will repose, the plate under the bowl, the spoon beside the plate, the table linen and the table itself are all "a *little* above the average taste, but not all the way over into the gourmet end that would put it out of the reach of the general public." A home economics staff bakes the cakes and cooks the meat for food advertisements; dress designers will create creations, and have them executed by costume shops or "little dressmakers," for those ads (mostly cosmetics) which require what is called high style.

A number of technical talents go into the final print advertisement, which would be much less professional without them. Most larger agencies have a staff typographer, who picks the type face which fits best into the general "feel" of the campaign. (It is amazing how passionately art people and typographers will argue about the relative merits of serif types—those with ornamental touches, such as little vertical lines coming down from the ends of the top bar of a T—as against the more stark sans-serif style. David Ogilvy, who employs two typographers, feels this sort of discussion is easily overdone; he likes to visualize two smartly dressed women walking down Fifth Avenue, one saying to the other, "You know, I'd have tried that new toilet soap if only they hadn't set the body copy in nine-point Garamond.") At every agency, large or small, there is a production department or a production man who works with an outside photoengraver to make sure the art work will reproduce properly in the newspapers or magazines in which it will appear.

Copywriters and art directors often want big, black newspaper ads to help establish a "masculine" image; but ink will smudge on a newspaper page. (This is especially so if the ad is to appear on a page which is printed on the "first impression," when a blank roll of newsprint goes through the press, which prints one side only. The paper then twists over a roller and comes back under another press which prints the other side, or "second impression." The action of the roller on the still wet ink of the first impression may make a mess of any ad which tries for a solid black effect in any part of the art work. Newspapers cannot tell an agency in advance whether an ad will be printed first or second impression, so the illustration must be light enough to reproduce well either way. These problems have been multiplied by the introduction of color printing in newspapers; "first impression" color ads, unless very carefully planned by production department and photoengraver, can come to look like a sloppy painter's palette rather than an illustration of a product.)

Even magazine reproduction, though infinitely better than anything a newspaper can offer (because a magazine is printed on coated paper, which fits more evenly against the printing plate than newsprint does, and does not have newsprint's ugly habit of absorbing and spreading the ink), presents grave problems to the production department. A full-color advertisement is made up of numberless little dots, as many as 28,000 to a square inch of paper, each dot in one of only four colors (yellow, red, blue and black, printed in that order from four separate plates). Some colors—shoe-leather brown, for example—are extremely hard to reproduce from the standard four-color palette. Even more serious are manufacturers' off-color packages, which, everyone feels, should appear in print in precisely the right hue. Where the company is a big enough advertiser, the magazines may be extra co-operative: thus Campbell's Soup—which has had the premier position in the *Saturday Evening Post* since the memory of man runneth not to the contrary (the position is the first ad after the central reading section) —has arranged with *Life* and the *Post* for a separate red ink, the color of the Campbell's package, in the printing of Campbell's ads.

When artist and copywriter wish to achieve subtle effects, shading pastels and a romantic mood, they are often licked by the high speeds at which magazines print their issues. Subtle color effects are produced by the adjacency of the little color dots (which do not print one on top of the other, but side by side, as examination of a color advertisement through a good magnifying glass will quickly demonstrate). For the effect in the original color photograph to be reproduced exactly, there cannot be so much as a millimeter of tolerance in the angle and position of the four separate printing plates: each one must strike the page at precisely the same point. The mass circulation magazines, printing five and six million copies a week, use presses which turn out upwards of seven hundred copies a minute, and at such speeds precise "registration" is impossible. Every once in a while the registration goes off completely (double lines around the automobile, or the shadow of a second pair of lips on the girl's chin), in which case the agency may ask, and may receive, a cash rebate from the magazine, or a "make-good," a rerun of the advertisement at no charge. ("You never," says production director Eli Gordon of Thompson, somewhat grimly, "get a make-good from *Life* or the *Post*.") But the registration may be off so slightly that the naked eye cannot see anything wrong with the picture—and yet the saddened production man and the miserable art director note the muddy ruination by inexact registration of a delicate piece of art work, lovingly hand-finished at the photoengraver's by a retoucher who is an artist himself ("And why shouldn't he be?" argues Grey's Ralph Froelich, "why should he ruin a good Ektachrome by rubbing down the eyebrows when they ought to be bold?"), proved on the magazine's own paper stock by the photoengraver's own high-speed press, guaranteed to the client as perfect . . . There is nothing to be done about it, just as there is nothing to be done when the picture of an elephant's backside, printed on the other side of the page, strikes through the pale Bahama waters of the bathing-suit advertisement, placing the bathing beauty in a position as uncomfortable as it is unglamorous. Nobody knows what an advertising man suffers.

4.

For television advertising all the rules are different. The campaign theme must be visualized not as an illustration but in terms of what Rosser Reeves calls the "video gimmick" (he used to call it the "video device," but shorthand at Bates reduced this phrase to VD, which he felt gave the agency an unhealthy look). The creative reference frame is not prose composition ("I don't think," says George Gribbin, "that a television copywriter particularly needs a feeling for words"), but dramatic timing. Excellent print copywriters with a gift for static illustration, who had no trouble tossing off forensics for radio announcers, found themselves unmanned by the combination of moving pictures and spoken words. Often they lack even the most elementary sense of timing: "You'll get instructions," says Rex Cox of Sarra, one of the half dozen largest producers of television film commercials, "which tell you to show a man coming home, kissing his wife, sitting down in the easy chair, putting on his slippers, reaching for a glass of beer—and that's going to take eighteen seconds, even at a dead run

—and on the audio side, all the announcer has to say is, 'Always reach for So-and-so's beer.' Or it will go the other way: the screen is just supposed to show a man reaching out his hand for a glass of beer, while the audio has a long spiel for the product."

At the beginning the agencies generally handled this problem by turning over to firms like Sarra and Transfilm a set of rough ideas for a script, which the television film company was to "work up" into a commercial. Meanwhile, the agencies beat the bushes for new personnel, impressing recruits from the drama schools and the ranks of unperformed playwrights, and forming them together in rough marching order as a "television copy department." This experiment in the managing of a new form turned out not to be entirely successful, partly because it produced different approaches for television and print copy, vitiating the strength of the campaign theme, and partly because the dragooned playwrights often had little instinct for selling.

The next step at some agencies (especially those which concentrate on broadcast commercials, like Ted Bates and William Esty) was to consolidate the two copy departments, with television work channeled to the more salesmanlike of the new talents and the more dramatically facile of the old copywriters. At others, the separate television department was maintained, but with television copywriters firmly slotted under the thumb of the group head, a print copy man. A few of the largest agencies absorbed their new television writers into over-all television departments, which worked on programs as well as commercials; and a man from the television department was slipped into each creative group, to act as technical counsel to and occasional substitute for the copywriter who wrote the print advertising. Thus, the wheel turned full circle, and the print copywriter, as the experienced planner of approaches to the sales argument, became once again the man who decided whether the TV commercial should show "real" people or prominent personalities or cartoon characters or the product itself in motion (like the marching Lucky Strike cigarettes which provided an opening for *Your Hit Parade* for more than six years.) But now the print copywriters knows—or can easily find out—what he is doing.

What goes to the television film company these days is a complete shooting script, plus a "story board," a set of rough drawings placed in television-screen-shaped boxes, which are to guide the film director in putting together the commercial (or the television director if the commercial is to be broadcast "live"). Usually the script is submitted to several companies—there are dozens of them now, including all the major Hollywood studios—and bids are solicited for the job. (Cartoons cost more than commercials which use live action, but they can probably be shown more often before the audience gets sick of them.) Over to the television film studio when the deal has been made traipse the agency's stylists and home economists, casting experts and a director from the agency's television department, and the copywriter, who must be present to change lines if it appears that an actor is uncomfortable with the script, or that the sound track runs 62 seconds instead of the required 58 seconds. In the textbooks it says that 125 words a minute will do just about right, but the copywriter cannot be sure his script will come out on the button until he sees an actor read it in synchronization with the relevant pictures. Getting everything to come out exactly on time—60 seconds of picture, 58 seconds of sound—is the simple, nagging problem that takes all the time in the studio.

In and around the shooting stage, usually a room two stories high, hung with Klieg lights and microphone booms and cameras on infinitely adjustable pedestals, stand the actors and actresses, half a dozen people from the agency, the film company's own producer and director, two cameramen, a sound engineer, assorted stagehands and lighting engineers, and perhaps even somebody from the client's advertising department. This great assemblage of expertise watches and coaches and makes suggestions, and finally it all goes perfectly—except that it's 1½ seconds too long, in a place that the film editor won't be able to cut. So everything starts over again; Hollywood figures five "takes" for every finished scene, but a television commercial demands ten. In advertising, it's always what looks easiest, and least-worth-doing-anyway, that causes the most anguish.

Part III | GETTING THE
MESSAGE OUT
TO THE PEOPLE

CHAPTER 9

OYSTERS AND PEARLS:

Media Selections

1.

"Markets make media," writes Neil Borden; a bald but complete, apparently simple and unquestionably true statement. The problem is: there are too many markets, and they overlap. There are local markets, regional markets, national markets. There are male and female markets. There is an upper-class market, a middle-class market, a lower-class market. There are urban, rural and (definitely, now; painstaking research has proved the visible fact) suburban markets. There are old-folks markets, middle-aged markets, young-married markets, teen-age markets, children's markets. And, of course, there are the markets segregated by common interests: the home-furnishings-and-decorations market, the sport's-car market, the high-fidelity market, the baby-products market, the gourmet market, the fashion market. To reach these many markets there are many media: some 1,750 daily news-papers, 450 television and 3,300 radio broadcasting stations, 600 consumer magazines, 325,000 billboards, and several million car cards in vehicles of public transportation. Only the blind and deaf or utterly comatose (who rarely spend much money anyway, or some method would be found to reach them) can avoid daily contact not with just one but with dozens of advertising media. No company—not even General Motors, with some 4 per cent of the entire national output rolling through its factories—can hope to make a splash in all of them. The advertiser's problem is one of selection; and standing in serried ranks, waiting to help him make that selection, are thousands upon thousands of media salesmen, carrying literally millions of facts and figures, real and alleged.

In no other area of his work does the advertising man find so much information, so much apparently logical basis for his decisions. Circulation and audience figures, combined with rate cards, give a "cost per thousand" figure, which tells the advertiser how much he must spend to put his message before a thousand people by the use of this particular medium. Breakdowns of the circulation number enable the advertiser to compare his sales in a market to the circulation delivered in that market by each advertising medium. Often a medium will even deliver an analysis of the brand preferences, economic status, personal habits and psychological quirks of its audience, which the manufacturer can then compare with the characteristics of the people who buy his product, as developed by the consumer research companies. And yet, media buying remains as personal a matter as anything else in advertising—a business of hunches and intuitions, of favors done and favors received, of calculated threats, denunciations and punishments. "Anybody who tells you that media buying is entirely scientific," says senior vice-president Jim McCaffrey of David Ogilvy's agency, "is either a liar or a coward."

The problem is that all media purchases represent a choice of alternatives, and only rarely are the alternatives really comparable. No advertiser can know for sure that a $3 million network television program will do more or less for him than the same amount of money put into local television, or radio, or newspapers, or magazines, or billboards, or a combination of all of them—or even a different network program. He can, it is true, get relative cost-per-thousand figures if he insists:

he can discover that his $65,000-a-week television program went into 9 million homes, at a cost of $7.22 per thousand homes; that his $22,242 full-page black-and-white weekly ad in *Life* went to a paid circulation of 6 million, at a cost of $3.71 per thousand primary readers; that his one-minute announcements on radio station KWK St. Louis, running thirty times a week for $21 each, cost about $1.27 per thousand households listening; that his 1,000-line ad in the Louisville *Courier-Journal* cost $830, or $2.08 per thousand homes receiving the paper; that his 20-second spot announcement on WRCA-TV, New York, appearing Monday through Friday at 7:29 P.M., all year long, cost $880 every night, or about $2.80 for every thousand viewing households; that his 46 billboards in Portland, Oregon, cost him roughly $48 each every month, or 25 cents per thousand for the 192,000 pairs of eyes which will pass by during the month.

Unfortunately, when the advertiser knows all this (and he can find out most of it easily enough, by checking survey data against the figures in the Standard Rate and Data Service monthly books), he still knows nothing. Even as a matter of statistics pure and simple, the figures are meaningless. The audience for the network television show is extrapolated from a study of the viewing habits of some 930 families which happen to have Nielsen Audimeters in working order attached to their television sets, and this procedure does not give an exact measurement. (Measurements of audiences for local stations are even more inexact; they might be described as sound guesses.) Moreover, the sponsor of a half-hour network show gets three one-minute commercial cracks at his audience, reducing the cost per thousand *per commercial minute* to $2.42 a home. This figure for a minute compares favorably with $2.80 per thousand for a 20-second spot announcement on WRCA-TV, a local station. And, finally, two and one-half people are watching every television set (it says here; perhaps the half is a nitwit), so the cost per thousand *people* per commercial minute is only $1. Demonstrably, though it costs $3 million a year, the television show is really very cheap; on the bandwagon, everybody, please.

Life's circulation, as compared with the TV audience, is very directly measured, the final figures sworn, certified and examined by the Audit Bureau of Circulation. (How the circulation was obtained, of course, is another matter; people turn on their television sets more or less voluntarily, while somebody sells them magazine subscriptions, often forcibly.) But the paid circulation is obviously not the full measure of *Life*'s audience: several people live in the home which subscribes, Uncle Joe comes visiting and riffles through, the copy is thrown in the dustbin and picked up by the garbage man, who carries it home for the baby to cut up. Studies by Alfred Politz Research tell *Life*, which tells the world, that no fewer than 28,033,000 Americans over ten years old see any given issue of *Life* magazine. On this basis, the cost per thousand readers of the magazine is only about 86 cents—and a magazine ad doesn't flash right off the screen and gone for good, it stays around the house for a while. Truly, a bargain.

Then there are the intangibles. Billboards may be very cheap, but how much of a selling message can you put on a billboard? Most American families do a good part of their shopping browsing through the newspaper, looking at the grocery store and department store ads: what is the value to a manufacturer of being there on the page with the retailers while the lady shops? Radio time is so cheap that you may be able to hit the lady on the head with your jingle over and over again, until you get it so firmly implanted in her noggin that she will remember it until the day she dies; what is the commercial (ignoring the moral) significance of making your brand name part of a customer's mental climate? Sponsorship of a network television show associates your product with an entertainment feature and perhaps a well-beloved personality, and there must be *some* money in this "gratitude factor." Appearance in a magazine associates a product, however dimly, with that magazine's editorial prestige, and people tend to believe what they read. But who are people? And what does any manufacturer care about how many *people* he reaches with his ad? He needs prospects, customers; and to separate the active, extravagant, upper-middle-income younger wheat from the tired, thrifty, low-income older chaff, all bound up together in the one mass-audience statistic, is a task beyond even the panjandrums of the research business (though they try; God knows, they try). Lots of women watch the championship prize fights and World Series baseball games sponsored by Gillette Blue Blades; what use are they to Gillette?

Even when the *type* of medium is clearly dictated by the nature of the product—a women's magazine for a baby food, for example—the advertiser has some hard choices ahead of him. He can aim directly at his market with a page in, say, *Baby Talk*, at slightly more than $6 a thousand, going to half a million recent mothers but going to them in a peculiar way, arriving free of charge, wrapped up in a package of diapers from the diaper service. Or he can hit at the lower-class young women's market, buying a page in, for example, *Modern Romances* at a cost of $2.55 a thousand, reaching a circulation of more than a million (82.4 per cent of them married, runs the litany; 72.5 per cent with children; 22.4 per cent with children under two years old), presenting more editorial matter on baby care than any other nonbaby magazine except *Parents'*. Or perhaps he should buy *Parents'* at $4.85 a thousand. Or hook his wagon onto one of the three big general women's magazines, with their high prestige value: *Ladies' Home Journal* ($3.65 a thousand), *McCall's* ($3.60 a thousand), *Good Housekeeping* ($3.40 a thousand).

Each magazine offers more or less different readers, though there is obviously some overlapping (try to find accurate statistics about overlapping, someday; it isn't easy). And each offers something more than readers—an editorial approach, an atmosphere, a position in the community. Different agencies take different attitudes toward these immeasurable factors. David Ogilvy's agency would not wish to put money into *Modern Romances* because it feels, in Jim McCaffrey's words, "that a product is judged by the company it keeps." Grey Advertising, on the other hand, sees no reason not to spend clients' money in the "romance books," because they offer prospects at a low cost per thousand. "If a lady's reading *True Story* magazine," says Grey's Larry Deckinger, "does she think she's reading junk? No. She reads it because she believes in it." The final decision may boil down to a choice between the *Ladies'*

Home Journal and *Good Housekeeping*, "LHJ" with its big page, high-quality coated paper, superior printing job; "Good House" with its small page and lesser printing job—but with the "Good Housekeeping Seal of Approval" to offer any advertiser who buys at least two pages a year. "What's the Good House Seal worth?" asks president Bill Kearns of Ted Bates & Company. "I don't know. I think it's worth something— I *know* it's worth a good deal to *Good Housekeeping*. But I can't measure it."

And yet, somehow, after much anguish and analysis, the allocations are made, the client's money is spent. In 1957 the allocations among types of media, in terms of money spent by national advertisers, were approximately as follows:

$150 million on billboards and car cards;

$300 million on radio commercials and programs;

$1 billion on television commercials and programs;

$1.2 billion on newspaper advertisements, including ads placed by local retailers under "co-operative" arrangements whereby the manufacturer paid the bills (this figure is most inexact because of the difficulty of estimating co-op money spent);

$1.35 billion on advertisements in the three main categories of magazines: consumer, farm and business.

The largest single advertising medium was the CBS Television Network, with sales estimated at $210 million; the NBC Television Network trailed about $40 million behind. In third position, with $130 million of advertising sales, came *Life*. No other single medium took in more than $100 million from advertisers; and the great majority of media, of course, took in less than $10 million.

2

There are perhaps 2,500 media salesmen in New York, and they form a separate community in the advertising business. Alone among advertising men, they owe no debt of fealty to a brand name or to a manufacturer; they work as individuals, with individual records of accomplishment and failure; and they can usually prove with facts and figures the value of their selling services. Like account executives and salesmen in other industrial fields, they tend to be personable, articulate, and highly convincing while they are talking. Many of them were once employees of advertising agencies, who left to become "reps" (for representatives: the word "salesman" is infrequently used in the trade) because the hours were shorter and the pay was better. Some reps, however, came into the media business from manufacturers' sales forces, since selling is selling as pigs is pigs; and some, particularly in the newspaper area, have put their entire working lives into selling space to advertisers. Competition among them is conducted on a not particularly elevated plane, since most reps are fanatically loyal to the *type* of media they represent and will seize any opportunity to denigrate its rivals. "I have no enmity toward television," says Jim Gediman of the Hearst Advertising Service, "merely lifelong hatred, economically based."

Media back up their salesmen with extensive advertising campaigns in the trade press, in the New York newspapers read by advertising men, and in *The New Yorker* ("Togetherness"; "Solid Cincinnati Reads the Cincinnati *Enquirer*"; "Who Could Sell Her Anything Now . . . Except The Nation's Voice?"; "The Influential"; "In Philadelphia Almost Everybody Reads the *Bulletin*"). Media also produce reams of promotional literature—announcing new circulation gains or program ratings, new studies of the audience, new advances in the economic condition of the local market—and bombard everybody in the advertising business with bundles of the stuff. And the salesmen reinforce this printed pressure on media buyers with incessant personal calls: the New York office of Young & Rubicam receives 2,500 of them every month, ranging from elaborate presentations with charts on easels to mere scouting expeditions over lunches for which the salesman pays. When he is not badgering the agencies, the media salesman is visiting with the agencies' clients, keeping them in touch with news from the world of space and time. Nobody in an advertising agency much likes media ads, media literature, visits from media salesmen—or the idea that the media salesman is closeted privately with a client. But it is recognized that every salesman has a duty as well as a right to make a pest of himself, and the media rep can usually get in to see anyone he seriously wishes to talk with at an advertising agency.

"I was brought up under Raymond Rubicam," says Thompson's Garrit Lydecker, "and he'd fire you if you refused to see a rep. So I'll see anybody, I'll see the rep from the *Southwestern Sheep Grazer*. He'll tell me things I don't know and maybe I ought to know." The media salesman's knowledgeability is valued for itself alone, independent of the magazine or newspaper or broadcasting station which he represents. Agency people live in a fairly sheltered world, bounded by the account groups in which they work; but media salesmen get around. It is the media salesman who spreads the gossip of the advertising business, and he is remarkably efficient at the job. A media salesman was in the Biow agency waiting room on the morning Milton Biow let his account supervisors and group heads know that he was planning to close up his agency; before lunch every vice-president in every agency in New York had the news.

Since media reps visit with clients as well as with agencies, they are often in a position to retail important information. "Some of the brightest guys I know are salesmen," says John Crichton, the young editor of *Advertising Age*. "They get antennae, know when an account is loose. A good relationship with space salesmen can be very valuable to an agency." Not infrequently, agencies receive reps for the purpose of selling the salesman on the quality of this particular agency: in the spring of 1957, Foote, Cone & Belding held several dozen formal morning conferences with groups of media salesmen, at which the agency presented the bare bones of its standard new business pitch—just to keep the trade informed.

Most media sales staffs are organized so that salesmen spend their time selling to one or two large or a handful of smaller agencies, exploiting their close and continuing contacts with a few well-placed agency people. Thus, at Peters, Griffin & Woodward, one of the larger firms of radio and television station representatives, each of the thirteen New York area TV salesmen (all Kentucky colonels, via the sponsorship of Kentuckian H. Preston Peters) works "an agency list," soliciting business from all the accounts handled by the agencies on his list and knowing that no other salesman from his firm will be calling on these agencies. Other media sales staffs may be composed of specialists in products. John Stewart, for example, who sells *Esquire* space to the liquor industry, was an account executive on liquor accounts and advertising manager for National Distillers before he went to *Esquire*. Stewart calls on all the agencies that have liquor accounts, and solicits nothing but liquor business; other *Esquire* salesmen will go to the same agencies to solicit apparel business, shoe business, travel business, etc. Sometimes media arrange to give their salesmen special training in product areas: thus, Gilbert Lea of *McCall's* worked a week in the back areas of a supermarket to learn the grocer's point of view.

Both the personal-contact and the product-expertise system have obvious advantages—personal contact in feeding to an agency just the sort of information that this agency requires in its planning procedures, product expertise in giving an account group an informed but outside view on the significance of new developments in the product field. (The product expert is also likely to have better access to client companies, which must do his medium some good. Clients rarely make their own media decisions, because only the very largest advertisers can afford to maintain their own media departments: they must assume that the agency knows best. But a good rep whose medium has been left off an advertiser's list may be able to provoke the client to ask the agency the reason for the omission; and this is more than half the battle.) "An intelligent rep," says John Stewart, summing up the situation, "can be a great help to an agency."

It is difficult to put a finger on the rewards which a media salesman receives for being a help. But there is little question that a rep who does an agency a service finds as time goes on that the intangibles of media valuation are being shaded in his favor. There is always a reason for buying any advertising medium; what keeps media off advertisers' lists is the fact that better reasons exist for the purchase of other media, and money is limited. No agency is so rigidly committed to a buying formula that exceptions cannot be made for cause. So the media salesman spends his expense account wisely (some of it at Joe & Rosa's, a pleasant and unpretentious if noisy restaurant on Third Avenue, which has become a media hangout), keeps an ear to the ground, and passes out the news as fast as he can to as many people as he can reach.

3.

To handle the complicated and time-consuming job of selecting and buying media—and receiving visits from media salesmen—all agencies except the very smallest maintain a separate media department. Because of the great quantities of clerical work involved in buying space for a single ad in 300 newspapers, or time for a single commercial on 500 radio stations, the media department is usually one of the biggest divisions in the agency. At Young & Rubicam, which has the largest and probably the most adventurous media department in the business, it accounts for 175 of the 1,500 people in the New York office. Historically, the media buyer has been one of the most poorly paid employees in an agency, and there is some disagreement among advertising men about the amount of skill involved. "Media buyers are clerks," says the head of one agency; "media buying," says a senior vice-president in the same agency, "is the frontier of this business, today."

There is considerable justification for both points of view. In some agencies senior buyers, and in all agencies junior buyers, will simply be handed a list of cities and space measurements, and told to get busy with the slide rules and forms. Even on this level, however, the really first-class space buyer makes genuine contributions to the success of his agency's advertising. He knows more than rates and circulations: he knows how to wangle. Newspaper space is ordered "r-o-p," for run-of-paper, but the experienced and skilled buyer will know how to handle matters so that his ad is placed on page 5 rather than on page 31. He knows for each city which days of the week are the big department store days (advertising a new kind of pop-up toaster, he wants to be in with the department stores), which days are the big grocery store days (advertising frozen orange juice, he wants to be in with the A & P and the Safeway). He knows (by reference to *Media Records*, a service which gives the total lineage in each of 114 product classifications carried by each newspaper) how much money advertisers of similar products are putting into the newspaper; and he also knows (by reference to the *Neustadt Service*, which supplies data on prices advertised by local retailers in the different categories) how the paper rates on the economic scale with local shopkeepers, who daily observe the results of their advertising. Often, the account group will allow him to learn, even though he is a clerk, the audience at which the ads are aimed, so that he will be able to choose papers according to their audience characteristics.

There is still nothing in this job—or in the highly comparable job of the time buyer handling local radio and television stations, wangling the best time with the biggest audience for his spot announcements—which is beyond the resources of a high-school graduate with a year's training. But not everybody can absorb such training.

At the frontier of the business, to use the picturesque phrase offered by a thoughtful media director, the media man is juggling so many variables and assuming so considerable a responsibility that his job may accurately be called creative—as media directors like to call it. Here the media man is in on the work of the account group from the beginning. He knows what percentage of the client's sales falls in each city, each metropolitan area, each state, each region. He knows what the client's share-of-market is on a nation-wide basis and in each division and subdivision. He knows from consumer research the demographic characteristics of the people who buy the product—male or female, rich or poor, young or old, homeowners or tenants, with or without children, and so on ad infinitum. He knows how they use and regard the product —in the home or in public, as a luxury or a necessity, as something that is fun or something that is work. He has been made privy to all the client's marketing problems and to the way the account executives and group heads, copywriters and artists hope to solve these problems.

With all these factors in mind, the media man at the frontier looks over the range of possible media in which the ads could appear—newspapers or magazines, spot announcements on local radio or television stations, network radio or television shows, billboards, car cards, match-books, the panoply of approaches to the public eye and ear. He decides whether the product and the campaign call for reaching everybody once in a while or a segment of the population over and over again. He determines whether the advertising should be steadily applied over the course of a year, or pushed out in recurrent waves which die down into periods of relative inactivity. Analyzing what each medium has to offer in terms of what the product requires, this theoretical paragon of media buyers with sure and steady hand spends the client's budget.

Such thoroughgoing examination of the thousands of factors which should, ideally, influence the choice of media is still some distance beyond the frontier. Since virtually all the factors are intangibles—saving only the geographical breakdown of the client's sales and the media costs-per-thousand—it seems unlikely that anyone is ever going to achieve a completely logical and indubitably correct media plan for an advertiser. But the choice of media is an extremely important factor in the success of an advertising campaign: mediocre advertising which reaches a million prospects probably helps the client's sales more than brilliant advertising which reaches only half a million prospects. (Procter & Gamble, which regards advertising as a form of sales *pressure,* will do without creative brilliance if necessary, but always insists on the most detailed imaginable sort of media planning.) The media departments which have at their fingertips the necessary vast quantities of information about product markets and media audiences, and the media buyers who are intelligent and skilled enough to juggle several different ideas in their heads at one time, give the agencies which employ them a considerable competitive advantage in serving clients.

But the customary division of the media department into space buyers and time buyers confuses the issue from the beginning. Where the split continues, as it often does, all the way through the department—so that the only media man responsible for both print and broadcast is the director of the department himself—key decisions on allocating the client's budget must necessarily be made either by the account executive, who knows relatively little about media, or by the media department head, who has only a skeleton knowledge of the individual client and his needs. The result is "formula buying," whereby a single pattern of media purchases—to achieve the lowest cost-per-thousand—or the widest possible broadcast of the advertising message, or the heaviest usable concentration of the message on a certain section of the community—is enforced on all the agency's accounts, regardless of circumstances; and media are chosen for certain products because they have always been used to advertise such products rather than because anybody has thought about the subject.

An interesting example of the results of formula buying can be found in the *New York Times* every day and in the *New York Times Magazine* on Sunday. The daily *Times* carries virtually no grocery advertising, although it ranks high in department store and home appliance advertising, both of which go after the same housewife market. But the *Times* never has carried grocery advertising, and agencies which handle grocery clients have no intention of starting now, no matter what facts and figures the *Times* may be able to show them. (The *Times* research staff once stopped 50,000 women coming out of grocery stores with bags of purchases to find out what newspaper they had read most recently; the *Times* ranked third in the survey, but last of all New York's eight papers in actual grocery linage. Of course, since the *Times* is New York's prestige paper, it is possible that the ladies were fibbing.) On the other hand, the *Times Magazine* is stuffed full of clothing advertisements every Sunday, partly because clothing manufacturers want to balance their advertising pressure with their regional sales figures in each type of media. Some 17 per cent of national apparel sales occur in New York State, but New York accounts for only 13 per cent of *Life's* circulation, only 9 per cent of *Look's* or the *Post's*. Looking at the audiences reached by their magazine advertising, media directors add the *Times Magazine* to the clothing advertiser's list to match up the circulation pattern with the sales pattern.

As a first step in breaking away from established formulas, Young & Rubicam in 1952 did away with space and time specialists and converted them to "all-media" buyers, assigning each buyer directly to account groups. This system was presently adopted by Foote, Cone and a few other agencies, though it is still the exception rather than the rule. Some agencies, among them J. Walter Thompson, have created a number of "associate media directors," who have no media specialty and who serve as senior members of account groups, participating in account planning from the start. The ideal associate media director, according to Thompson's Art Porter, "should be a cross between a good market research man and a good account executive."

The argument against the all-media buyer is, essentially, that he must be less efficient than the specialist: nobody can know as much about print and broadcast as the specialist knows about one or the other. The argument for him is that he can apply his media knowledge to the big problem of allocation for an entire account rather than to the little problem of media purchases in a single area. Moreover, the all-media buyer is free to think to some purpose about the primary decision which must be made in allocating the client's money: shall we apply our advertising pressure *locally* (via newspapers or spot announcements on the local radio and television station) or *nationally* (via magazines, network radio or network television)? In advertising those products which nearly everybody buys—cigarettes, soaps, foods, drugs, toiletries, cars, gasoline—it usually makes little difference whether the agency buys print or broadcast advertising; in most cases, either will probably do the job. What *is* important is the decision to buy local coverage, to apply advertising weight in proportion to the client's local market (but leaving some areas with very skimpy advertising help) or to buy a national blanket which will settle down all over the country, even in areas where the client's brand is hard to find.

This decision is often a very difficult one, forcing the media planner to think about the other factors—type of product, type of purchaser, and so forth—from the beginning. Sometimes the answer is obvious: Johnson's Baby Products must aim at the readers of the women's magazines; Hamm's Beer is not distributed outside the Middle West, and would receive no benefit from selling itself to most of the members of a magazine or network television audience. But sometimes an agency will decide that the obvious answer is not the correct one, as Earle Ludgin put Rath meats in *Life,* even though distribution of the product was thin or nonexistent in many eastern states; or as McCann-Erickson staged one of the most expensive of television spectaculars for Esso gasoline, which is not sold at all in some areas. Or the agency may go the other way, as Ted Bates often does, advertising Kool cigarettes, for example, primarily by local spot announcements, even though the product has full national distribution.

In either case, of course, severe disproportion of advertising pressure and sales can be remedied by adding local spots to coverage in national media or by throwing an occasional magazine advertisement over an essentially local campaign. Sometimes this need to fill the gaps produces the otherwise inexplicable appearance of what seems to be the wrong ad in the wrong medium. Thus, Viceroy was advertised in *Commentary,* the American Jewish Committee's sociological-intellectual magazine, an expenditure rationalized by the fact that Bates's television show and broadcast spots did not even begin to reach the highbrow Jewish audience, which smokes.

CHAPTER 10

HITTING THEM
WHERE THEY
LIVE

"Radio is about the only way you can reach some markets. Take teen-agers. They don't watch television, everybody knows that, it's been proved over and over again. They certainly don't read. But they listen about three hours a day."

Spokesman, Radio Advertising Bureau

"When a sales manager *really* gets in trouble in a market, they have a meeting and somebody from the advertising department will say, 'Let's merchandise our TV show.' But in the end it's always, 'Oh, hell, let's get into the newspapers and knock the town loose.'"

Spokesman, Hearst Advertising Service

"We do research studies, match up markets with television viewing habits. The food companies wanted to know about people who buy frozen foods; we found that the heavy purchasers of frozen foods are also the heavy viewers of television. Gasoline and oil manufacturers—we found that the heavy drivers are the heavy viewers. The heavy cigarette smokers—the two-pack-a-day people—are heavy viewers, but you get them mostly late at night. Don't talk to *me* about overcom-

mercialization on television. Just open your god-damned newspaper: it's
seventy per cent ads."

Spokesman, Television Bureau of Advertising

1.

The local advertising medium is, of course, the newspaper. Newspapers are the oldest advertising media, and they are still, in grand total,
by far the biggest. Though they receive only 27 cents out of the manufacturer's media dollar, they take nearly 78 cents of every dollar spent
by retailers and grocery stores to advertise themselves and the wares
they sell. (Some of this money comes from manufacturers, too, via "co-
operative advertising programs," by which the retailer advertises that
the manufacturer's products are for sale in his store and the manufacturer
pays part or all of the advertising bill—usually all, whether he planned
it that way or not.)

Advertising space in newspapers is sold at so much per agate line per
column (there are fourteen agate lines to an inch, roughly 22 inches of
type, usually eight columns wide, on a standard-size newspaper page;
a full page runs 2,400 to 2,500 agate lines). Sometimes the line rate is
"flat," and will not change however much space an advertiser buys;
sometimes it is subject to quantity discounts, which may range up to
25 per cent for the advertiser who takes the equivalent of forty or so pages
a year (a considerable requirement: forty pages of national advertising
in the Chicago *Tribune*, for example, costs $162,489.60 at full discount).

The basic line rate applies to an ad placed "r-o-p," for run-of-paper,
meaning that it can appear anywhere at all, on any page, at the top or
the bottom of a column, buried in among other ads or next to reading
matter, as the luck falls. A good agency space buyer ought to be able
to protect his client against a really evil fate, but if the advertiser wishes
a complete guarantee, he may order specific pages or positions, at an
extra charge. Thus, the basic national rate of the daily *New York Times*
is $2.05 per agate line ($4,920 a page) before discounts; an advertiser
who wants to guarantee a position at the top of a column and next to

reading matter must, however, pay an additional 85 cents per line; an advertiser who insists that he must be on the society page pays an extra 25 cents a line; an advertiser who demands a specified position on page 2 or page 3 pays an extra $1.50 a line. In practice, these charges are at "publisher's option," and apply only if the advertiser insists on his position. If his agency merely asks for it nicely, and he is a regular customer, he will likely get what he wants at no extra charge.

Many national advertisers feel that they are already paying an extra charge—indeed, that they are being held up on the highway—because the newspaper's line rate is always far lower for the local retail store than it is for the manufacturer. On the average, the retailer pays less than half what the newspaper will charge a national advertiser for the same space. This argument is quite old now, and to all practical purposes it was settled in St. Louis in the 1930's, when the newspapers cut their national rate to bring it level with their retail rate and gained virtually no additional national advertising for their pains (which were considerable: the first reaction was a howl of rage from retailers, who wanted corresponding cuts in *their* rates).

The national advertiser's complaint was never entirely legitimate anyway, since a considerable rate differential is clearly justified by the facts. The newspaper keeps every penny of the retail rate, while 15 per cent of the national rate must go to an advertising agency. Newspapers do not need to maintain large sales staffs to convince the local retailer that he needs them, while the national advertiser and his agency must usually be wheedled and wangled, wined and dined, and sold. Local ads are a positive asset to the paper in the eyes of its readers, who look for retailers' announcements of sales, bargains and specials, while the national ad is just something on the page. Finally, the local merchant advertises week in, week out, at all seasons, while the national advertiser usually schedules his appearances only in the heavy buying seasons of spring and fall. "The retailer signs up for a year," says Herbert Moloney of Moloney, Regan & Schmitt, which represents such papers as the Denver *Post*, the Cincinnati *Enquirer*, the Portland *Oregonian*, the Houston *Post* and the Toledo *Blade*. "If the copy for his ad doesn't arrive on time, the paper simply puts a box around his space and writes, 'Compliments of John Smith's Store.' A national advertiser who comes in and goes out can't expect the same rate. I live in Rye. When I take the train to and from Rye, I pay a commutation rate; if you want to visit me once in a while you pay much more for your trip. That's fair, too." Often, however, newspapers which give considerably reduced "commutation rates" to the heavy local advertiser will refuse to give any quantity discount whatever to the national advertiser, even if he runs his ad every day, all year long; and then the national advertiser's gripe carries conviction.

Media reps like Moloney, Regan & Schmitt sell the great bulk of newspaper space which is bought by national advertisers, and are ordinarily the advertiser's and the agency's only regular contact with the newspaper. (Somebody from the paper will usually come to town once a year, and the rep sets up a cocktail party for him; and he may sell too.) New York newspapers handle their own national advertising sales to Madison Avenue agencies, and a few out-of-town papers maintain their own national sales offices in New York. Usually, however, a salesman representing a number of papers can do a better job for less (the newspaper rep's commission customarily though not always runs around 10 per cent), and the paper relies on its rep. Though reps solicit each other's papers once in a while, the relationship between newspaper and national representative is a highly stable one, and shifts occur very rarely.

The rep's job is threefold: to sell newspapers as a medium, to sell the markets in which his papers are published, and to sell his specific newspaper against competing journals in the same market. Even in big cities, the second part of the job may be the whole battle, because there is only one paper in the market—in three of the nation's twenty-five largest cities, Kansas City, Atlanta and Providence, the newspaper business is a monopoly. "But sometimes it's more difficult to sell a single-paper market," says Leonard Marshall of Cresmer & Woodward, the firm handling, among others, the Los Angeles *Times,* which carries more advertising linage than any other newspaper in America. "You're the only one shouting, 'Tucson! Tucson!' When there are two of you shouting, you seem more important."

Selling a market to an advertiser whose sales in the market are low is usually a hopeless task, but the reps will try it if their papers give them sufficient statistical material to make a good case. Some markets, for example, are expanding rapidly by the stimulus of new industry; the rep offers the advertiser a chance to win a dominant position "in the fastest-growing market in North Carolina." Often a brand which is important nationally sells poorly in a given city; the rep for a newspaper in that city (arriving with a study of brand sales in the market, ordered by the newspaper) urges the advertiser not to let his competition run away with this "A" market, but to push forward via newspapers to his rightful place. At the same time, the rep is selling the competition on the need to advertise more heavily, to hold a leading brand position. Some newspapers have gone to considerable trouble to organize their medium-sized cities as good "test markets" for new products or new packages, arranging with retailers for inexpensive store audits and supplying certain research services at low fees or without charge. The Springfield (Mass.) *Union-News-Republican* advertises the slogan, "Test Effectively, Test Efficiently, Test Springfield." For the convenience of manufacturers who want to try something out in several medium-sized cities scattered through the country, there is a special organization, the Burgoyne Test-City Group, which advises on proper balancing and on technical aspects of the test.

Competitive selling in a market often involves a good deal of infighting. Paper A may have a larger circulation than paper B, or a lower cost-per-thousand; or it may reach a section of the community which is more desirable from the advertiser's point of view. "Suppose we're running a grocery ad, and the budget gives us only one paper in Cleveland," says J. Walter Thompson's Art Porter. "The Cleveland *Press* has the big, family circulation. But if we have an ad for the New York Central or for F. I. du Pont [a stock-brokerage house], we want to reach men readers, we'll put it in the morning *Plain Dealer*, get the commuters." Often, two newspapers make completely conflicting claims: page 607 of a recent issue of *Newspaper Rates and Data* contains a full-page ad announcing that "Dallas *News* readers have MORE . . . spend MORE . . . and there are MORE of them!"; on page 608 the Dallas *Times Herald* claims that it "Reaches More People with More Money to Spend!" The explanation is that the *Times Herald* has a larger circulation in the Dallas metropolitan area ("where 57.9 per cent of the families have 68.8 per cent of the buying power in the whole Dallas Retail Trading Zone"), while the Dallas *News* has a large circulation in the surrounding country-side ("Out-of-town customers are responsible for 35.2 per cent of Dallas' retail sales volume!").

Newspapers, capitalizing on their important position in the community, sell an advertiser more than just space: they also sell "merchandising help," offering to broaden a manufacturer's distribution in local stores and convince local retailers that they should put their best efforts behind a brand advertised in the local paper. Representatives from the newspaper will work with the manufacturer's sales staff in analyzing the local market, and may even go along with the salesmen to pep up a presentation to local buyers. The case is stated most simply by Jim Gediman, a lean, traditionally cynical, dedicated newspaperman who is executive vice-president of the Hearst Advertising Service, which acts as a national rep for nearly all the Hearst papers: "Nobody will ever know a market like a newspaperman; it's a relationship like a parish. Even if he's a dope he can't help being an expert, better than an Einstein if Einstein's perspective is the Biltmore bar and the Westchester route. A rabbit, to put the matter crudely, knows more about warrens than an eagle."

Newspapers love to publish case histories of what their merchandising staffs have done for advertisers, without charge. One big booklet, called *The Big Plus* in honor of what newspapers give advertisers, described half a dozen such cases—among them a set of seven mailings sent to all salesmen at local appliance stores by the Indianapolis *Star* and *News,* to back up a Frigidaire campaign; a free carton of cigarettes and a free silent butler (somewhat gaudy, this) sent to the *wives* of executives and buyers at major local tobacco outlets, distributed by the Toledo *Blade* in honor of a Philip Morris campaign announcing a new package; a set of Squibb "Open House Specials" displays physically set up in drugstore windows by members of the Seattle *Times* advertising department. (The displays, of course, were provided by Squibb, and bold as brass on each of them appears the common box, "as advertised in *LIFE*.")

It is general practice among newspapers in medium-sized and smaller cities to send a weekly newsletter to all drugstores and grocery stores, notifying proprietors that certain brands will be advertised by their makers in the newspaper during the coming week. Often, for a larger campaign, special mailings will be sent, including some gimmick to remind the retailer that he ought to stock up now, to be ready for the big demand that will follow the newspaper ads. (If the retailer stocks up, the manufacturer has already won the battle: "inventory pressure" always moves merchandise.) And, of course, the newspaper's retail advertising staff will suggest "tie-in" ads to the retail stores, to accompany the big national campaign; this activity, while useful to the manufacturer, cannot be counted as a favor to him by the paper.

In their efforts to help the manufacturer while helping themselves, some newspapers make great expenditures on market and consumer research. The Chicago *Tribune* runs a Consumer Purchase Panel similar on a local scale to J. Walter Thompson's national operation. The Los Angeles *Times* and the Cleveland *Press* conduct home inventories, sending members of their staff to a selected sample of households to check personally on the contents of the pantry shelves; they also look around to see if a newspaper is in the house. Other papers, among them the New York *World-Telegram,* the Cincinnati *Post,* the Boston *Herald-Traveler* and the St. Louis *Globe-Democrat,* conduct regular store audits in a carefully selected sample of local stores, to determine the effective distribution of nationally advertised products in the local market.

The most elaborate such program, by far, is run by the Hearst Advertising Service, which supplies national advertisers with "an operating sales control" for each of the twelve markets in which there is a Hearst newspaper. These "control" plans include complete detail maps of each city and its suburbs, subdivided into sales districts according to traffic flow, with the different kinds of stores clearly marked on the maps. Pittsburgh, for example, has 20 sales divsions; Baltimore has 27. Experience has taught the Hearst people that by keeping an eye on a few of these districts a manufacturer can predict what will happen throughout the entire city; if desired (for a small fee), the Hearst merchandising staff will watch these districts for him. When a Hearst merchandising man, checking through a retail store, finds that an advertiser's product is out of stock, he will kindly call the distributor; if he finds the advertiser's point-of-sale posters and display cartons reposing quietly in their shipping box, he will (bullying the retailer if required) put them up himself. Little things like that can make a great difference.

Not every newspaper likes the idea of merchandising support to advertisers. "Many papers feel," says a spokesman for the Bureau of Advertising, the central promotion agency of the industry, "that they're selling white space, plus the prestige of the paper, and that's enough." The *New York Times,* for example, does not believe that the advertiser is entitled to merchandising just because he buys space—or that merchandising help is worth much, anyway. "What does the paper really do?" says Irvin Taubkin, head of the *Times* promotion department. "It takes some kid fresh out of school, or still in school, a part-time junior in the ad department, and he trots around to grocery stores with proofs of the ad. Well, here you have a manufacturer, spending millions of dollars on advertising, but neglecting the final job with the grocer, leaving that to some kid from the newspaper; it doesn't make sense." Nevertheless, the *Times* will support its advertisers, "when there is a mutual advantage"— that is, it will send letters to the trade, informing people that national ads are to break in the *Times.* "I sit up here," says Taubkin somewhat gloomily, "trying to think of ways not to say NO."

And not every advertiser is sold on the value of the newspaper's merchandising support: as some clients would rather dispense with fancy agency services and pay less than 15 per cent commission, agencies would often like to eliminate the merchandising help and pay a lower line rate. "These guys," says one media buyer, "put more money into preparing the reports of what they've done than they put into actual work on the job." Others feel that a distinction must be made between work done by the newspaper on its own initiative, in a disorganized way, and work carefully planned by the paper, the agency and the advertiser in conference to determine what this brand really wants in this locality and what this newspaper merchandising staff can really do to help it.

There is another problem about newspaper merchandising support, too, which most people in the business would rather not discuss—the question of when the nice offer to help the advertiser becomes a nasty threat to hurt the company which does not advertise or (worst of all) withdraws its advertising from the paper. In *National Advertising in Newspapers,* a book published in 1946, Neil Borden reported on the pressure which newspaper publishers have brought to bear on reluctant advertisers and their agencies—floods of inspired mail from local re- tailers and distributors, queries from local bankers, planted questions at board of directors meetings, even letters from congressmen. Borden's book was too pessimistic about the future of newspapers as national media. He did his research in wartime, and used as his reference figure the newspapers' 28-cent share of the national advertiser's dollar in 1941, the last prewar year. With television on the horizon and magazines show- ing spectacular circulation gains over 1941, Borden clearly felt that the newspapers would be unlikely to hold on to their 28 per cent share; in fact, however, despite the emergence of television, newspapers in 1957 had held even, at 27 per cent. But Borden's contention that many adver- tisers are reluctant to buy into newspapers, for fear that they will have terrible trouble buying out, still held true eleven years after his book was published.

2.

Advertisers who put their local budgets into radio and television stations, buying "spot announcements" on local programs, receive neither the rewards nor the punishments that may come from close association with so powerful a member of the community as the newspaper publisher. Most broadcasting stations do offer merchandising services (some of them swap free announcements for chain stores against a guarantee by the stores to favor advertisers on the local station in putting up point-of-sale material), but the broadcaster cannot pretend to the expertise of the publisher. Considerably less of a broadcasting station's revenue comes from local advertisers, and the station staff is not nearly so closely in touch with the retailing community as a newspaper staff will be. What the local broadcaster sells is, essentially, his audience—plus the special selling values, if any, of locally originated programs.

Though both must sell their local markets, the newspaper and the broadcasting station have essentially different selling problems. Newspapers, as the Sunday *New York Times* and Chicago *Tribune* prove every week, are almost infinitely expansible: a newspaper can make space for all the ads it sells. The broadcasting day, however, has specified limits, and it is considered bad business as well as bad public relations to sell more than seven minutes an hour for advertising messages. There is some disagreement as to the values of forward placement in a newspaper, but even those who believe that there is a difference between an ad on page 7 and an ad on page 15 will agree that the difference is slight. The difference between being on a television station at 9:30 P.M. and being there at 9:30 A.M. is on the order of five women to one—ten to one if you are aiming at both the male and the female audience. Moreover, a newspaper's circulation is known to the last integer, verified by the Audit Bureau of Circulation on sworn statements; and a newspaper's audience is loyal, taking the same paper day after day, so an advertiser can be told with some exactness what he is buying. The audience for a local station flows in and out by twists of the dial, with loyalty to programs rather than to stations, so the composition of the station audience changes from half hour to half hour. (Though people do appear to have some loyalty to *radio* stations.) And the number of people in that audience at any minute is, simply, undiscoverable. Four research services try to measure these matters, and they come up with four different answers.

Many television stations have very little time of their own to sell. Of the nation's five hundred stations, one hundred (all of them among the 150 largest) are members of the "basic" CBS or NBC network, which means that any advertiser buying a CBS or NBC network show automatically buys time on these stations. (Another 50 are on the "must-buy" list of the ABC network.) Of the 18 possibly valuable broad-cast hours, the two big networks "option" nine hours from their basic affiliates, which means that these stations cannot without damned good reason (and not too often, even then) carry anything in these nine hours except sponsored network programs. For giving the network the use of its facilities during these hours, a station receives from the network roughly 28 per cent of its charges for time, plus the right to sell some 60 seconds an hour, 30 each during the on-the-hour and on-the-half-hour breaks for station identification (most stations charge about 60 per cent of their full hour rate for these two spots). In addition, of course, the local station receives the immensely popular network pro-grams which draw the big audiences.

Though the networks can (by Federal Communications Commission rule) compel their affiliated stations to accept no more than nine hours of network programming during the 18-hour broadcast day, both NBC and CBS offer another five to seven hours a day of network television shows. Provided the network shows are sponsored and produce revenue, most affiliated stations will accept them, taking the sure 28 per cent (plus 60 per cent for the spots, which are easier to sell when the station offers "adjacencies" to network programming) rather than going after the full-time rate and assuming the costs of independent programming. On these key network affiliates, which have the biggest audiences and cover areas accounting for two-thirds of the nation's total retail sales, the national advertiser looking to buy local markets finds only a limited list of "availabilities." Still, there are the "chain breaks" (the 20-second spots and 10-second "ID's," so called because they appear with the station identification), the occasional local programs, the "syndicated" non-network half-hour film show (*Zorro, Whirlybirds*), and the late movie, a few remaining bits of merchandise for sale.

All but a handful of the nation's 500 television stations are affiliated with one network or another, and during the peak viewing hours (7:30-10:30, more or less, depending on time zones) more than 400 of them will be broadcasting network shows. Nevertheless—despite the limited amount of time for sale on the best stations—advertisers in 1957 paid some $400 million for television spot announcements, local programs, half-hour films and "participations" on local movie shows.

3.

The sale of local television time is handled mostly by the same sort of organization—the national "rep"—which handles newspaper space. (The NBC and CBS networks both maintain "spot sales" organizations for the five stations that each of them owns and operates, and these organizations also handle spot sales for a handful of key affiliated but independently owned stations. The national reps feel—and feel strongly —that the networks have pressured their key affiliates into giving the spot representation business to the network's own office; as one of them puts it, "There's no question that some stations which wanted network affiliation badly were told that affiliation and representation went hand in hand." ABC does not maintain a sales office for the stations it owns; ABC's spot business is handled mostly by Blair-TV, partly by the Katz Agency.) In one respect, the station rep's assignment differs from that of the newspaper rep: an advertiser who wants to reach the entire newspaper-reading public will have to buy space in every paper in town, while the flowing nature of the broadcast audience gives him the chance to reach just about everybody with several TV spots on a single station. "When we hear that an agency has money for one of our markets," says Wells Barnett of Blair-TV, "we want it all." Possibly for this reason the station rep receives a higher commission—a customary 15 per cent instead of the newspaper rep's customary 10 per cent.

Stations divide their broadcast day into periods which carry different price tags, according to the estimated differences in the size of the audience. In some smaller towns there may be only two categories—"A," for 7 P.M. to 11 P.M., and "B," for 6 A.M. to 7 P.M. and 11 P.M. to midnight. In the bigger cities some of the most prosperous stations have managed to make five and even six divisions of the broadcast day, to soak the last few hundred dollars out of the very peak listening hours. Thus, WCAU-TV, Philadelphia, charges $750 for a 20-second announcement between

8 P.M. and 10:30 P.M., $500 for the same announcement just before or just after this choice period, $350 after 11 or before 7:30 P.M., $225 during weekday daylight hours, and only $150 before 8 A.M.

These neat pricing divisions are obscured, however, by a bewildering overlay of quantity discounts, frequency discounts, special plans, and the like. Thus, on WCAU, an advertiser who buys an announcement for twenty-six consecutive weeks receives 5 per cent off the rate; 10 per cent if he buys it for a whole year. Or he can buy a "six-plan," which gives him six announcements in a week, before 6:45 P.M. or after 11:30 P.M., at 25 per cent off the usual rate; or a "twelve-plan," on the same terms, at 45 per cent off. Few stations have so simple a system as this one; at most, spots per week, spots per year, dollar volume, "anchored" spots (where the time slot is guaranteed), "floating" spots (where the station merely guarantees to put the announcement on the air at some time during the broadcast day), combinations of programs and spots all give different discounts. A few smaller stations offer advertisers a pure gamble: all the spots not sold today for, say, $1,000, which may buy a minimum number or ten or twenty more than the minimum, as the ball bounces. Scientific media buyers do not like this sort of thing.

Almost every station also has some time to sell in larger than 20-second pieces. "The cross we bear in this business," says Daniel Denenholz of the Katz Agency, an unusual representation firm which handles newspapers as well as broadcasting stations, "is that people think of spot announcements only. We can offer film shows, live local shows, too." About three-fifths of station revenues from non-network sales to national advertisers comes from spot announcements; the rest comes from sponsorship of local programs or film shows bought individually from film producers, or of segments of Hollywood movies which the stations broadcast more or less full length. Many stations try to give their movie presentations a local flavor—"at least," says Wells Barnett, "the best of them do. They take an announcer and make him a kind of film jockey, 'Your host for Bacchanalian movies, every day at this hour.'"

Until 1956 only a limited amount of modern feature movie material was available to local stations; then the Hollywood studios suddenly opened the floodgates, selling off great quantities of former box-office triumphs. Television rights to the films were bought by syndicates organized for this purpose, and the syndicates peddled packages to the local stations. For the stations feature films have been an audience bonanza, and occasionally a business headache, because a promising film package will often cost more money than a station has on hand. There has been a good deal of bartering, the station giving the syndicate a certain number of spot announcements in return for a showing of the feature film. (The syndicate then sells the spot to advertisers at bargain prices.) In a few cases advertisers have bought the film rights themselves, supplied films to the stations, and taken big spot campaigns in trade. Station reps watch such shenanigans with mingled emotions— but their arrangements with the stations give them some commission, usually at a reduced figure, on the bartered spots; and, as Dan Denenholz says, living with the situation while not accepting it, "the stations have got to have product."

Feature films also have promoted a little jiggery-pokery in the measurement of station audiences. Several of the most widely used "rating" services make their audience surveys during the first week of each month, so the stations make sure they put on their most attractive feature films, the Clark Gable and Humphrey Bogart pictures, for that week. Some media buyers, estimating the size of the local audience for a feature film program in the three unserviced weeks, deduct 25 per cent from the rating numbers, "to give a more reasonable figure." Station reps try to avoid opinions on ratings as much as they can. They discover which of the rating services each advertising agency prefers, and use only that survey when talking to the media buyers from that agency. But, says Wells Barnett, "we don't sell ratings. We can't do it. Some of our stations have good ratings and some don't; if we talk ratings, how are we going to sell the stations that don't have good ones?" Most station reps regard Barnett's attitude as wishful rather than real; a station has nothing to sell but its audience, so there is no way of escaping audience ratings, even though nobody really believes that local ratings are accurate. "Hell," says George Castleman of Peters, Griffin & Woodward, "we *have* to sell ratings. They won't listen to us otherwise."

4.

One of the reasons why station reps must pay so much attention to admittedly inaccurate ratings of local audiences is the fact that many advertisers are currently using spot television for full-scale national campaigns and not merely for local purposes. Expensive as spot announcements are, they still cost less than network shows. "It's contrary to all history," says Clifford Parsells of Ted Bates, which puts something more than half its total billings into spot announcements and is the largest spot buyer in the country. "It always used to be true that syndicate buying was cheaper, a page in the *American Weekly* cost you less than a page in all the newspapers that carried *American Weekly*, a radio network show costs you less than spots on all the radio stations. Today, television spots give you a big price advantage over a network buy." Network salesmen would quarrel with Parsells' analysis, arguing that a half-hour network show gives the advertiser *three* one-minute commercials, and that the cost-per-thousand for the three together is slightly lower than the cost-per-thousand of *three* spot announcements on the same line-up of stations. But Parsells and many other media directors feel that there is far more value in three spots reaching different audiences at different times than in three one-minute commercials during a single program. "If your story is good," Parsells says, "you can do a lot more than one-third of your sales pitch in the first minute."

If spot television is reasonably priced, however, spot radio is the discount house of the media business. Six one-minute announcements a week at 12:00 noon will cost an advertiser $903, after all discounts, on Philadelphia's WCAU-TV; for the same money he can buy 25 minute spots on WCAU radio. A four-to-one ratio is common in the television/radio comparison (it cuts down to about three-to-one for those television spot advertisers big enough to take advantage of "twelve-plans" instead of "six-plans"). The realization of this big numerical difference—plus the realization, which dawned suddenly on many advertisers, that people still listen to radio—has produced a continuing boom in radio time, which will probably last until the demand for radio spots has raised radio rates to a level where the medium no longer commands so considerable a competitive advantage.

The word is "saturation": radio spot campaigns are saturation campaigns. Exactly how many radio spots must be thrown into a market to saturate it is a question nobody can answer. Daniel Denenholz of the Katz Agency, speaking very conservatively, mentions a minimum of 24 spots per week per station, or 120 every week in a five-station market. BBDO, introducing Hit Parade cigarettes, bought 96 announcements plus 24 news broadcasts a week on each station—600 performances of the Hit Parade jingle going over the airwaves every week in a single five-station city. Ogilvy's Jim McCaffrey thinks that 600 a week *must* be too many spots to throw into a single market. "There must be a point of diminishing returns somewhere," he says. "People get fed up, and they're no longer interested in what you have to say." Nevertheless, McCaffrey feels that 200 spots a week is the minimum size for a saturation campaign in a larger market. As Thompson's Art Porter sees it, the question is one of what the competition is doing rather than one of diminishing returns: "If I reach you once, and he reaches you three times, he seems more important than I do."

Perhaps the greater contributor to the present prosperity of spot radio is Henry I. Christal, a cheerful, nervous, broad-shouldered older man with a fringe of gray hair and big black eyebrows, who in 1952 retired from Edward Petry & Company, a station rep which handles both radio and television stations, "and looked around for what I ought to do next. Radio seemed the most exciting field." Christal was virtually alone in that opinion in 1952, when radio was cringing away from the very sight of television's monstrous growth, and published rate cards were being undercut by 70 per cent and more to try to get some business. Setting up his own office as a rep, to handle radio alone, Christal took some radio stations from Petry and lured others to his side by the sheer confidence of his manner. By the end of 1952 he was selling time for eleven major stations in eleven major markets.

Christal felt that radio's first need was to establish the fact that it still had an audience, and there was only one way to do it: a research study, preferably by the most respected and incorruptible research organization in the business. That meant Alfred Politz, whose audience studies for *Life* were agitating the media world. Christal took his proposal for such a study to the board of what is now called the Radio Advertising Bureau, and its members turned him down flat. Among the opinions expressed was one that radio could not afford to have its weaknesses exposed by impartial research. So Christal himself, with his eleven stations, put up all the money for the Politz study; as he likes to point out, 3,000 AM radio stations have benefited from the expensive initiative of these eleven.

Briefly, Politz took a sample of some 5,000 people in 26 areas where television was already strong in 1952; of his sample, 72 per cent owned a television set. He asked them whether they had listened to radio yesterday, and found that nearly 70 per cent of them had; he asked them to break their listening into seven periods—before breakfast, during the three meals, between meals, and after dinner. He asked them where they listened (kitchen, dining room, bedroom, living room, car, etc.) and why. He asked people what they liked about radio (42 per cent said music, 32 per cent said news), and what they didn't like (24.6 per cent said too many commercials). And then he asked them a question with truly spectacular publicity value: "Suppose you were at home and heard a sudden rumor that war had broken out. What would you do to find out if the rumor was true?" Sure enough, more than half the people interviewed said they would turn on the radio. This question and answer, though irrelevant to an advertiser's needs, helped bring the Politz study to the attention of almost everybody in the advertising business, and radio was suddenly on its way up again.

What the Politz study proved was that radio had listeners all day long. Politz found that about 15 per cent of all American women listened to radio in the kitchen while preparing dinner, and that about 15 per cent of all men listened to the radio in their cars while driving home from work. The almost immediate result of the study was to sell out the 4 to 7 P.M. period, a circumstance that Christal views with grim humor. "Five years ago," he says, "you couldn't *give away* time between four and six—everybody was supposed to be watching television with the kids." These days the station reps are having a little trouble selling the 9:30 A.M. to 3:30 P.M. stretch (and the evening stretch, when everybody really is watching television), but they're working on it. So is Politz. What troubles advertisers is not fear of a small audience but concern that their commercials are appearing too close in time to other commercials; Pall Mall, for example, has asked all radio stations to be extra careful not to put Pall Mall spots too close to spots for competing cigarettes, or for "objectionable" products, like mouth washes.

Radio stations sell more than audience: they also sell the personalities of their disk jockeys and announcers. "We tell advertisers," says Wells Barnett, stepping out from under his Blair-TV hat and donning his John Blair, Inc. (radio representatives) hat, "that this man on the radio station is your local salesman. He's on from seven to nine in the morning, every day, and he's a known quantity in town. He goes to teen-age proms, runs his show sometimes from a glass-enclosed trailer in the heart of town, everybody knows him." The Radio Advertising Bureau (now revivified and capable of some spectacular promotions, such as the broadcast of a hundred spots for the Brooklyn-Staten Island ferry over radio stations in Omaha, Nebraska, deliberately driving listeners crazy to prove to advertisers that radio spots are heard) makes the claim in an even stronger fashion. "There are maybe three or four hundred guys in this country today," a spokesman says, "who may not be as good as Arthur Godfrey, but they're doing the same thing, and you can buy them for peanuts."

The great Godfrey himself started off, of course, in just such a role, as a local radio announcer; and by good fortune there exists a record of the first time his name was ever heard in the offices of a Madison

Avenue advertising agency. The occasion was a complaint from the advertising manager of the Bulova Watch Company, who called up and told an agency person who had better be identified as X that the company wished to withdraw its spot announcements immediately from station WTOP, Washington.

"I asked him what had happened," X recalls, "and he said he'd had ten thousand letters from Washington, complaining about a foul-mouthed announcer who was making dirty jokes about the Bulova spot. That sounded serious, but I calmed him down. I told him WTOP was one of the CBS owned and managed stations, and we bought all five of them as a package, and we couldn't just cancel one. I suggested that he send over all the letters, and I'd look at them and speak to the people in Washington about it.

"So he sent over the letter," X continues, "there was only one letter, if there'd been two he'd have said twenty thousand, and it was a peculiar letter. The man who wrote it wasn't mad, he was just curious. He wanted to know who this guy was who had used the most standard radio announcement in America as a slightly off-colored joke. At this point it began to look more genuine than the usual client complaint, even though there was only the one letter, and I called down to Washington to speak to the manager of WTOP.

"I said, 'We've got a client complaint about one of your men making fun of the Bulova Watch announcement,' and on the other end of the phone he broke up. When he finished laughing I told him it wasn't a joke, his station was about to lose some business, and he apologized. He said, 'We've got this kid announcer named Godfrey, and I guess he got bored just saying, "Seven o'clock Bulova time," every morning. He went down to the library and got a sound-effects record, a cow giving off a big, loud Mooo-ooo-oo. Then he played it on the air and said, "What'samatter, cow? Did you have a bulova time?"'"

From here it was only a brief step to immortality.

CHAPTER II

ALL ACROSS THE COUNTRY:

Magazines

"The thing that amazes me about magazines is that they still sell against each other. Here's this thing that's come in and taken this big chunk of dough, television, and they don't sell against it, they sell against each other. They'll come in here to show me how much better *Look* is than *Saturday Evening Post*—which is academic, because this account isn't using either. Then there's *Life*—well, *Life* is so goddamned rich you cancel ten pages they don't even call you up to ask why."

Account supervisor, J. Walter Thompson

"Just tell me the name of the man who said that, so I can go over there and call him a liar. Any cancellation, one of our salesmen gets a memo on his desk, he has to report back on it within forty-eight hours."

Richard Wilson, Life Magazine

"What you may have heard on Madison Avenue about magazines selling against each other is nothing next to the agonizing about it that's being heard within the magazine industry."

L. Philip Ewald, The New Yorker;
chairman, public relations committee,
Magazine Publishers Association

1.

More manufacturers advertise in magazines than in all other media put together. Most products are not, after all, of interest to everybody. Only gardeners and exotic cooks want grass seed, only adolescent girls want slave bracelets, only sportsmen, soldiers and criminals want rifle bullets. To the manufacturers of such products, magazines can offer what no other medium can supply: a selected audience, every member of which may be assumed to have some interest in the manufacturer's product. Magazines thus make it possible for companies with very small advertising budgets to cause a considerable splash in the limited markets at which, by the nature of their product, they must aim. The costs of full-page advertisements in specialized magazines are often under $1,000, and the cost-per-thousand can be (though it usually is not) low. *Popular Gardening, Seventeen* and *The American Rifleman* (necessaries, respectively, to the grass seed maker, the slave bracelet confectioner and the bullet manufacturer) all come in for less than $3.90 per thousand of circulation; if the advertiser can make do with a quarter page, as most advertisers to specialty markets can, his cost-per-thousand drops below a dollar. No other medium can reach certified prospects anywhere near so cheaply.

On the other hand, people who read specialized magazines are often themselves specialists, opinionated, cussed, somewhat unamenable to advertising. Though the manufacturer usually must go after them, if only to keep his name before the most articulate group of people in his market, he may find better sales results with an audience less belligerently interested in his product but still within his market potential (*Living for Young Homemakers* for grass seed; *Field & Stream* for rifle bullets). Some of the circulation of these magazines will be wasted—

on apartment dwellers, for example, who read Milly's *Living,* on fishermen in the *Field & Stream* audience—but by and large the bulk of the readership is in the advertiser's market. Or the manufacturer may wish to reach out to a market segregated only by sex, the grass-seed man advertising in *Ladies' Home Journal* or *McCall's* to interest women in new ways to achieve a beautiful lawn, the rifle-bullet company advertising in *True* or *Esquire.* Here the waste circulation will begin to run to more than half the total audience—but there is a chance of making new customers for this kind of product. Or the manufacturer may decide to go after everybody who uses grass seed and everybody who buys rifle bullets by advertising in the three mass-circulation "general editorial" magazines, *Life, Saturday Evening Post* and *Look.* Any one of these will probably give him more product users than any of the specialized books—but since the bulk of the vast circulation will be wasted, he will have to pay much higher cost-per-thousand for his customers. On the other hand, his retailers will be impressed with his prosperity and his importance and may give special prominence in the store to a brand which appears "as advertised in *Life.*"

Again, a manufacturer may have a product which appeals to a market segregated by attitude: a man selling a high-quality liqueur or an imported sports car wants people who consider themselves sophisticates, and advertises in *The New Yorker*; a man selling a home ice-cream maker wants people who do *not* consider themselves sophisticates, and advertises in *The American Legion* magazine, in *Grit*, in *Farm Journal*, all of which go primarily to rural and semirural America. Here, too, *Life* or the *Saturday Evening Post* may reach a greater absolute number of prospects; as always, at much higher cost.

To the media buyer, therefore, the magazine market appears as a great set of eccentric and overlapping circles. The three great circles of *Life*, the *Post*, and *Look* fill nearly all the market, reaching nearly two-thirds of the households in America—five-sixths of the households with more than $7,000 annual income—during any given month. Partly inside each of these circles, and covering small sections of the market which the mass-circulation magazines do not reach, are the magazines aimed at major categories of the population—men or women, urban or rural, upper income or lower income. And dotted mostly inside, a little outside, and all around the bigger circles are the specialist magazines, for hobbyists, limited age groups, limited interest categories. New advertisers with new products usually start in the little circles and work out eventually, if they are successful, to the mass media. Big advertisers with widely consumed products like to spend their money to reach the great audiences.

In selling their space only the small, specialized magazines have a market to themselves, among advertisers whose budgets are too small to attract salesmen for major media. Otherwise, every magazine sells in competition with other magazines that have roughly the same sort of audience (*Newsweek* must sell against *Time* and *U.S. News and World Report*), in competition with smaller publications covering a product market more directly (*Newsweek* must fight for a piece of the liquor advertiser's magazine dollar against class magazines like *The New Yorker*, men's magazines like *Esquire*, leisure-time magazines like *Sports Illustrated* and *Holiday*; for a piece of the "corporate" advertiser's dollar against business magazines like *Fortune* and *Business Week*), and in competition with the three giants (any of which can offer an advertiser a big chunk of *Newsweek's* circulation among their own readership, plus much, much more). Hence the roughhousing which so disturbs the leaders of the magazine industry: each magazine salesman, knowing that other magazines are constantly in the advertiser's mind as alternatives to his own, feels positively obliged to denigrate his rivals.

2.

Magazine space is sold in theory on a per-line basis, but actually on a basis of pages, half pages, quarter pages, and so on. Three sets of rates are quoted: for black and white, black and one color, or four colors. Thus, the *Saturday Evening Post* charges $23,475 for a black-and-white page, $29,340 for a two-color page, $35,000 for a four-color page (all these prices are subject to quantity discounts ranging from 3 per cent for the advertiser who spends roughly $150,000 a year in the *Post* to 16 per cent for the advertiser who spends about $2 million). Fancy special effects—a fifth color for the manufacturer's package, or a "bleed" effect, with the ad running out to the end of the page instead of maintaining the usual margin—cost extra. Except for the back cover (which in the *Post* costs $12,600 more than an inside four-color page; it is much in demand, because people reading the magazine usually display the back cover to everyone around them), position is not sold in magazines: the advertiser buys his page and takes his chance on where it will appear. But any position can be earned by the regular advertiser. The most prized position is one of the two inside covers, which advertisers earn by steady appearance in the magazine. Once an advertiser has been given an inside cover, he will keep it for that issue every year, provided he maintains his advertising schedule. Among the few selling advantages which a new magazine has is the fact that it can promise inside covers to every advertiser its salesmen approach.

Most magazines sell their circulation figures, the sort of people who make up that circulation, the individual editorial "feel" of the magazine (which must rub off to some extent on its advertisers), and some variety of national merchandising support. The circulation figures are absolutely accurate and audited, and the magazines break them down for advertisers into states, cities and even counties to enable the media departments to keep their statistical tallies. The sort of people included in the circulation is something which the magazine has to prove to the media buyer's satisfaction; among the factors which led to the downfall of *Collier's* was its inability to prove that it held a particularly strong position with any one desirable segment of the community.

Every media buyer uses a copy of the "CMR" (*Consumer Magazine Report*), issued semiannually by Daniel Starch and Staff and containing a breakdown of the paid circulation of each major magazine into age groups, occupations, income categories, ownership of hard goods from automobiles to iceboxes, and so forth. The CMR is the result of interviews at some 26,000 households scattered throughout the country ("probably," says Daniel Starch, "the largest probability sample in the country"). But only a relatively small proportion of the sample buys any one magazine; data on any magazine with less than a million paid circulation will be drawn, by statistical likelihood, from less than 500 purchasers. So a salesman who does not like the Starch results can present to the media buyer a study made by his publication, which has sent out a mailing (asking age, occupation, income, etc.) to every twentieth name on the circulation list, and has received back some 8,500 completed questionnaires. On the basis of this study, involving many more subscribers than the Starch sample could turn up (but conducted, perhaps, with somewhat less impartiality), the salesman supplies the buyer with a new and more comprehensive analysis of the market he will buy when he buys this magazine.

Almost every magazine mails out such questionnaires to its subscribers every once in a while to help the salesmen. (One exception is *The New Yorker*: "Harold Ross would never allow mailings," says L. Philip Ewald, head of the magazine's promotion department. "It was Ross's position, honored by the people who took over after he died, that when a subscriber put down his seven dollars he didn't expect to get ding-donged by all sorts of people.") From the media buyer's point of view, however, all such surveys are suspect, if only because the group which fills out its questionnaires (usually less than 25 per cent and never more than 50 per cent of the total mailing list) is not necessarily typical of the magazine's readership as a whole. To get around this objection, *Harper's* and the *Atlantic*, which are joined together by a single sales office, once went after *all* their subscribers in a single city, Rochester, New York. The sales office sent out the usual questionnaire, followed it up with a letter and another copy of the questionnaire to everybody who had not answered on the first round, and then made telephone calls to all those who had still not replied. "We got answers from seventy-seven per cent of our Rochester circulation," says C. B. Crockett, the gray-haired, distinguished and aggressive president of the joint sales office. "But the most useful thing about the survey was the other twenty-three per cent. This was a winter survey, and the reason they were unavailable was because they were all out of town, in Tucson or Florida."

The editorial "feel" of a magazine is more difficult to pin down and thus more difficult to sell; and this question brings the salesman up against the advertiser's or the buyer's tastes in national media. Media buyers on Madison Avenue do not as an ordinary matter read the Fresno *Bee* or listen to station WCCO, Minneapolis: all they know about the contents of local media is what somebody has told them. Like everyone else, however, they are consumers of national media, and they have opinions about editorial content and television programming which must in some way color their attitudes. (Though the best of them try hard: "I like *Sports Illustrated,*" says Ogilvy's Jim McCaffrey, "so when the *Sports Illustrated* rep comes in here I give him a real hard time, he has to prove it to me. Prejudices about media are not the sort of thing you're unaware of, and I think good media buyers lean over backwards not to let their tastes interfere with their job.") There is one objective measurement in this area: the *Lloyd Hall Editorial Reports,* a service which measures the editorial lineage devoted by each magazine to each of some forty-odd topics. In theory, a magazine prints pieces on subjects that interest its readers, and if some kind of product has been receiving "support" in a magazine's editorial section (beauty care, music, furniture, fishing), this magazine should be a good medium for that product's advertising. In fact, of course, a magazine is quite capable of running articles on a subject simply because it would like to get some advertising money out of manufacturers in this area.

Emotional reactions by the advertiser himself are probably more important here than in any other area of advertising. An ad in *Life,* or a television show of his own, can make an advertiser glow inside with the warmth of his own importance, while an ad in *True Confessions* may not add to his self-esteem. This emotional situation is put to its most obvious use by billboard salesmen, who take a client out in a car to "ride the showing" and let him see what he is getting for his money. One salesman remembers the time he took a small local advertiser to Columbus Circle and showed him his new, spectacular (and unduly expensive) billboard in what was then the second choicest location in New York, right after Times Square. "Look," said the client in tones of awe, "There's Coca-Cola. There's Chevrolet. And, right between them, there's Katz."

Often an advertiser will develop an irrational loyalty to one magazine and will refuse even to listen to sales talks from its competitors. *Life* had great difficulty cracking the automotive market because most automobile people were intensely loyal to the *Saturday Evening Post*. One *Life* salesman remembers a trip to Chrysler headquarters in Detroit, and the senior executive who broke into his spiel by taking his arm and leading him over to the window. "See that factory?" the executive said. "Know what built that factory? *Saturday Evening Post* built that factory." Another salesman wooed Chevrolet into *Life* for the first time, after much elaborate presentation had failed, by noting that Chevvy was advertising itself as the nation's number-one car in the same newspapers that *Life* used to advertise itself as the nation's number-one magazine. He tore out the two ads, roughened the edges convincingly, and pinned them together with a handwritten note: "Why isn't the nation's number-one car in the nation's number-one magazine?" The last great support of *Collier's* in its final, fading year was the alcoholic beverage industry, still grateful for *Collier's* uncompromisingly wet stand throughout the prohibition years.

Agencies, too, may have strong media preferences. David Ogilvy, for example, told a convention of British advertising men about *The New Yorker*: "What an amazing medium that is! There can be no other magazine in the world which begins to approach *The New Yorker* in terms of pulling power in relation to circulation. They only sell about 370,000 copies [this figure is actually 50,000 too low], but those copies go to the key people in every community." To another audience, making a bow to the fact that *Harper's* and the *Atlantic* between them outsell *The New Yorker* in forty-five of the forty-eight states, he described these two magazines as "the natural extension of *The New Yorker* market." Though Ogilvy's agency was only the forty-fifth largest in the country in 1956, it bought more space in *The New Yorker* than any other agency except BBDO.

The most remarkable job of building an editoral "feel" has been done by *McCall's* magazine, using the slogan "Togetherness." It is strongly denied at *McCall's* that the slogan was coined with advertising sales in mind. "You may get confused on this thing," says Gilbert Lea, *McCall's* vigorous, good-looking and very young advertising manager, "a lot of people do. You'll understand it if you will buy the concept that the criterion of a successful publishing venture like this one is to keep at least abreast and probably ahead of the trends of the time. Now, our editor and publisher, Otis Wiese, has four kids, and he likes to spend time with them. He found out everybody else was doing it, too. He took his family with him on vacation, ran into similar family groups on vacation in Bermuda, Yellowstone, everywhere he went.

"Around 1900, it was not unusual for a woman to refer to her husband as The Governor. Somebody said that if you put men and women together around the turn of the century all you got was children. Today, there's a ninety per cent overlap, a man and his wife share the same life. Otis gave it the word 'Togetherness,' didn't expect the word to stick. He announced it first as an editorial philosophy, began editing the magazine for a woman with a family instead of for a woman as an individual. In fact, we didn't realize the marketing overtones, ourselves."

Without casting doubt on Lea's exposition, it would be well to note that Togetherness solved a number of selling problems for *McCall's*. Of all the women's magazines, *McCall's* offers the oldest audience: the median age of the women who buy it is 40.7 years, according to the Starch CMR. Politz studies of the *McCall's* audience indicate that the magazine is in its field the most heavily read by teen-agers (who do not buy it; they live in the homes of women around forty years old). Every successful mass-media sales story, for reasons psychological as well as economic, was youth—which *McCall's* subscribers did not have. The Togtherness theme, implying the existence of children old enough to participate in family decisions (including buying decisions) gave the sales staff a "feel" to sell, a "feel" which matched exactly with the known audience characteristics of the magazine and had an attractiveness all its own.

3.

Merchandising services by magazines are a fairly new development, pioneered by *Life* in the years shortly after the war when it appeared possible that newspaper merchandising helps would persuade manufacturers to shift some of their budget from magazines to newspapers. *Life* sales trainees were sent around to stores all over the country on missionary duty, to tell them about *Life* and how much *Life* valued the retailer, and to push the idea of featuring products which bore the tag "as advertised in *Life*." (These tags, printed and punched with a string through them, are available to advertisers in *Life* at roughly 2 cents each; stickers are much cheaper; easels displaying a copy of the ad itself and a legend, for store display, can be ordered at *Life*'s cost of producing them.) The promotion was immensely successful, revealing again to advertisers the blind faith which people tend to place in a magazine they read. Although most analysts believe that the bloom is now off the rose ("As in all these things," says Everett Braden, former vice-president of Kroger's food chain who is now Foote, Cone's New York director of merchandising, "there is a fatigue factor"), a survey performed for *Life* in November, 1956, indicated that 26 per cent of the nation's grocery stores, 30 per cent of its drugstores and 14 per cent of its appliance stores were using display material tied in to advertisements in *Life*. "In calendar 1956," says *Life*'s Richard Wilson, "retailers bought thirty-seven million lines of newspaper advertising to announce that they carried products 'as advertised in *Life*.'"

Magazines have for some time capitalized specifically on public willingness to trust print media. "People do not expect an advertiser to lie," Claude Hopkins wrote in *Scientific Advertising* in 1923. "They know that he can't lie in the best mediums." And it is, of course, true that no magazine ever wants people to be unhappy about purchases they have made as the result of an ad in the magazine. Three magazines particularly have accentuated this possibly naïve public faith by granting advertisers a specific recommendation in return for a certain minimum advertising schedule: the *Good Housekeeping* Seal of Approval, the *Parents' Magazine* Commendation Seal, and the *American Medical Association Journal* Seal of Acceptance. In all three cases some testing of the product is performed by a special section of the magazine staff to determine that it will not actually harm people who buy it (there is a possible legal liability in these situations if the new blood-iron remedy, for example, turns out to be poisonous). Other magazines simply give away a kind of recommendation as one of the benefits an advertiser buys for his money: the *Saturday Evening Post* will supply tags announcing "A *Post* Recognized Value," which means that there doesn't seem to be anything much wrong with the product so far as a space salesman can tell by looking at it.

Other magazines specialize in industry-wide promotions, a big burst once in a while—like the joint *Post*-NARGUS (grocers' association) promotion of September, 1957, which involved more than 100,000 food stores and a special section in the *Post* reprinted for distribution as a pamphlet—or steady contact with the trade. *McCall's*, for example, publishes no fewer than seventeen monthly, bimonthly and quarterly little magazines sent free of charge to retailers, buyers, salesmen and executives: "pocket letters" for floor covering buyers, furniture and bedding buyers, hardware and lumber dealers and builders, tableware buyers, linen buyers, drugstore beauty products buyers, and (separately) supermarket beauty products buyers, food buyers, restaurant executives, home economists, and appliance stores. In addition, the magazine supplies sample catalogues of advertising art work to independent supermarkets to help them prepare their newspaper advertising and runs an annual contest to choose the best local advertising by a food store. Each "pocket letter" aims to give its recipients some information of value that they may not yet have picked up; and, of course, tells everybody what is coming up in *McCall's.*

4.

Such selling arguments are sufficient to carry a magazine through competitive battles with other magazines and with newspapers; but they have been relatively ineffective against the national broadcast media, radio and television. The problem first arose in the mid-1930's, when "rating services" for radio programs, estimating the total audience of each major program, began to influence media buyers. Aside from the ratings there were no figures whatever for the calculation of cost-per-thousand on the purchase of radio time. Magazines found that their audited circulation figures were being compared with the survey-based ratings of total broadcast audiences and that the magazines were doing very badly in the comparison. *Life,* then brand-new and seeking to find out something about its audience anyway, organized the Committee for the Continuing Study of Magazine Audiences, consisting of recognized market researchers (among them George Gallup of Young & Rubicam, which was more heavily involved in radio than any other agency, and Archibald Crossley, whose program rating service was the most widely used in the industry). The committee, later reorganized as the Magazine Audience Group, was to establish criteria for the investigation of magazine "readership" as distinguished from paid circulation.

Obviously, magazines are not read only by their purchasers. They litter dentist's offices and barbershops, where a number of people read them; several members of a household read them; people who don't buy them take them away from friends who have finished with them; people leave them on seats of public conveyances and strangers pick them up. *Life* especially, in those early years when there was not enough coated paper or high-speed press facility to meet the demand for the new weekly news-picture magazine, had a very heavy "pass-on" circulation in addition to its basic paid circulation. Agencies had been conscious of this fact (Kenyon & Eckhardt had run its own little survey in the city of White Plains and had come up with a statement that each copy of *Life* had *twelve* to *thirteen* readers), but until they had comparable statistics they would have to compare audited magazine circulations with estimated broadcast audiences. Working under conditions established by its highly reputable committee, *Life* (with an assist from *Look*) went out into the market to make surveys and estimates of magazine readership. Conceivably from motives of curiosity, conceivably from motives of competitive selling, the picture magazines also developed readership figures for text magazines such as *Collier's* and the *Post*. Inevitably, the picture magazine, which could be read cover to cover in an hour by even a fairly slow-witted subscriber, showed a greater pass-on circulation than the text magazine, which offered some hours' worth of reading.

Opposition from the text magazines and from the Audit Bureau of Circulation, plus certain inconsistencies in the survey data (between one survey and another; for example, one magazine showed a 144,600 increase in readership in a state in which its audited circulation had *dropped* by 9,088), restricted the usefulness of magazine audience studies. In 1949 it appeared likely that the Advertising Research Foundation (a nonprofit service organization with advertisers, agencies and media equally represented in its board of directors) would step in, dissolve the Magazine Audience Group and undertake the supervision of magazine audience studies. Though the ARF plan fell through, its existence served to discredit all the surveys which had gone before. *Life*, confronted with the danger of a return to the days when it had no effective argument to make against the "treasury numbers" which the broadcasting networks were throwing around, went looking for the most accurate and scientifically responsible research firm it could find, a firm which could redefine the techniques of audience measurement and carry out a research study that might win general acceptance. All paths led to the door of Alfred Politz Research, Inc., in business less than seven years but already regarded by research directors at agencies and advertiser companies as the most reliable firm in the field.

Not wishing to admit the demise of the Magazine Audience Group statistics, *Life* in 1950 put Politz to work on a separate question, the

question of *accumulative* audience—the number of people who saw
one or more issues of *Life* over a period of time, rather than simply
the number who had looked at one given issue. This study, with Politz's
lengthy description of it, was extremely well received in the advertising
business—not least because it stated *Life's* single-issue readership at
about 5.2 readers per copy, which yielded a final figure more than two
million below the figure in the most recent Magazine Audience Group
report. *Life* immediately began planning with Politz a more ambitious
project, to compare the one-time and accumulative audiences of four
magazines (*Life, Look,* the *Post,* the *Ladies' Home Journal*), one
Sunday newspaper supplement (*This Week*), four leading radio programs (this study was done in 1952, before nighttime network radio
had collapsed), and five leading television programs. The survey was
published in 1953 under the title *A Study of Four Media,* a bound book
176 pages long, full of bar graphs and pie charts in three colors, plus
brief, wide-spaced, easy-to-read statistical tables. It still ranks second
only to the *Standard Rate and Data* books as indispensable equipment
on a media buyer's desk. Since this first monumental project, Politz
has done other studies for *Life,* plus work for *Look, Better Homes &
Gardens,* the *Reader's Digest,* and the *Saturday Evening Post.* The
Digest job fulfilled a prophecy made when the *Digest* in 1954 first
announced it was going to accept advertising. "They won't find it so
easy as they think," said a media salesman out loud. "They'll have to
pay a higher postage rate, they'll have to hire a sales force, and they'll
have to pay for a Politz study."

A Study of Four Media was the result of visits by interviewers to the
homes of some 8,060 people whose households had been chosen for
investigation after rigorous probability analysis of the entire population.
(To the layman, nothing seems simpler than the choice of a random
sample: you just go out and pick people at random. In fact, however,
one of the most complicated jobs in mathematical statistics is to "randomize" a small sample of human beings from a large, spread-out population. The "probability" sample is an attempt to approach a random sample—by using random-number tables to choose among equal categories.)

Home-office statisticians, working from Census data and detailed maps of each area, gave Politz's interviewers instructions as to exactly which houses were to be visited, and no substitutions were permitted. If the occupants of the house or apartment were not at home, or were too busy for such nonsense, the interviewer was under instructions to try again, and again, at least eight times per house, until he received either his interview or a flat rejection. Rejections were merely to be reported to home office, and the interviewer was to go about his other assignments. This procedure is now standard practice in all high-budget research jobs, and everybody is deadly serious about it. (In one project, which Archibald Crossley's Crossley—S-D Surveys performed for the U.S. Government, a California interviewer found that the house she had been told to visit was no longer there: a flood had carried it some two miles down the canyon, into the next county. She called New York with her problem and was told to get down that canyon and visit that house, and no excuses. She rented a jeep, got to the house and—much to her surprise—found the people still in it.) Of the 8,060 households in the original Politz sample, 7,141 were willing to co-operate at the beginning. The interviewing proceeded over a period of a year, with each household visited six times by the interviewers, and at the end 5,236 families had survived all six interviews. The final data was drawn from 99,052 visits which accomplished 33,686 completed interviews. The cost of the survey has been variously estimated, but $350,000 is regarded as rock-bottom minimum and $650,000 as likely.

Politz felt that one of the failings of the previous Magazine Audience Group studies had been the fact that all the people interviewed knew they were being asked about their magazine reading habits. Asked whether he reads *Life*, a man may well think about whether he *should* be reading *Life* (and whether the interviewer thinks he should) before he answers. To avoid this chance of bias, the Politz interviews were set up as a study of what sort of articles, stories and picture stories *interested* readers of magazines. This fiction was carried to great lengths; in fact, the interviewers themselves were never told that the study had as its primary purpose the simple measurement of audiences. Interviewers first asked respondents whether they had read any issue of any of these magazines during the past six months. Those who said that they had not were simply marked down as nonreaders and not subjected to further questioning. With the others, the interviewer produced a copy of the magazine in question, two weeks to eight weeks old, and told the respondent that he wanted to find out what sort of items, appearing in this magazine, seemed most interesting to *him*. The interviewer then leafed rapidly through the issue, asking the respondent to stop him whenever any item appeared particularly interesting. "The respondent was made to feel," Politz wrote in his technical appendix to the study, "that the chief purpose of the interview was editorial and that his interview was valuable, regardless of whether or not he had seen the issue before."

Soliciting people's opinions about whether items are interesting automatically opens a wide field of conversation. To make sure that the interview did not drag out to unmanageable lengths, the interviewers were supplied by Politz with a "canned" admonitory comment, something to be memorized and used verbatim whenever an interview got off the track. Not infrequently, a respondent would announce that he had seen or read this particular item, to which the interviewer replied, "Suppose this were the first time you had seen it, does this item *look* especially interesting?" As Politz wrote in his appendix, this question "carried the implication that the interviewer was more concerned with what the respondent thought about the item's appearance than with whether or not he had seen the item." Only at the very end, more or less in passing, as a side issue related to the already expressed opinions on interest, did the interviewer ask the respondent whether or not he had, in fact, seen this particular issue before. When the questionnaire came back to tabulating center, all the material about what seemed interesting was thrown away and only the simple yes-or-no readership fact retained.

Politz employed 207 interviewers steadily on this project for more than a year. Slightly more than half of the interviewers were men, 98 per cent of them were over 25 years old, and two-thirds of them had been to college. They were selected only after careful screening (one of the major qualifications was an ability to speak the "canned" comments in a natural way), and subjected to intensive training by 35 instructors, who traveled back and forth across the country to work with them. Before anyone conducted any interviews that would be counted in the survey he conducted at least two dry runs that were thrown away—one under the eye of an instructor, the other independently. His reports on both were analyzed at home office before he was formally hired for the project. While the interviewing was proceeding, supervisors checked the work by calling or visiting respondents and sending them stamped-addressed postcards on which to comment on interviewer and interview. In short, every precaution was taken to ensure maximum possible accuracy.

This technique was impressive for the pains taken, the money spent, and the obvious honesty of the approach; and the results of *A Study of Four Media* were very much along the lines that experienced advertising men thought an honest survey would produce. (That is, two of the television shows were seen by more people than had seen any single copy of *Life*; today, with television more common that it was in 1952, there are probably a dozen weekly shows with a wider one-time audience than *Life*.) It was also impressive that *Life*, when printing up the results, arranged the tabulations in such a way that each magazine and each medium appeared separately, in its own section of the book; people could make comparisons, of course (that was the purpose of the research), but the comparisons were not to be flung in their faces.

It was *Look* which decided that the Politz data should be used for competitive selling *among magazines*. Always the most intensely and destructively competitive of the magazines in its space-selling policy, *Look* advertised the results of *A Study of Four Media* (which showed *Look* second only to *Life* in almost all audience categories) in the trade press and in the New York newspapers. Meanwhile, *Look* commissioned from Politz a second study, which was published in 1955 under the title *The Audiences of Nine Magazines*. The big difference between the 1955 study and the 1953 study, from *Look's* point of view, was the fact that the new survey included *Collier's*. *Look* printed up the new Politz data in tabular form, the nine magazines listed one under the other to facilitate immediate comparison; then advertised and sent its salesmen around to brag that *Look* had a far bigger audience than *Collier's* in every category—and could be bought for about the same price, since both had about the same paid circulation. The most damning single statistic for *Collier's* was the statement that of the people who read only one of the nine magazines, *Look* could supply 3,800,000 and *Collier's* only 2,000,000. It is widely believed among media buyers (none of whom thought much of the pitch himself, of course) that *Look's* vigorous use of this statistic was what greased the skids under *Collier's*. This judgment may be questioned—any coroner's jury would have to bring in a verdict that *Collier's* jumped rather than a verdict that it was pushed—but certainly *Look* was out after *Collier's*, and used the Politz study as ammunition.

At this point the text magazines became seriously concerned about the prospect of unending audience studies, each proving again, with more and more elaborate statistics, the obvious fact that people finish with picture magazines and pass them on more quickly than they finish with text magazines. There was only one thing to do: hire Politz to demonstrate that there were advantages to a text magazine which a picture magazine couldn't claim. The first such counterattack came from *Better Homes & Gardens,* which commissioned from Politz a noncompetitive study (that is, no other magazine was investigated) to show that people kept *Better Homes & Gardens* around the house for a while and referred back to it every so often to look up something they had read. The resulting report, with bar graphs printed in decorator colors, included one evaluation that went a step beyond factual research into uncharted, statistically dangerous but promotionally auriferous ground. Among the reader characteristics which Politz examined was a psychological attitude labeled "venturesomeness," willingness to try new products; Politz said that out of the 123,800,000 people over ten years old in the United States at the time of his survey 40,100,000 could be called *venturesome*; and of these 40,100,000 some 17,400,000 read at least one issue of *Better Homes & Gardens* during the course of a year.

The *Reader's Digest*, being new in the advertising business and competing directly with *Life* and *Look* for advertising revenue, required something with greater sex appeal; and Politz suggested to them a measurement of "Reading Days." In his introduction to the finished report, Politz wrote: "We know that the particular way in which the public finds itself in contact with a medium has a bearing on the usefulness of the advertising it carries. The superficiality or the intensity of contact with the medium, the respect, the indifference, all play important roles. . . . *Reader's Digest's* hope . . . was that a given copy stays in contact with a particular reader for a long time. If this is true, then the likelihood of building up a great number of readers per copy is reduced. . . . It is hoped that this study adds still another measurement for [the advertiser] to consider." Finding out the number of different days on which people actually pick up and look at a magazine is by no means an easy research assignment. Politz tackled it by approaching an unusually large sample (19,117 households, of which 14,515 completed the interview) and asking them to reconstruct the previous day. What did they do before breakfast? Did they listen to radio? Look at television? Pick up a magazine? If so, what magazine? And after breakfast? . . . The result, not surprisingly, was the discovery that people picked up a monthly magazine on four different days or more (5.3 for the *Digest*), while they picked up a weekly magazine on fewer than two days (1.3 for *Life*).

During the course of this study for the *Digest*, Politz took the opportunity to sew up the last statistical hole in his procedure—the argument that people who considered themselves regular readers of a magazine might say they had read a particular issue even though, in fact, they had not. Since the final statistics for readership in the earlier reports had been arrived at by multiplying the actual number of self-proclaimed readers in the sample by a factor as high as 25,000, only a few such errors would be necessary to inflate the Politz audience estimate by hundreds of thousands of nonexistent readers. To test the question,

Politz conducted a pilot study involving 275 interviews and presented to people advance issues of a magazine—issues which had not yet gone on sale to the public. Altogether, 12 of the 275 people interviewed claimed to have read magazines which they could not have seen.

Politz investigated further, and found that seven of these twelve impossible readings had come via two interviewers who had never worked on media studies before. "Follow-up on these seven claimed readings," Politz wrote in his technical appendix to the report, "were made by an experienced trainer of interviewers.

"Of the 7 people, 6 were finally contacted and re-interviewed.

"—2 respondents on the second interview admitted making a mistake.

"—2 respondents were over 70 years of age and adamantly insisted they read every single issue of the magazine they claimed reading.

"—1 respondent was also over 70 and still claimed reading the issue although the trainer felt the respondent did not understand the meaning of the question. . . ."

It is moments such as these that justify the verbosity, the differential equations and integrals of technical appendices. Research is *not* all dull statistics; it is also *scenes*, openings for the imagination: the belligerent old man, the cool trainer of interviewers becoming rattled from the shock of his insistence. . . .

Finally, there was the *Saturday Evening Post*, the last holdout against the Politz magic. "My staff hated Politz," said the late Morton Bailey, who was the *Post*'s advertising director. "They didn't believe a picture magazine could have so many readers, they thought Politz was inventing them." (In fact, the *Post* at one point hired National Analysts to do an audience survey which, it was hoped, would shoot Politz full of holes; but National Analysts came up with almost exactly the same results.) The *Post* picked up part of the bill for the *Reader's Digest* study, hoping that it would come out with a bonus of Reader Days to hold as a war club against the audience statistics of the picture magazines. Actually, the *Post* scored best of all the weeklies (1.8 Reader Days, as against 1.3 for *Life*, and 1.5 for *Look*, which comes out every other week), but not so far in the lead that a salesman could make hay from the statistics. So the *Post*, somewhat regretfully, assigned Politz the job of a purely psychological attitude study among *Post* readers. If the *Post* could not make a concrete claim of audience or Reading Days, it could demonstrate through research that its readers considered it a very special sort of magazine, and that the readers themselves were very special, very desirable people. Since they read words, they would be articulate; since they read the *Post*, they would talk about what they had seen in the *Post*. Politz did his study, the *Post* published it in a luxurious white leather binding, and spent $250,000 advertising its results, which proved the *Post* reader to be "The Influential." (Bailey had picked this phrase out of a book by Paul Lazarsfeld of Columbia University, one of the first advertising research psychologists in the trade. He was somewhat concerned that Politz would feel the word went too far in describing the results and very hesitantly asked Politz's permission to use "The Influential" as the theme of a big *Post* advertising campaign for the study. Politz listened to him, sat for a moment without saying anything, then pronounced the words, "I *love* it!")

Basically, the Politz study for the *Post* was an extension of the usual poll-by-questionnaire which virtually every magazine sends to some of its subscribers every year. But it did develop a good deal of information of a kind never before supplied to advertisers. Thus, for example, Politz broke down the readership of the *Post* by "Special Room Where Most Recent Copy is Kept," listing living room, bedroom, den or playroom, dining room, kitchen, and "other." By careful examination and analysis of the statistics the advertiser could discover that 1,300,000 of the *Post*'s 14,219,000 readers kept their most recent copy of the magazine in the bathroom.

CHAPTER 12

ALL ACROSS THE COUNTRY:

Television

"Up to recently, if you wanted to buy prime evening network time for your client, it wasn't *what* you knew that made the difference, it was *who* you knew."

Broadcast media buyer

"I may have a program with a 20 rating that's doing a whale of a job for me, but the network won't let me keep it. They've got another program which they think can pull a 35 rating. Even if it does, I know it won't do as good a job for me, but I don't have any choice. They'll make me give up my program and take theirs."

Television department director

"These guys, they don't really care about the program, they care about the fifteen per cent."

William Hyland, executive vice-president in charge of network sales, CBS Television

1.

It is impossible to overestimate the value of the Politz studies to the great mass-circulation magazines. Except for a trick question (about "venturesomeness") or an occasional question which brings the respondent's self-esteem too prominently into play (the *Post* study showed 10,392,000 readers of the *Post* attending the opera in 1956, a figure at least four times as great as actual opera attendance in the United States during the year), Politz's results are accepted as accurate throughout the advertising business. The magazine industry, moreover, has benefited by the fact that one research organization dominates its audience surveys, so that there are no conflicting claims, each backed by a different researcher, to befuddle the already confused media buyer. By comparison with the magazines, the television networks, fortunate in every other way, have had extremely bad luck with their audience ratings. Since these audience estimates vitally affect the business standing and the earnings of the entertainers whose programs are rated, and since these entertainers are newsworthy fellows one and all, the argument over television ratings has exploded into the public press and aroused a good deal of simple nastiness.

There are five different television audience ratings services, applying four different techniques to the problem of national audience measurement:

1. By far the most widely accepted is the Nielsen National Television Index (NTI), using an electronic measurement device, the Audimeter. Developed at MIT in the 1930's and vastly refined by Nielsen engineers, the Audimeter is a plain metal box about the size of a small bedside radio, containing some $350 worth of fancy electronic gadgetry and a clock mechanism which will keep it in working order through a power failure and enable it to pick up its duties when the power comes on again and the television set returns to action. The Audimeter is attached to the family's set or sets and registers the hour and minute at which each set is turned on, the channel tuned, and the length of time

the set remains tuned to each channel.

There are about 1,000 Audimeter-equipped TV homes in the country, but 5 to 8 per cent of Audimeter-equipped sets or Audimeters are out of order (or registering their data improperly) at any given time. The people who allow Audimeters to be attached to their sets are paid for their trouble at the rate of 25 cents a week, plus a contract by which Nielsen agrees to pay half the cost of repairs if anything ever goes wrong with the set. On the newest Audimeters even the payment of quarters is automatic: the machine takes a film cartridge, which drops two quarters to waiting hands as it is slipped into position. ("This helps assure," Nielsen says, "that whoever picks up the mail will immediately put the new cartridge in the Audimeter.") The old cartridge is then mailed off to Nielsen in Chicago, where the film undergoes a fanatically elaborate inspection, the data it contains is decoded, checked against a list of the actual programs carried on the various channels in this locality during the two weeks, transferred to punch cards, and tabulated. Except for the check on what was actually broadcast on the channels (which takes the full-time attention of a staff of twenty-six people), every operation is done on machines specially designed to handle Audimeter film. Nielsen says that IBM has told him his job is the most complicated continuing process using IBM equipment in private industry anywhere in the world.

The Nielsen system has two overwhelming advantages: it does not depend for its results on the always fallible human memory, and because it uses a fixed sample it can more accurately measure audience trends over a period of time. It also has one serious disadvantage: the expense of Audimeters and tabulation is so extreme that the sample must be kept very small—so small that the data from Audimeters cannot be analyzed down into market-sized slices. Advertisers can receive no very good idea of what sort of people are in the audience, or where they live, from Audimeter data alone. To supply such services, Nielsen must supplement the NTI panel reports with information gathered by a partially verified diary system from an additional "Recordimeter" panel of another 1,000 TV homes.

2. Second only to Nielsen in acceptance is the Trendex service, which measures the popularity of network programs in twenty cities, each of which has several television stations. The Trendex method is known in the trade as the "telephone-coincidental"—that is, interviewers call up names in the telephone book and ask the person who answers the phone what television program he is watching at this moment (or was before the damn telephone rang). The great advantage of this service has been the fact that it can give a rating the next morning, while Nielsen requires at least three weeks; the great disadvantages are the telephone bias (the fact that only people with listed telephones can participate in the sample), the city bias (the fact that the service tends to make local calls from the heart of town, and falls off in the suburban market), and the limited time period to which the technique is applicable (since you cannot call people up at all hours of the night). And, of course, twenty cities do not make up the entire United States: the Trendex reports leave great gaps of unmeasured audience.

3. Another method, used by The Pulse, Inc., involves personal interviews à la Politz: interviewers (all women) call on homes and ask the people who answer the doorbells which television programs they saw the day before. The technique is "aided recall"; that is, each interviewer carries with him a roster of the programs shown the day before and lets the householder look at the roster while answering. There is a reconstruction of the previous day, again à la Politz, but not nearly so detailed or complicated; in fact, each interview is supposed to be over within eight minutes. At the end of the interview, the interviewer asks a few questions to pin down "demographic" data about the household—age, income, occupation, education, etc. The advantage of the Pulse method is the fact that it supplies such demographic data for a very large sample—7,800 homes a day for the previous night's viewing. The disadvantage is the obvious potential inaccuracy of relatively unplanned house-to-house surveys relying on "aided recall."

4 and 5. Two firms—the Audience Research Bureau and Videodex, Inc.—use a "diary" method of measuring television audiences. A pre-

selected panel of homes is given a diary in which to write down each program watched by the family—or any member of the family. The diary sits on top of the television set, and in theory everybody writes down what he is watching when he turns the dial. In fact, of course, the more conscientious of the respondents write down their viewing for the day just before they go to bed, relying on immediate memory; and the less conscientious of them simply fill in the blanks at the end of the week, to the best of their recollection. As much as one-third of the two thousand diaries sent out every month are not returned. The advantage of the diary method is its cheapness, since there are no machines to be built and maintained nor interviewers to be paid; the disadvantage is substantial inaccuracy.

In early 1958, ARB launched a new service, which will provide *instantaneous* audience measurements in seven cities, sending data via leased wire from a meter on the TV set to a central headquarters.

The differences between these systems are not merely matters of measuring technique; the four methods actually measure different things. The electronic devices measure tuning, pure and simple: they testify that the television set is on and tuned to Channel 2, but not that anyone is watching it. An early study of nonattendance at an operating *radio* set was made by Archibald Crossley in 1939, and he found that at any moment as many as 25 per cent of the blaring radios in the United States could be playing to the walls of the room, with nobody listening. Other studies have shown this problem as far less serious, and even at worst it would seem likely that television has cut the percentage, but some media men estimate that in the daytime 40 per cent of the housewives are not watching the tuned-in television sets.

The telephone-coincidental method measures watching as of the moment of the telephone call, and at no other time. Before the advertiser's great moment has arrived, the broadcast of his commercial message, the man who said he was watching this program may have turned it off or tuned to another channel. Nevertheless, telephone-coincidental methods do measure viewing. Diary methods at best measure only that viewing which the diary keeper is willing to admit in writing (thus, diary services unquestionably understate daytime viewing by housewives, because the lady of the house is unwilling to write down, in a place where her husband is likely to see it, the fact that she had two hours' free time during the day to loaf around and look at television). And personal aided recall measures only the programs people remember seeing and, again, will admit (not everyone who drooled over the wrestling matches last night wants to give out this piece of information to an utter stranger in the cold light of the morning after).

So it is not surprising that, in the sedate words of the Advertising Research Foundation, "different program audience size measurement services have often reported widely divergent measurements for the same broadcast." In fact, it is generally true that a man with a moderately successful program can find an audience measurement indicating that he has an extremely successful program; while a man selling against a big hit can find some audience survey with which to assure his victim that the hit is really not doing very well. Since statistics are very important in the advertising business, and no media salesman ever has any scruples about how he uses them (because he doesn't believe in them, anyway; it is an occupational failing), advertisers and agencies soon found themselves foundering in a sea of contradictory numbers. A "Radio-Television Ratings Review Committee" was constituted by the Advertising Research Foundation to rescue the drowning advertisers. The committee labored for something more than a year and in 1954 produced a report on "Recommended Standards," which was to be followed, committee chairman Larry Deckinger said in mid-1957, "by further investigation, experimental work and recommended procedures. It is, I think, a legitimate criticism of the committee," Deckinger added, examining his cigar carefully through his big horn-rimmed glasses, the expression on his round, young face composed to reveal nothing, "that we have been somewhat slow about arriving at the second step."

Basically, to avoid technicalities, the committee came down for Nielsen, on the grounds that the Audimeters were accurate measures of tuning, and that tuning was, as Deckinger puts it, "the only thing you could hang your hat on." The research services themselves were

invited to comment on the report, which they did with varying degrees
of grace. "What ARF blandly recommends," wrote Pulse, "is a mono-
theistic worship of the machine . . . not to be cutely remote—your
analysis boils down to an excellent promotion piece for the A. C.
Nielsen Audimeter." The late C. E. Hooper denounced the report
as "Research by Proclamation," made cynical reference to the fact that
the president of the Advertising Research Foundation was a consultant to the Nielsen organization, and ended with a suggestion for
disposition of the committee's findings: "That all copies, save one, of
the ARF report be destroyed. One should be retained as an example
of what not to do."

Despite the controversy, and despite the committee's failure to proceed to the rest of its job, the ARF report established the Nielsen ratings
as the only ponderable force in network audience measurement. The
other services still continue, and even thrive, mostly on their measurements of audiences for local stations and on their measurements of the
radio audience (which does something like one-quarter of its listening
out of doors). Today, however, television network programs can survive
on the air only if they receive a fairly good Nielsen rating (15, indicating an audience of 6 million households, is about bottom for a nighttime show); otherwise the networks will toss them out and shop for
something new.

To the people employed on these programs, this situation is a tragedy;
to the critics who like the programs which disappear, it is a serious
annoyance; to the ten or so million people who have been watching and
enjoying the unsuccessful shows, it is a sad commentary. But, as one
of the victims of the rating services has often commented, "them is
the conditions which prevail." A television network has nothing whatever to sell an advertiser except the size of the audience that will watch
his show. If one program has a low audience, the program that follows
it will also, in all likelihood, have a low audience. (Many people who
watch television are either too lazy or too uncaring to turn the dial.
There have been a few occasions when program A was moved from
9:30 to 9, and program B from 9 to 9:30, with astonishing increase
in audience for both. People tuned in to see program A and hung

around to watch B; while in the old days they had ignored the less-appealing program B and had not cared enough about the more-appealing program A to get up and change the station. The switch of the Phil Silvers Show and Navy Log, on the CBS network, produced exactly this result.) Networks are in vigorous, not to say vicious, competition with each other for the advertiser's dollar; and if a less popular program stands in the way of victory in this competition, the program will be ruthlessly sloughed away, whatever its quality.

Disregarding the morality (or admitting the permanence) of this procedure, the question often and bitterly asked by television personalities and television critics is whether the ratings are really accurate. There are only 1,000 Audimeters in the whole country, only 930 of them in working order; there are only three Audimeters in the city of Portland, Oregon. How can 930 households state the actual viewing habits of some 40 million-plus American homes with television sets? How can a "sample" of 930 homes give an accurate measure of a "universe" of more than 40 million?

Well, oddly enough, it can—within certain predictable ranges of error. The fact that people look different, dress differently, live differently, and think differently is not important to the man measuring the total size of a television audience—provided that lots of these different people watch the same television program, as they do. "Sampling" is a valid technique for gaining information whenever the "universe" to be sampled, however diverse in other respects, contains a reasonably high proportion of whatever it is you are measuring. Mathematical statistics, given its logical assumptions, is an exact science. When Nielsen says that the Ed Sullivan show reached 35 per cent of all television-equipped homes, or 14,420,000 households, the odds are almost 19 to 1 that it reached more than 13,370,000 homes and fewer than 15,470,000 homes. (The odds are about even that it reached more than 14,070,000 homes and fewer than 14,770,000.) Obviously, a possible error of 1,050,000 households is not to be taken lightly by anybody, but it is not so extreme as to cast doubt on the fact that the Ed Sullivan show is an immensely successful program.

And when Nielsen says that *Omnibus* reached 12 per cent of all television-equipped homes, or 4,945,000 households, the odds are 19 to 1 that it reached more than 4,225,000 households and fewer than 5,665,000 households. The possible error here of 720,000 is more serious than the apparently larger error on the Ed Sullivan show, because it involves a greater percentage of the estimated audience. Even so, at the maximum reasonable level of error, Nielsen has demonstrated that *Omnibus* has considerably less than half the audience of the Sullivan show.

At the level at which networks begin to want badly to ditch a program—15 "points," for percentage points—Nielsen's inaccuracy is limited (19 times out of 20) to 1.92 points. What the network hopes to substitute is not a program that will hit 18—where it might or might not have a larger audience, in reality, than the program rejected—but something that will reach a rating of 30, just under the very top shows. Giving the old program the full benefit of the maximum plausible error (and, considering that the rating comes out every two weeks, that maximum error is unlikely if the program shows a steady run of 15's), the show is still well under the average for nighttime network programs, and the network by its own lights cannot be blamed for casting it aside.

All these figures are predicated on a true "random" sample, which Nielsen does not have because it cannot be achieved. But his efforts in that direction have been noteworthy. Politz sets up his magazine audience studies in "clusters" of interviews, so that interviewers will not have to travel great distances on their assignments, which means that Politz samples are some distance removed from an ideal random state. (Nevertheless, because his sample is ten to twenty times the size of Nielsen's, Politz on pure statistics is at least as accurate in his measurements of magazine readership as Nielsen can be in his measurements of television audience.) But Nielsen need not worry if his Audimeters are fifty miles apart, since the machines need only occasional servicing. And he can spend almost any amount of money to "randomize" his sample, because he intends to use this sample as a fixed panel: he can amortize the costs of randomizing over dozens of research reports.

The fact that there are only three Audimeters in the city of Portland, Oregon (there are ten others in the suburbs), does not mean Nielsen's sample is weak; on the contrary, it means his sample is strong, because the television-owning population of the city of Portland, as a proportion of all television owners in the country, would call for only three out of one thousand Audimeters. When his data comes in, Nielsen does not have the vaguest notion of how programs rate in Portland. His possible error in each locality is infinite. But the patterns of mathematical statistics virtually guarantee that these errors will mostly cancel themselves out across the country, leaving him with a national rating accurate enough to justify its use as a basis for network decisions.

2.

Granted that the Nielsen ratings are accurate on a national basis, however, and that the networks are right to take them seriously, there remains some question about the importance of ratings to an advertiser. Knowledge of the total audience reached by the advertising message is, of course, very important, but it is merely the beginning of the media problem. The Dell Comic Group, with 15 million paid circulation and virtually unending pass-on readership, can offer an advertiser an audience at less than 70 cents a thousand for paid circulation, probably less than 10 cents a thousand for total audience. But the audience is composed of kids with only a few quarters jangling in their pockets (Dell's comics are not the horribilo-sadistic type that appeals to the military market), and not many advertisers want to go after the kids alone. It is possible for a television program to have a very large audience of people who are not in the market for the product advertised.

Advertisers who wish to know the kind of audience they are reaching must depend on other research services (most frequently Nielsen's own diaries, or Pulse or ARB). There is no strong feeling in the industry that any of these services are notably accurate by Audimeter standards. Nevertheless, they are the only wheel in town, and advertisers who cannot afford to pony up for their own research studies of these matters (most of them could, but shrink at the very thought) must draw their conclusions by weighing what the services say against what the network salesmen say. When commissioned research *is* done to determine audience characteristics, it often turns up some startling results: thus, Philip Morris abandoned the sponsorship of *I Love Lucy*, then the most popular show on television with a rating consistently over 40 points, because audience analysis indicated that relatively few heavy cigarette smokers watched the program; while CIBA pharmaceuticals was delighted to find that its *Medical Horizons* program, with a rating rarely over 7 points, reached 40 per cent of the nation's doctors at least once a month. (Nevertheless, CIBA finally gave up the show.)

Networks are not particularly concerned about the composition of the audience to their programs, because an audience that ill suits one advertiser will probably fit another one quite well. What the networks want is, simply, to maximize the total audience watching their programs, and in pursuing this aim they have followed with remarkable thoroughness Professor Hotelling's classic prescription for "duopolistic competition" (monopoly means one supplier; duopoly, two). The standard case in economics deals with a street twenty blocks long, containing a single grocery store on the downtown corner of block 5. A second grocer comes along: where shall be place his store? Public interest calls for placement on block 15, guaranteeing that no resident of the street will be farther than five blocks from a grocer. But the new grocer can secure the biggest market by placing his store on the uptown corner of block 5, right across the street from the competition, which will make him the more convenient of the two stores for the residents of fifteen blocks.

Operating to maximize market rather than to serve the public interest, the television networks have often followed this model, programming Phil Silvers against Milton Berle, *Robert Montgomery Presents* against *Climax*, Steve Allen and guests against Ed Sullivan and guests. The habit of identical programming is ingrained in the networks. The late Leonard Hole, who was in charge of NBC's new-program department, commented with interest in early 1956 about a CBS departure from form: "Seven-thirty to eight has always been for news programs. Now CBS has put an adventure program in the slot, reaching for the children just before they go to bed. We haven't changed, but if they begin to steal the ratings, we'll probably have to go to an entertainment show, too." In the event, NBC did drop the news shows from their historic place, substituting quizzes, music and mysteries: it was too dangerous to let CBS get the jump.

The extent to which this procedure operates against the public, which is certainly entitled to a choice between different kinds of shows, has been well demonstrated by television critics; what is less well understood is that it works against advertisers, too. An advertiser wants a particular kind of show because he feels that the market he wishes to reach will watch this sort of program more than any other; when the rival network programs the same thing at the same time, his effective penetration of his market is reduced. It would be false to imply, of course, that advertisers always accept low ratings with a good grace because they are pleased with their program; some advertisers bow to the rather foolish tyranny of the ratings and will pressure a network to drop a show which the network feels has potentialities, because the current rating is too low. "There have been occasions," says Y & R's Pete Matthews, "when we have withdrawn our client's support, and we were wrong. An advertiser can say, 'I'm paying the freight and I'm not getting the value. As near as I can tell, it's the program that's at fault.' Well, he isn't necessarily right."

Generally speaking, however, it is the networks rather than the advertisers who have been driving for the top ratings, regardless of other factors. The advertiser needs not only the right market, but also the right program, one which is "compatible" with his selling message. "It's quite possible," says Foote, Cone's Roger Pryor, "that a program might be ten points lower on Nielsen and still better for the selling message." Scott Paper, selling the idea of a luxury toilet tissue, would not wish to set its commercial against a real-life drama of the slums; and researcher Horace Schwerin found that Borden's commercials for strawberry ice cream produced a profoundly wrong reaction when set inside a gory murder show. To the networks these matters mean nothing; but even an unsophisticated advertiser, whose dream in life is to see his program atop the Nielsen Index, can understand the need for a program that sets the right mood for his product.

In the days of big radio the agencies themselves controlled the programs: they bought the time and put their own show in it. Today the networks maintain a fairly strict editorial supervision of what goes out over their facilities. On the face of it, this shift of responsibility seems to represent a social good: networks have no axes to grind (in theory) and are subject to indirect government regulation; and the stations that form the networks are legally obligated to act in the public interest, which advertisers are not. And, in practice, the networks have offered a number of public service programs and special events which advertisers would never have planned on their own hook. But the overall result has been disappointing: in their desperate competition with each other (a competition based as much on personal enmity as on financial logic) CBS and NBC have progressively lowered the *class* of their program lists to win the top ratings. There is no record that either network has ever refused to continue a cheesy, tasteless show which was receiving a high Nielsen; while NBC has bounced from its nighttime line-ups such superior attractions as the *Alcoa-Goodyear Playhouse*, the *Armstrong-Kaiser Circle Theater* and the *Voice of Firestone*—although, in every case, the advertiser was extremely pleased with what he had. Most of the quality shows on ABC, which until 1957 was too busy keeping alive to worry about pleasing the selective minority, are cast-offs from the two squabbling giants.

Most disappointing of all, from a public viewpoint, the assumption of programming authority by the networks has not led to any increase in courage in the handling of controversial material. While agencies ran programs, it was impossible that any issue or person conceivably obnoxious to any segment of the community could make an appearance on the air: advertising agents are servants of clients, with an almost fiduciary duty; they could not in good conscience agree to place the client in a possibly compromising position with part of his market. Networks, however, are their own boss, and their willingness to throw advertisers out the window whenever they wish to put a cheaper program in the advertiser's time slot argues that they do not live in terror of what advertisers will think of them. Nevertheless, they have acceded to blacklisting and harkened to all the old voices from minority and special interest groups.

In effect, network control of programming has made life more difficult for the advertiser (who fails to get the programs that reach his market in his way) without improving the over-all quality of broadcasts. The only beneficiaries have been the show business people whose price has constantly gone up as the networks compete with one another. Among the claims made by the networks to support their position as program controllers is the fact that they lose money on their own shows, because they put such fantastic sums into program development (presumably for the public good; they easily make up these losses on the sale of time). Foote, Cone's Roger Pryor, a bandleader and Hollywood personage before he became director of an agency television department, will have none of this. "Anybody who would issue 20- and 25-year contracts to talent has got to lose money," he says. "Metro-Goldwyn-Mayer in their palmiest days never did *that*."

3.

Despite all the conflicts, the two top television networks have little real trouble selling all their nighttime broadcast hours, every night of the week. (In fact, of course, it is the existence of this sellers' market which has enabled the networks to push the advertiser around.) Television is undoubtedly the greatest selling medium ever devised, for those relatively few advertisers whose market is so large that they do not waste most of television's enormous audience and whose advertising budget is big enough to carry television's enormous costs. The combination of the moving picture and the speaking voice, both in the consumer's own living room, gives the television advertiser something that is almost the equivalent of a door-to-door sales staff—which makes its visits at a cost considerably less than one cent per call. When the personality presenting the sales pitch is himself a great salesman—a Godfrey, a Steve Allen, a Tennessee Ernie Ford—the advertiser's cup runneth over. But he must make sure that the right stuff is in the cup —that the sales argument is an effective one in television terms and that the audience reached provides enough prospects for the product.

The differences in values between broadcast and print advertising can be put rather simply. Broadcast reaches a large section of the community which print advertising never touches. "Before radio," says Clifford Parsells of Bates, "it was theoretically true that you could reach everybody with your advertising, but you never did. There's 35, 40, 50 per cent of the population who may be literate, but reading is so difficult for them they don't do much of it." Broadcast sales messages can scarcely be escaped; few people can go out of earshot, physically or psychologically, when the commercial comes on. And an advertiser who buys a regularly scheduled broadcast program buys heavy "frequency"—that is, he is sure to reach many of the same people over and over again with repetitions of his sales story.

This repetition factor is undoubtedly important in advertising, and it was the secret of the success of the old radio soap opera, which had a relatively small but extremely loyal audience. Guy Richards, who recently retired as media director of Compton Advertising, recalls the early years of daytime radio, when Procter & Gamble "put together its own radio network for Oxydol, there wasn't any network in those days, and pounded home the message every day of the week. Well," Richards says, shaking his head at the memory, "strange things began to happen with Oxydol." Even those advertising men who most cherish originality will grant without question the importance of repetition. "Just the fact that you're there all the time," says Bill Bernbach, "makes people feel they can trust you. Psychologically, you're somebody who can be depended on."

On the other hand, the fact that you are reaching the same audience over and over again means that the total number of different people exposed to the message is somewhat lower than it would seem. Magazines will reach more people than a television show, per advertising dollar invested. "Our basic premise for Johnson & Johnson's Baby Products is that we have to buy large amounts of circulation," says Y & R's Matthews, "in fact as much circulation as possible in magazines read by women from eighteen through thirty-five. The reason is obvious: we never know when one of these women is going to become a customer." It is easy to escape reading an ad in a magazine, but a print ad, unlike a television commercial, will almost never arouse resentment and added consumer resistance. Moreover, though only one-fifth of a magazine's readership is likely to notice any given advertisement, that fifth will probably include the great bulk of the prospects for the product in this particular audience: when people are thinking of buying a new icebox they notice all the refrigerator ads. And print advertising at its best carries a conviction that the spoken voice—always slightly distrusted, too directly associated with selling—can never quite achieve.

The kind of sales argument to be used is important, perhaps crucial, in deciding whether print or broadcast media will give better results. "You may be advertising a new car model," says Paul Gerhold of Foote, Cone, "and you have something in which people feel a substantial interest. Or you may have a *legitimate* product improvement, or a *bona fide, honest-to-God* emotional appeal. Or, on the other side, you may have a product story that has been told very often, or an uninteresting product, or a factual rather than an emotional approach. Generally, when the interest is high, the media that give the prospects a chance to dream over the ad, respond to it at their own pace and on their own time, will be it; that's print ads in monthly media. When interest is low, something like television, which requires a physical act by the respondent to avoid the advertising, is obviously more appropriate." Jingles or hypnotic slogans (which can be used for institutional as well as selling purposes: "Better Things for Better Living, Through Chemistry") make a far greater effect on the air; image-building campaigns are almost invariably more successful in print. "Somehow," as Gerhold puts it, "when the product moves, you lose

that defined image of the brand." Similarly, the advertiser will be best
off with television if he has a single product feature that can be demonstrated convincingly (the one minute from snap to picture with the
Polaroid camera, for real; or the quicker action of Bufferin in the
stomach, for kicks); best off in print if he has a complicated or subtle
selling argument.

Radio and billboards function today mostly as reminders, ways of
calling back to the prospect's attention the idea of buying a product
he already knows about. Both are most used where there is no real
selling argument, but where a catchy jingle or an odd, bright picture
may stick a brand name firmly in the consumer's mind. And both, of
course, are particularly valuable for automotive products, because they
catch the man in the car (Edsel ran a very heavy billboard showing at
the beginning, "to put the car on the road"). Gasoline companies sponsor broadcasts of the local baseball games, because many men like
to listen to the ball game while driving and because nearly all filling
station operators tune in the baseball broadcast while sweating out the
long summer day.

So, at any rate, run the rules, and rules are disobeyed only at the
risk of unknown perils. But in media as elsewhere in advertising the
man who breaks the rules and gets away with it is the man who sends
his client spinning away on the high road: briefly; until the fact of
his success changes the rules, and everyone gets together in the new
rut to start all over again.

Part IV | FINDING THE
FACTS OF LIFE

CHAPTER 13

FROM THE FARMER'S WIFE TO THE INTEGRAL CALCULUS

"The problem with research is, people *lie* when you ask them questions. I remember, checking on why people drop out of book clubs, we sent a questionnaire: did you read these books? We put in three or four phony titles and as many people checked those as checked the big sellers."

Maxwell Sackheim

"Almost no researcher has realized all the things he can get from respondents with the right *kind* of questioning."

George Gallup

1.

Albert Lasker told the Columbia University Oral History project that Claude Hopkins had been the fastest worker he ever saw—that Hopkins could go down to see a client one day and come back with the answer to the client's problem the next day. Hopkins himself credited his youthful poverty, in the 1880's and 1890's, for his ability to *know*, almost immediately, the most likely advertising approach. Poverty, he wrote in his autobiography, "took me among the common people, of whom God made so many. I came to know them, their wants and impulses, their struggles and economies, their simplicities. Those common people whom I know so well became my future customers. . . . I love to talk to laboring-men, to study housewives who must count their pennies, to gain the confidence and learn the ambitions of poor boys and girls. Give me something which they want and I will strike the responsive chord. . . ."

Those, of course, were the days. But it is probably true that one of the reasons for Hopkins' great success was his willingness—even when he was making nearly $300,000 a year—to go out on the back roads and talk to farmers' wives about toilet soaps. Hopkins was a great believer in getting what he called "data," and hired people to do product research for him (what's in this product? how is it made?) whenever he had a new and particularly difficult job. It would not have occurred to him, however, to hire people for the purpose of finding out what consumers thought of a product. He could do enough of *that* himself, by personal interviews and by personal analysis of coupon returns from mail-order ads.

In the 1920's and early 1930's the copywriter who went out and talked to people had a great advantage over those who, in Hopkins' scornful phrase, "gained their impressions from golf-club associates." Ringing fifty convenient doorbells will not provide a scientifically accurate answer to a corporation's marketing problem, but it will very likely give a copywriter a number of ideas he would not have thought up by himself. Perhaps even more important, it may enable an advertising man to find out what is *wrong* with the product or with the current selling approach. When Benton & Bowles (then a new agency) was first assigned the Maxwell House Coffee account, it sent a few copywriters out to ask people why they *didn't* buy Maxwell House. A good proportion of the people questioned said that they thought Maxwell House was a good coffee, but it cost too much. Bill Benton's final recommendation to the client (General Foods, which owns Maxwell House) was to cut the price, taking the money *out of the advertising budget* if necessary, to put what advertising money was left into a weekly nighttime network radio show, and to slam across the coffee's old slogan, "Good to the Last Drop." A quarter of a century later, Benton & Bowles still has the Maxwell House account and will probably have it forever. General Foods is one of the few client companies that will reward an agency for a first-class piece of work by continuing loyalty through good years and bad.

But copywriters ringing doorbells could speak with only a few housewives living near the copywriters' homes or offices—and these housewives might be the wrong people to approach with questions about a brand. Obviously, it would do little good to ask a New York housewife about a regional brand sold only in the Gulf Coast states. And it soon appeared equally obvious that position in the wrong demographic group —wrong age, income, education or family status—might disqualify a housewife just as completely as position in the wrong geographical area.

"Brands tend to seek their customers rather than customers seeking their brands," says Peter Langhoff, research director of Young & Rubicam (a title virtually equivalent to president of a research company, since Y & R maintains its own research operation, complete with field interviewers and tabulators). For each brand of a product there is a certain maximum potential market, which is considerably smaller than the total market for this sort of product. Nobody can sell all of the people all of the time. One of the most important functions of advertising is, simply, to present the *existence* of a brand to the consciousness of the brand's potential customers. Advertising is wasted if it is directed (by a wrong choice of media) to people who do not live where the product is sold or (by a wrong choice of selling approach) to people in an age or income group which for some reason is not attracted to this brand. An advertiser hoping to increase his sales must know the groups to which his present customers belong and must concentrate his selling artillery on the people in those groups—plus the people in the groups demographically adjacent, who may be more susceptible to his persuasions.

Moreover, people do not consume equal quantities of a product: some customers are heavy users and some buy only occasionally. A customer converted in the light-user group may scarcely pay the cost of advertising, while a customer converted in the heavy-user group may contribute a steady stream of profits. Again, it seemed possible to break down the market into its parts, geographically and demographically, to isolate the heavy users at whom the advertising should be aimed. (Though it is more important to hit the potential customers, who are likely to fall down, if the heavy users fall into a different, and apparently less tractable, group. Thus, the J. Walter Thompson Company found that 5 per cent of the population, representing 13 per cent of the nation's beer drinkers, bought 52 per cent of all the beer. But Thompson's client was Schlitz, a light, premium beer which appeals to the occasional rather than to the steady beer drinker. On this basis, Thompson decided to go after the 87 per cent of occasional beer drinkers with lightweight ads stressing Schlitzness, and to let the heavy users go.)

Such detailed information cannot be developed by a copywriter who takes a few hours away from his desk to ring doorbells; nor can it be developed by a manufacturer sitting atop his factory and listening to optimistic reports from his salesmen. Somebody must send out teams of investigators to make a thorough survey of the market and to report back with their findings.

Much of this had been foreseen as early as 1908, when Harry Dwight Smith began to propagandize the advertising business in the interest of formal research; and Archibald Crossley was actually conducting formal surveys as early as 1919. It was not until the mid-1930's, however, that the industry as a whole caught up with the need for such systematized information. Thompson's Garrit Lydecker, recalling his apprenticeship under George Gallup of Y & R, says that "in those days we had a hell of a time convincing the people in our own agency to pay any attention to us, let alone the clients." The dawn came as a revelation: if market research could perform what it seemed to promise, it would virtually eliminate the risk from advertising. Market research firms sprang up like so many bright wildflowers from the otherwise barren soil of the 1930's, and while there were probably no more than twenty of them when the war came, these twenty were flourishing mightily.

Today there are nearly seventy market research organizations operating on a nation-wide basis; a 1957 directory in *Advertising Agency* magazine listed twenty-seven such firms with five hundred or more full- or part-time employees. A few of them, most notably the A. C. Nielsen Company and the Market Research Corporation, offer continuing studies of the national market for package goods, and tell manufacturers how much of what the public is buying. (This is not so simple as it seems, and most manufacturers cannot find out their sales to the public without such a service. Manufacturers sell to wholesalers and retailers, who maintains inventories, and these inventories may fluctuate without relation to consumer sales. It is quite possible that a manufacturer's sales to retailers will rise at a time when consumer demand for his product is falling, because retailers are increasing their inventories. In 1957 manufacturers' sales to retailers in many lines decreased even though public consumption went up, because higher interest rates made it more expensive for retailers to carry stocks of unsold goods and they therefore cut down on their inventories.) Other research firms measure aspects of the market—customer characteristics, selected store sales, consumer brand preferences, advertising effectiveness—either under long-term contract or on a one-job basis. Hundreds of thousands of citizens are interviewed and scores of thousands of stores are audited every month by the market researchers, tons of IBM punch cards pour through their automatic calculators, reams of statistics, graphs, charts and analyses pour across the desks of their clients, sales managers, advertising managers, employees of advertising agencies, and others.

But the risk has not yet been eliminated from advertising.

2.

Market research measurements in the 1930's were crude and commonly wrong. It is obviously impossible for any research firm except the United States government to investigate the entire market, and even the government undertakes such a job only once every ten years. Each researcher had to select a sample from the market, learn what his sample had to say, and then project the data to fill out the full dimensions of the market. Clearly, the final report could not be accurate unless the sample was truly representative of the market to be measured, and at the beginning no one had the foggiest notion of how to obtain a representative sample.

The most professional method of approach in those days was to set up "quotas"—so many doctors, so many bricklayers—according to Census information on the number of people in each occupation, and to spread the interviews more or less around the country. Statistically valid information cannot be drawn from a quota sample, however (quota sampling problems were probably the reason for the bad guess in the 1948 Gallup Poll of the presidential election), because the totals can be no more than an adding up of individual results within each biased occupational group, and the sample size for each group is never large enough to give accurate answers. It was not until 1943 that statistician Lester Frankel of the Census Bureau (later vice-president of Alfred Politz Research) conceived the "area probability" sample, enabling market researchers to apply the developing science of mathematical statistics in analyzing their results. Area probability samples have now been adopted for almost all serious research work, where high standards of accuracy are desired, but a surprising number of firms continue to bumble along with quota samples.

The honesty, intelligence and training of the interviewers also are major factors in the accuracy of the final research report. In the 1930's interviewers were easily and cheaply recruited from the ranks of the unemployed and were all, by definition, amateurs at the work. Faking was by no means uncommon, and "interviewer affect" (that is, conscious or unconscious guidance to the respondent by the interviewer) was almost universal. This problem persists and always will persist, but the extent of the damage has been greatly reduced by training programs and interviewer control procedures (which include calling up the people who were interviewed and asking them what happened). Nevertheless, some firms still hire interviewers on the most casual application, trusting them to know what they are doing and to behave nicely to their employers.

Finally, it was believed in the 1930's that an interviewer could find out almost anything from a respondent simply by asking him a straight question, and it was not for some time that analysts of the reports realized they were being fed malarkey by the people of America. Sometimes the fault lay in the questionnaire itself, which asked people for information they could not reasonably be expected to give (Do you prefer a strong mouthwash or a mild mouthwash? The subject admitting a preference for a strong mouthwash would also be admitting—to an utter stranger, too—that she suffered from what Gerard Lambert had taught the world to call halitosis). Often, however, a straightforward question about a matter with no particular emotional overtones would draw large quantities of obviously false replies. Investigation of these errors produced what was then the rather startling conclusion that many people simply did not know the answers to easy questions about their own tastes and buying habits.

Only an occasional housewife has thought through her reasons for buying or not buying a product (except, of course, for the simple, "Tried it once, didn't like it," which is scarcely to be remedied by advertising). Confronted with the straight question, many women do not even know which brands they buy. In Denver a few years ago researchers stood beside clerks at checkout counters in a supermarket, wrote down what the ladies were putting into their shopping bags, then followed the shoppers home and (after giving them enough time to put the stuff away) rang the bell to ask which brand in each of a number of product lines the lady had most recently purchased. A wrong answer came back nearly one-quarter of the time. Asked to concentrate her attention on the reasons why she buys or neglects a given brand, even the housewife who knows very well what she buys will often pull out a rationalization which may or may not have anything to do with the case. People usually want to be helpful.

And even when results were gained which appeared to be highly accurate, advertisers found themselves puzzled as to the next step. The mucilage that bound together a market for a brand was usually not to be found by simple analysis of demographic classifications: most brands drew at least some of their market from nearly all ages, incomes, family responsibilities, and so forth. Still, it seemed an obvious truth that people who buy brand A must have some other characteristics, apart from the mere brand preference, which distinguish them from the people who buy brand B. The common failure to deduce market characteristics from breakdowns of demographic data, coupled with the discovery that many housewives actually did not know why they bought one brand rather than another, produced a demand for *psychological* classifications, for discovery of the "real reasons" which guided consumers in their choice of brands.

Much of the pioneering work in this area was done at McCann-Erickson, under the direction of Marion Harper before he became president of the agency. Harper had studied psychology at Yale, and among his assistants was Dr. Herta Herzog, Paul Lazarsfeld's first wife and a psychologist in her own right. Borrowing techniques from the clinical laboratories, the McCann researchers set certain standard tests, used to diagnose mental illness, before more or less normal consumers, checked the consumers' brand preferences in various product groups, and then sought for correlations between scores on the tests and consumption of brands. Every once in a while they came up with a spectacular finding, most notably when they applied Rorschach tests to cigarette smokers. (The Rorschach test presents the patient with a set of actually meaningless black-to-gray ink blots on a white page and asks him to tell the doctor, please, what the ink blots seems to him to represent. All sorts of interesting notions about the patient can be drawn from the results of this systematized parlor game by an experienced practitioner, but the responses are usually regarded as most significant in establishing the patient's patterns of submission or dominance: that is, does he tend to accept his lot or to control his surroundings?) "You could put cigarette brand personalities on a scale," says Donald Armstrong, who worked with Harper and Herzog on the tests and is now McCann's director of research, "all the way from Lucky Strike, LSMFT, aggressive, to Philip Morris, the gentle smoke, hypochondriac. Herta and I passed Rorschach test results back and forth across a table, and just looking at them you knew immediately the brand the poor devil *had* to smoke. We were right eighty times in a row."

Harper, Herzog and Armstrong were working largely from "brand personalities" indicated by other research work, and verifying their assumptions by testing consumers. Elsewhere, independent researchers were working at a similar problem from the other side, seeking to determine the subconscious significance of products and brands in the minds of consumers as a group. Here, too, a number of techniques were imported from the psychiatric clinic, but the central tool was the long, rambling, "unstructured" interview, during which the housewife spoke freely of herself, the way she spent her time, what she thought about products and brands, and how she used them. The interviewer was to function as a psychiatrist-substitute, making sympathetic noises and occasionally directing the talk back to an unusually promising area. These two- and three-hour consumer research sessions were described as "depth interviews" (a promising brand name) by Ernest Dichter, Ph.D., head of the firm which has the largest single slice of this business and of the publicity attending it. It was Dichter's contention that by analyzing the verbatim transcripts of these interviews, a psychiatrically trained person like himself could discover the sexual symbolism with which, in the theory, the id has endowed the commonplace objects of daily life. Quite possibly, thereafter, an advertising approach could be found which would tie a brand name to the fundamental human urge with which the product is associated. "The right slogan," Dichter says helpfully. In this context, use values and product features are secondary to the purchaser; his "real reason" for buying is the satisfaction of deep drives which he does not consciously understand.

Except under the severe pressure of new business solicitation, Dichter and his associates do not claim that the sexual imagery of a product is always—or even commonly—a motivating factor in consumer purchases. They believe it is always there, and that any research designed to find selling approaches must begin with an understanding of the relationship between the product and the fundamental human drive, but that the sexual symbolism is often too deeply buried under the consumer's ego to influence brand preferences. As Dichter himself puts it, "the knowledge of basic motivations is necessary, or else you will not see any significance in an important phenomenon. But the *manifestations* of these basic motivations change, and usually you have to appeal to the manifestations." The search for manifestations leads Dichter into fields far removed from theoretical psychology, into areas of "the brand personality" which cannot be related, by any stretch of the dialectic, to basic sexuality.

These other areas are often sociological rather than psychological, referring to status symbols rather than to sexual symbols. Products that are consumed in public—most notably automobiles, of course, but also houses, furniture, clothing, liquor, books and records, tableware, food (as served to friends at dinner), and so forth—unquestionably testify in one way or another to the social standing, aspirations and origins of the people who buy them. This testimony is not, however, taken under oath, and the subject is an extraordinarily tricky one. Social aspirations may conflict with social status, and either or both may disagree with social origins.

Assuming for the sake of argument that individual patterns of buying are, in fact, dictated by social forces, these forces will operate very differently in the parvenu oil areas of Texas and in the disintegrating enclave of Tuxedo Park, in the open working-class suburbs of Los Angeles and in the nasty slums of Chicago. Emphasizing the social symbolism of a product may influence the market for the brand in a way which the advertiser did not necessarily desire. The Lord Calvert "Men of Distinction" campaign produced a great increase in the consumption of the brand by Negroes; Cadillac's insistence on ownership of a Cadillac as proof of position has degraded the car in the eyes of the small community which needs no proof of its position and rather resents being lumped with the *arrivistes* from the prize-fighting, popular music and manufacturing worlds. Bishop Fulton Sheen, who has specialized in the conversion of the upper classes, is chauffeured about in a Mercedes-Benz. Finally, in the great stretches of the middle class there are communities in which the old saw about keeping up with the Joneses has been transfigured to the new power tool of keeping *level* with the Joneses. In these communities it is the worst of bad form to behave or consume in such a way that one may be suspected of snooting one's neighbors—to drink Scotch, for example, when all the boys are drinking bourbon. In this area, distinctions between otherwise identical brands may be made by the "brand image," which is at least in part created by advertising. To advertise effectively, the argument ends, a manufacturer must know his present brand image, the community it selects, and the opportunities for increasing the market offered by the facts of social stratification.

Research on these matters fits easily into the amorphous area which sociology has staked out for itself in the colleges, and a good deal of the work on brand images is done on a fellowship basis by graduate students, especially at Columbia and the University of Chicago. The big names in the field are Burleigh Gardner, Lloyd Warner, David Riesman and William H. Whyte, the last two serving as apostles to the gentiles. Gardner has largely abandoned his academic career and devotes most of his time to his own research firm, Social Research, Inc., which has grown to the point where it now employs a professional staff of fifteen and a core group of full-time interviewers. It is the organization of choice for those advertising men—most notably Edward Weiss and Pierre Martineau, research director of the Chicago *Tribune*—who regard sociological phenomena as the background against which advertising must do its work.

"What is killing off the Freudians in this business," Edsel's David Wallace remarked casually, "is David Riesman's theory of the 'other-directed' person," the individual who draws guidance from a "reference group" rather than from childhood inheritance. The psychological and sociological researchers use some of the same tools—sentence completion,

"thematic apperception," "semantic differential"—and often a firm with
an essentially psychoanalytic bias, like Dichter's, will keep sociologists
on hand to come up with analyses of status symbols or (more frequently) to interpret the Freudian analysis in more widely acceptable
sociological terms. Advertisers are impatient with the niceties of difference between theoretical disciplines, and any research firm which
announced that it could do one branch of "projective" research but
couldn't do another would shortly find its clients dribbling away to a
firm which offered both for the price of one.

It must be observed, however, that the Freudian and the new
sociological attitudes are not compatible. Both are self-enclosed theoretical systems claiming an eventual explanation for all human relations.
Both are deduced from scattered insights rather than developed from
general propositions, and in the interstices of the insights they may
find no quarrels. But their perceptions are different, often completely
contradictory. There can be no reconciliation between Riesman's peer
group and Freud's paternal authority; in announcing the repudiation
of what they like to call "the Protestant ethic," the sociologists (though
some of them are not conscious of the fact) have proclaimed the death
of the conditions which underlie the Freudian analysis. It is unimportant whether either is right, whether there are elements of truth in
both, or whether both are wrong (indeed, in advertising research
generally it is unimportant whether the researcher's theoretical bias
is sound or not, provided the theory is distant enough not to get in the
way of the facts). What is important is that any man who understands
and professionally practices one cannot intelligently or thoroughly practice the other.

Yet, through some remarkable confusion, both are subsumed by the
advertising business under the single name "motivation research."
Public confusion is even worse, since few people outside advertising
have had any contact with this phenomenon save in the pages of Vance
Packard's *The Hidden Persuaders*. Packard classifies as motivation research the entire work of the advertising business, from copywriters'
horse-sense hunches (Ted Bates's "Cleans Your Breath While It Cleans

Your Teeth," attributed by Packard to motivation research done some sixteen years after the slogan made its first appearance) through to Dichter's most rigorously Freudian analyses. And such confusions, of course, are the wellsprings of controversy.

Finally, through these years when the theoreticians have been selling advertisers on their theoretical certainties, a few firms have developed research techniques to solve specific problems in a specific way. They will ask direct, market-research questions or analyze long interviews if the problem seems to call for such tactics; but their essential approach is to regard each question as a *stimulus* and each answer as a *response*, neither true nor false, neither psychologically nor sociologically significant. They hope to set up questions or sets of questions which will not in themselves carry any emotional charge, but will draw answers indirectly revealing the true answers to questions which—if asked directly —would have put people on their guard.

The practice of this technique requires experience, a high order of cleverness, and a clear intelligence. The methods employed were pioneered in the 1930's for industry and during the war for the Army by Elmo Roper. Requested to investigate public attitudes toward the local power and light company, Roper went around and asked people whether they thought their electricity bills were too high. Requested by the Army to find out which units were psychologically most ready to go into combat in North Africa, which of them had the greatest faith in their regimental commanders and would most willingly follow their colonels, Roper sent interviewers to the camps to ask GI's how the chow was in their outfit. In both cases he knew that the answers he received to his apparently extraneous questions also told his employers what they wished to know. The outstanding practitioners of this technique in advertising research today are James M. Vicary in a small, rather relaxed and highly eclectic way, and Alfred Politz (who worked for several years in Roper's office) in a great, big way, with extraordinary emphasis on continuing studies and verifiable data.

CHAPTER 14

LOCATING THE MARKET

1.

Research theories come and research theories go, but, said Art Nielsen, sitting over a frugal lunch at the conference table of his rather plain office in The Nielsen Building, "I'd say our clients feel that the *Food-Drug Index* is more important to them today than it's ever been before." Nielsen at sixty is a tall, lean, athletic man (he and his son have several times won the national amateur father-and-son tennis championship) with a lean, Danish face, rimless glasses and a fringe of long hair that is still largely blond. An electrical engineer by training, he has been a researcher for some thirty-five years, a market researcher for more than three-quarters of that time, and the letterhead on his stationery states truthfully, "A. C. NIELSEN COMPANY World's Largest Marketing Research Organization." The lunch he was eating was a duplicate of the lunch being served downstairs in the cafeteria of The Nielsen Building, a large, five-story structure with the appearance of a well-kept old high school, which stands on the Evanston City Line at the northern edge of Chicago.

More than 1,350 full-time employees work for Nielsen in the Chicago office alone, and Nielsen has further offices in New York, San Francisco, Toronto, London, Oxford, Dublin, Amsterdam, Sydney, Wellington, Brussels, Lucerne, Frankfurt and Stockholm. Though the name is best known outside the advertising business for broadcast ratings, Nielsen's major efforts are concentrated in the market research divisions: ratings account for about $4 million out of a domestic revenue of roughly $15 million and a world-wide revenue of roughly $20 million. Nielsen also *likes* the *Food-Drug Index* because "in the food and drug business practically everybody wants the truth." So does Nielsen: alone among market researchers, he is basically more interested in his techniques—in perfecting them and defending them against any attacks from the ignorant rabble (anyone who doubts the accuracy of a Nielsen finding is *ipso facto* ignorant rabble)—that he is in proclamations of the information which his services produce.

The A. C. Nielsen Company was started in 1923 strictly as an engineering consultants firm, supplying evaluations of manufacturers' materials and equipment. Toward the end of the 1920's the company began to supplement these equipment reports with studies of the capital goods markets, performed for the same clients. In late 1929 and early 1930 the capital goods markets could be described by the single word "None"; and in 1931 it seemed quite likely that Nielsen, along with so many other businesses, would not survive the depression. Fresh life appeared quite suddenly, however, when a new type of client, a proprietary drug manufacturer, walked in the door with a new type of problem involving a survey of drugstores. Nielsen's success in analyzing this unfamiliar area quickly brought him other clients among the drug manufacturers and among companies which sold through drugstores.

Inevitably, Nielsen's field men found themselves calling over and over again on the same druggists, carrying each time a questionnaire which often took as much as an hour to complete. Their welcome wore thin, and one day an interviewer was told to get out and stay out before he had finished asking the druggist the last questions on his list.

In desperation, anxious not to throw away fifty minutes of accomplished interview, the interviewer dug into his own pocket, pulled out a dollar bill and offered it to the druggist for ten more minutes of his time. The druggist snatched the bill and gave courteous, careful attention to the rest of the interview. The interviewer reported this experience to Nielsen, partly as a joke and partly in the hope of getting his dollar back, and the conversation about it in the shop produced what was then an entirely original concept of market research.

Briefly, Nielsen and his associates decided to establish a permanent panel of drugstores, representative of the nation's drugstores as a whole, paying each druggist a nominal sum for his co-operation. Further, they decided to eliminate the interview procedure, which was likely to take up more than a nominal sum's worth of a druggist's time, and to ask instead for the right to examine his invoices and audit the stock in his store, to determine how much of each product he was selling. While auditing the store, which he would do every two months, the Nielsen man would also look around to see what products were featured in window displays, on the counters, at special prices, and so forth. Finally, Nielsen would offer this service to *all* drug manufacturers and drugstore suppliers, selling the same information to bitter competitors, on the grounds that everyone could use the data and could buy it a great deal cheaper if the entire industry footed the bill. Every step of this procedure was a success. The *Drug Index* was launched in 1933; a year later the service was extended to food products and grocery stores. Nielsen revenues in 1933 came to $52,000; by 1937 they had crossed the million mark, though the nation was still in the middle of a depression and businessmen could scarcely afford to throw money away on fripperies. To say that the service had proved itself is an understatement.

The *Food-Drug Index* grew despite the disappointment of its subscribers in what was probably their greatest hope—that it would enable them to measure accurately the results of their advertising. Instead, the *Index* proved beyond doubt that sales were dependent on so many factors that the effect of advertising could not often be isolated. But what Nielsen gave was even more important: the first accurate measure of all selling factors acting together, not only for the company examining the data but for its competitors as well. Total national sales could be projected from the sample, and each manufacturer could see at a glance his share of the market. Since reports came in every two months, on a continuing basis, he could find out whether he was gaining on the competition or whether they were gaining on him. Comparing his results with theirs, he knew whether changes would be necessary in his selling effort—usually in the advertising, too, even though he could not *pinpoint* the blame on advertising if sales were dropping. Moreover, the Nielsen figures were broken down by geographical region, by the client's own sales areas (if desired), into six different classifications of county size, by kind of store, and by size of package. A company could learn, usually for the first time, just how good its distribution was, in absolute terms and by comparison with its competitors, and received a figure every two months on how many stores were out of stock in each area, an invaluable check on the efficiency of the sales staff. Finally, as lagniappe, Nielsen told the company the extent of "dealer push"— how many dealers were using its point-of-sale promotional material, how many were displaying the brand, how many were offering it on sale or in combination with other items in a specially priced package, how many were advertising it in the local press. Departing from the United States after his first yearlong visit in 1938, David Ogilvy pronounced that "Nielsen has been to advertising in America what Galileo was to astronomy."

In 1957, as the two indices neared their twenty-fifth anniversary, Nielsen was undertaking audits in some 1,600 grocery stores servicing 500,000 families and some 700 drugstores servicing 750,000 families. His clients included almost every major food, drug, soap and toiletries company in the nation; some of them paid as much as $500,000 for *Food-Drug Index* information alone. Except for the A & P, every major grocery chain in the country co-operates with Nielsen, not merely for the few dollars but also for certain free marketing reports which Nielsen sends them. Grocers have no objection to an auditor fiddling around in their stock; indeed, they sometimes await the auditor's arrival impatiently. "Our man will come in," says E. P. H. James, Nielsen's British-born assistant, "and the storekeeper will say, 'I've been waiting for you. Do you know where I put that dozen dozen something?' And our man will say, 'Sure, it's behind the safe.'" Nielsen is not disturbed by the absence of A & P, the largest single food chain, from his list of co-operating stores. "We select our samples," he says, "and when we make up our lists of which stores should be audited a certain number of A & P outlets turn up on the list and demand to be included. So we take the nearest chain store most like that neighborhood's A & P."

Some 240 men work full time for Nielsen auditing the 2,300 stores in the national panel, plus 2,300 additional stores in certain test markets which Nielsen maintains as an added service for his regular clients. (Another service estimates advertising expenditures by each company in each product field.) Nielsen's field men go through a six-month course of training at a dummy store not far from the central office ("a Chinese copy of a real supermarket," says James, "except that it doesn't have any customers"), where they learn to use the forms on which they will report on 3,000-plus different branded items. Nielsen estimates that it takes one man one day to do a complete audit of invoices and stock in a small grocery, two men three days to perform the same job in a big supermarket. But the bulk of the work in this sort of operation is, inevitably, in the tabulating center where the forms are checked for completeness and their contents run through the serried ranks of IBM machines.

When the results have emerged from the chattering calculators they are sent up to the charting room, which prepares some fifty thousand charts a year. (The client to whom the chart will go always has the bar representing his brand at the left of the graph; separate charts are prepared for Colgate, Gleem, Pepsodent, etc., to give each client a feeling that he comes first.) Then the statistics and charts go off to the Nielsen "service representative," who will present the figures and analyze their significance every two months at a conference with the client and, usually, the client's agency. As an ordinary matter, the report takes three hours to present . . .

2.

Obviously, there are two ways to find out how goods are moving: to ask the stores what they're selling or to ask the people what they're buying. Nielsen follows the first of these paths; the J. Walter Thompson Consumer Purchase Panel follows the second. So does Sam Barton's Market Research Corporation of America, but in a far more thorough and complicated manner. A few large companies regard Barton's procedure as better than Nielsen's for most purposes; others, while relying largely on Nielsen for their total sales data, buy Barton's service for certain added values. (MRCA's monthly reports cost on an annual basis about half as much as Nielsen's every-other-month reports, with prices running up to about $50,000 a year, depending on the amount of data desired. Monthly Nielsen or weekly MRCA reports also are available to advertisers, at an extra charge.) Barton himself feels that he is very directly in competition with Nielsen. "If you have enough money," he says, "it's nice to have two doctors or two accounting systems, but if you have limited funds you'll take just one."

In person, as in technique, Barton and Nielsen are contradictory. Nielsen is the rather stiff engineer, working with store shelves and numbers, running a very formal organization with gold pins for five-year employees, gold pins with one diamond for ten-year employees, gold pins with two diamonds for fifteen-year employees, and so on up to the final accolade of the gold pin set with "2 Baguette Emeralds, 1 Diamond" for the forty-year man (nobody has made this level yet, since the firm has been in existence only thirty-five years). Barton, by contrast, is a casual sociologist who looks rather like a Wendell Willkie with straight hair, who works with people rather than with audited numbers and keeps them on the job by studied informality: everyone in his small New York headquarters office (tabulating center is in Chicago) calls him "Sam." Where Nielsen likes to talk about all the checks and certainties in his system, Barton relishes all the human problems that arise in running a consumer panel and all the human ways he has found to solve them—or most of them, anyway. The two men are not friends, and each will go some distance out of his way to criticize the other's services.

Barton's panel includes roughly seven thousand households scattered throughout the United States, each of which fills in a diary of pur-chases, including price and package size, by all members of the family. Diaries are mailed back to Barton every week, with a Sunday night or Monday morning postmark. (Since most families do the bulk of their shopping on Friday and Saturday, this procedure minimizes the chance that people will wait until sometime after their purchases to write down their recollections of what they bought. The Thompson panel, with *monthly* diaries, runs a far greater risk of this sort of sloppy work in the laboratory.) Within the panel, some four thousand individuals keep *daily* diaries, mailed out every night, reporting their purchases of foods and household supplies, some drugs and toiletries, towels, sheets and (of all things) phonograph records. Each member of the household must sign the weekly diaries, and each of them is paid separately (in "points" good for catalogue merchandise) to encourage everybody to keep his own records. The average payment per household is about the same as Thompson's ($50 worth of merchandise a year), but the scale is variable to enable Barton to tempt middle-class families who are repelled by the nuisance of keeping a purchase diary.

Virtually every other panel of any kind in the advertising business is composed exclusively of white, literate, English-speaking Americans, but Barton is interested in everybody with money to spend. Foreign-language diaries are sent to those big-city immigrant families which do not speak English, and foreign-language-speaking field staff work with them on keeping the diary accurately. Illiterates are a somewhat tougher nut to crack, but Barton has managed it by asking them to save the wrappers or labels from everything they buy; the field man comes along once a week, fills out the diary from the wrappers and from supple-mentary questions, and makes a trip to the family's local store to find out what prices were paid.

Barton's sample has been set up with attention to "area probability" techniques, but with modifications which are required to compensate for those households which turn up in the mathematical sample but which refuse on any terms to keep a purchase diary. The drop-out rate is roughly eleven hundred families a year, and replacements are chosen at random from within the same neighborhood. "Also," Barton says, "there's a million new families a year, and you have to keep up with them. It's harder to hold young families, especially when the wife becomes pregnant with the first child." To help hang on to the sample, Barton increases his payment per diary for every year the family is in the panel. Payment begins immediately when a family joins the panel, but data from that family will not be included in the totals until thirteen weekly diaries have been filled in under the questioning eye of one of MRCA's field staff of nearly two hundred.

Barton is quite sure that members of his panel do not become "professional consumers" and that they do not buy higher prestige items because they know somebody is watching them. "Maybe they'll buy sometimes to impress their friends," Barton says, "not to impress us. Only occasion I can think of along that line was a woman in a poor section, who bought a chicken, it was a splurge for her. She looked in her diary and found no place to write down that she'd bought a fresh chicken, and she wrote us. She was disappointed." Like Thompson, he is also sure that panel members have only the vaguest notion of the purposes for which their information is used. "They know they're members of the National Consumer Panel," Barton says, "and whenever there's any trouble they're to write Sam Barton about it. That's about all they care to know."

MRCA's sixty clients receive total national purchase data broken down à la Nielsen into regions, sales areas, by county size and (probably much less accurately) by type of store. Unlike Nielsen, Barton cannot testify to distribution, to dealer push, to out-of-stock figures or to inventories. On the other hand, he can supply information even more valuable to a client in planning his advertising (as distinguished from the rest of his sales effort, where Nielsen is a greater help). He can break down the market for a brand in terms of demographic characteristics, highlighting strengths and weaknesses. He can tell a client how many new customers he is winning and the extent to which new customers tend to keep buying his product. If a client is offering consumers a special deal, two-for-the-price-of-one, Barton can tell him (within twelve days or less after the deal begins) whether he is tapping a new market by his deal or whether he is simply borrowing from the future by persuading regular customers to buy more at the special price.

Where new products are concerned, Barton can supply the most vital single piece of information: how many *repeat customers* has the product developed? On the always touchy question of brand loyalties ("There is no such thing," says George Gallup; "it's the biggest delusion in the advertising business; the minute a customer thinks somebody else has more of something or a lower price, he's over there"), Barton can give the only answer in the business thoroughly backed by statistical data. He says that there are very marked loyalties, but not to a single brand; people will alternate their purchases among two or three brands, buying them in different proportions from time to time, but rarely venturing outside their own magic circle. Again, as in the Nielsen service, information comes to a client not only about his own brands but also about competitors (who may also, again, be clients of the same service). "I run a grocery store," Barton says, "any company can come in here and buy."

Given the conflict between the two men, Barton is particularly pleased about one piece of sales data that he can supply and Nielsen probably cannot—the prices at which the goods are actually moving. By gathering data continuously, Barton makes much more delicate measurements of market movements than Nielsen can deliver by probing into each store at most once a month. Barton's service, for example, is a major source of data for the Department of Agriculture studies on retail food prices. As 1957 came to a close, Barton was planning to challenge Nielsen in still another area—broadcast audience measurements—but, though he has run a number of experiments, one of them under the sponsorship of NBC Radio, he has not yet decided on the system he will use.

CHAPTER 15

HATS, RABBITS
AND MAGICIANS

1.

A few miles beyond the New York Central marshaling yards by the Hudson in Harmon, New York, a narrow side road leads off Route 9 up what is labeled Prickley Pear Hill. There is a single house near the foot of the hill, and then something more than a mile of private road, winding around the hill to climb some six hundred feet above the Hudson, the scrub and low trees opening up occasionally to give a vista of the river, other tree-covered hills—but no other houses. At the end of the lonely drive the road widens to an oval parking lot with a rough stone wall along the side, a gate opening through the wall. On second look the wall becomes part of a large fieldstone house with fewer than the usual number of windows and a semifortified appearance, and the gate is an archway through the house leading into an open courtyard. There is a view over the Hudson Valley hills for miles around, but not another human habitation in sight. Here, if anywhere near New York, is the setting for a mad genius; and it may have been with this psychological impression of the house in his mind that Ernest

Dichter in 1953 bought it to be headquarters of his Institute for Research in Mass Motivations (now called the Institute for Motivational Research).

From the beginning of his practice as an independent advertising consultant, in the late 1940's, Ernest Dichter, Ph.D. (the doctorate is in psychology), has sold himself as a kind of mad genius, and his service as something nobody else could or would do. This tactic and the publicity it gained for Dichter's Institute have furiously antagonized Dichter's fellow researchers. Some of them fear, distrust or dislike Dichter's originality; others have tried and rejected, or tried and used in a subordinate role, the great majority of the techniques Dichter introduced to advertising research and then violently publicized. This negative attitude of his colleagues bothers Dichter not at all. "I feel I'm better off building a better mousetrap," he says, "and antagonizing the conventional mousetrap makers."

Dichter's mousetrap begins operation, once a client has placed cheese in it, with a series of "unstructured interviews," round-table discussions or "psycho-drama" sessions (Dichter calls these impromptu pieces of play-acting his Motivational Theater) built around a product or a brand. Interviews are usually scattered throughout the country; the participants in group discussion and role assumers are drawn partly from a panel of families living in the surrounding towns of Peekskill, Harmon and Croton-on-Hudson. Interviews, round-table discussions and psycho-dramas are all tape recorded (the round-table discussions and the psycho-dramas may also be photographed), and from a basis of these transcripts of free conversation or role assumption Dichter and his staff develop hypotheses about people's "real reactions" to products, current advertising campaigns for these products, and especially the brand which has retained the services of the Institute.

The discussion panel has not been constructed according to customary sampling procedures; it has been solicited in part by members of the Institute staff (who give speeches at local clubs) and, on occasion, by commercial announcements on the local radio. Dichter's Institute has sponsored a radio discussion program which presented members of the panel talking over some local issue or some consumer product under the direction of an Institute research associate. At the end of the program listeners were told that if they wished to participate in similar programs they need merely drop a card to Ernest Dichter, Ph.D., President, Institute for Motivational Research. In recent years, with the increasing publicity given to the Institute, and the growth of local pride in possessing such a facility right at hand, more and more panel members have been bringing their friends. All are welcome, though old-timers sometimes must be dropped from the panel because they have become too knowledgeable. Each round-table session or psycho-drama session ends with the award of a door prize. Once a month a general drawing is held, and one of the panel families wins an evening in New York, with babysitter, railroad fares, dinner at a good restaurant, and tickets for a hit show all paid for by Dichter. It is a far more humane procedure than the usual gimlet-eyed interviewing.

In part, the "motivation" theory holds that the Colonel's lady and Judy O'Grady are sisters under the skin, so the Institute has not always seen the need to extend its work further than the confines of Westchester County. Usually, however, the usable "manifestations" of the motivations are fairly near the surface, and Dichter feels it desirable to look around and see if the same manifestations are cropping up elsewhere. For really elaborate jobs—such as the continuing study for Ford or the 1957 study for the Silversmiths' Guild, on motivations in the choice of silverware patterns—the Institute will attempt a full national sampling on a quota system. Sometimes the client will specify the type of sample desired. And those clients who cannot afford full-scale research projects may buy "creative memos," based on the experience of the staff and a few local interviews.

All interviews with fairly large samples must of necessity be partially "structured"—that is, question-and-answer rather than rambling response—but the structure remains psychiatric. The respondent will be shown a picture of two people performing some action and asked what they are doing, or consuming some product and asked what it is (one of the more charming of these drawings, for a children's panel, showed four young men in space suits in a space ship, eating breakfast; the question was, "What breakfast food are the spacemen eating?"). Or he may be shown a cartoon with blank balloons coming out of the mouths of the characters—who are, say, looking at an automobile—and asked to fill in the conversation. Or he may be shown an incomplete sentence and offered a choice of five completions for it, one of which will be "correct" in the terms of the motivation analysis which is being tested.

But the grist for all these mills flows largely from Dichter himself. Dichter or some senior member of the staff interviews the client and goes over the relevant facts and theories. Then Dichter may begin a self-analysis about the product. "There was a grass company that came to me with an advertising problem," he said, sitting out on the terrace beside the rather ill-kept grass at the Institute, "and first I asked myself, 'Why does anybody have a lawn?' You need the concept of a living lawn, rather than a decorative lawn. People like to stretch out on a lawn. Why? Look back to your childhood. As I was thinking about lawns, there came to my mind a play by Grillparzer, you probably never heard the name. At the end of the last act the hero stretches out on the lawn. When I stretch out on a lawn, nothing can happen to me, I can't fall out of this world. The lawn is an upholstered way of getting a direct feeling, direct contact with Mother Earth.

"This kind of insight," Dichter added, "you have to have *first*. Then, the practical application of it is, don't show people playing on a lawn, show a great expanse of lawn."

How can Dichter find out that this insight is *not* a true description of people's feelings about a lawn, assuming for argument's sake that it is not? "We say, 'Here is hypothesis number thirteen,'" Dichter explained. "Then we set up a number of projective tests. If we ask people to describe all their feelings about the lawn, and if nobody in fifty people said anything leading to the hypothesis, then I would say, 'This feeling about lawns is too deep, it would require a full psychoanalysis to get it out of people.'"

There was a pause long enough for another subject to be mentioned, and then Dichter added a second possibility to his explanation. "Or it might be," he said, "that Dichter is wrong, it's just Dichter's imagination."

Procedurally, the problem with motivation research is that there is usually no way to *prove* the researcher's insights (though Dichter would strongly disagree). If the analyst perceives something, the fact that the respondent does not perceive it becomes in a sense irrelevant. The heart of the Freudian theory is that people hide symbolisms from themselves and can release them to view only with considerable pain. It would be unreasonable to expect them even to approach such questions during a two-hour interview with an avowedly commercial purpose, and a sincere "motivational" researcher may without concealment stress what people really meant rather than what they really said.

The end result for Dichter's client, however, is a suggestion very similar to a copywriter's hunch, better than a copywriter's hunch in that it is partially verified by study of extensive comments by consumers, and better also in that it is the work of Ernest Dichter, Ph.D., widely regarded in the trade as the greatest copy idea man of our times—a veritable Claude Hopkins of the world of repressed symbolism. "He could quit what he's doing," says Norman B. Norman, "and get fifty, sixty thousand dollars a year as copy chief at any agency in the country. He can predict what people will answer. He doesn't know where half his ideas come from, but he's right." Dichter himself comments mildly, "It would be fair to say that I am consumer-oriented." Looking at a product, he has an instinct for seeing it as the consumer sees it. Sometimes he will suggest changes in a product or added features, usually something of which thousands of housewives who speak unheard had said, "Now, *why* don't they do this . . ." Looking over a tractor for a farm equipment company, for example, Dichter suggested that they put a rearview mirror on it, so the farmer would no longer have to suffer cricks in his neck from looking back to see if the furrows are straight. This is not "motivation research"; indeed, some of Dichter's most triumphant recommendations cannot be traced either to motivations or to research. They are just plain Ernest Dichter, Ph.D.

Interviews with several dozen advertising people who have worked with Dichter produced only one man (McCann-Erickson's Anthony Hyde, formerly president of the Tea Bureau, for which Dichter did one of his common-sense studies) who thought Dichter's reports were, in the terminology of the trade, "duplicable." The same interviews, however, failed to turn up anyone in a responsible position who did not believe Dichter was worth the money he was paid. "I tell our clients," says Richard Lessler, an experimental psychologist turned marketing and research director of Grey Advertising: "use this guy. Use his ideas. Milk him. But for Christ sake don't tell me it's research, because it isn't research as I understand the word."

Viennese by birth, Dichter studied psychology at the University of Vienna and at the Sorbonne, and came to the United States in 1938 as a young missionary anxious to spread the gospel. With the help of Paul Lazarsfeld, whose course he had taken in Vienna, he got a minor job at a minor market research firm, which he proceeded to terrorize by the originality of his insights. On Lazarsfeld's rather amused recommendation, the research department of Compton Advertising bought Dichter a lunch and asked him what he could do to help, for example, Ivory Soap. "Applying the Gestalt principle," Dichter says, "I told them I would not be interested in what people think of soap. I would be interested in what they think of *taking a bath.*"

Nobody at Compton had ever conceived such an approach to the Ivory Soap problem, or to any research, and Dichter found himself with an assignment. Further assignments for *Esquire* magazine and the Chrysler Corporation (it was for Chrysler in those early years that he developed his now-famous conception of the convertible as a man's "mistress," and the sedan as the sober "wife") led him to a job for J. Sterling Getchell, which handled the Plymouth account. After Getchell's death he went shopping for research jobs at other advertising agencies, none of which had the courage to hire him, debated starting his own research service, and wound up in the Columbia Broadcasting System promotion and later program department. In his spare time he wrote articles for magazines on popular psychology and a book called

Successful Living, which appeared just too early to catch the fad for such volumes; he was Norman Vincent Peale's predecessor in the advice to the world-befuddled section of *Look.*

After the war, egged on by friends in the agencies (he has hundreds of friends in the agencies; the men who most bitterly condemn his procedures are almost always personally fond of "Ernie"), he started his own consulting service, operating at first on a highly individual basis with a single research assistant. In early 1957, at the height of his influence in the advertising business, he confessed to an old friend that he often regretted the steady expansion of his Institute to its present size of sixty full-time employees and five hundred occasionally employed interviewers; although he had hired the best people he could find, many of his clients still insisted on talking to Dichter personally, and he found himself working harder than ever simply to meet the imposing payroll and take home the same money he made in his early years as a consultant.

A short, rather stout man of fifty, with a large head resting on a folded double chin, short neck, freckled skin and disappearing reddish hair, Dichter dresses even at the office in open-necked shirts and sports slacks, presenting to the visitor what might be called a sight. His office in the fieldstone house is homey, with a desk set in a corner beside a French window opening onto a terrace, and chairs and couches arranged against the far wall for casual conferences. Visibly tense but visibly controlled, as the psychiatrically minded should be, he speaks English with only a trace of an accent and in an aggressively colloquial style, avoiding whenever possible the jargon of his trade. He is a great salesman without any of the conventional salesman's attributes, but what he is selling is unusual, too.

What puzzles Dichter's friends when they speak of him is the question of which comes first in his thinking: the knack of seeing products as a consumer sees them or the Freudian symbolism. It is astonishing how often Dichter's motivational analyses lead to copy suggestions which a first-class advertising man should have found without any Freudian explanation. Many of Dichter's proposals could come right out of John Caples' primers for students in advertising courses; once he even urged copywriters, on motivational grounds, to use the word NEW in their headlines whenever possible.

Several of Dichter's most famous and apparently most Freudian research jobs have produced what can only be described as common-sense suggestions. When the airlines came to him for advice, they were trying to still the fear of death by advertising, presenting the argument that air travel was essentially safe and that nobody need be afraid to fly. Dichter reported back that the fear of death was not a major factor in men's reluctance to fly, that they were more concerned about their wives' disapproval of flying and the "posthumous embarrassment" which might result if their wives turned out to be right. But Dichter did not need any extensive Freudian analysis to support his advertising recommendation that the airlines abandon the safety theme and concentrate on selling to men the speed and convenience of flying, to women the idea that the airplane would get their husbands home faster. Any advertising man with a head on his shoulders knows that when you have a possibly dangerous product you do not tell people it isn't really dangerous; if you advertise *against* what people believe you simply reinforce their anxieties. The copybook rule that covers the situation speaks of the need to stress the positive approach, the product benefit.

Again, Ronson lighters came to Dichter with a selling problem arising at least in part from public belief that Zippo was more likely to work when you wanted a light. Ronson had been trying to crush this atti- tude under a weight of advertising which asserted that the Ronson was failureproof. Dichter's analysis of lighters said that flame was a sexual symbol ("erotic implications," he explains; "sexual symbolism of primi- tive fire-making devices, discovered at a small German university; Goddess of Light, associated with Eros"). But his advertising recom- mendation was, simply, that Ronson should show the flame-producing mechanism in close-up, rather than the lighter as a whole. By showing the guts of its lighter, Ronson expressed its confidence in its own device without making a claim that the market was not prepared to believe.

Probably Dichter himself does not know whether he sees the problem first in traditional advertising terms or in psychoanalytic terms; and since he is immensely adept at expressing the one in terms of the other, the answer would be of merely parochial interest. What everyone agrees on is that Dichter is a born promoter of Dichter and of Dichter's clients, and that once he gets a bone in his teeth he never lets it go. His sales literature to the trade provides some delightful examples of this characteristic, presenting a client list which is up to date in that it includes the Institute's newest clients, but somewhat stale in that it rarely drops a name, even though Dichter is no longer working for the organization cited. Today Dichter can find dozens of success stories for which his work was at least in part responsible, but in the spring of 1957 he gave a reporter a biographical press release which featured the sales story he used when he was starting out as a consultant:

"The Chrysler Corporation became interested in Dr. Dichter's new approach involving the 'depth interview.' . . . New, dynamic approaches were developed for a number of Chrysler products, including Plymouth, whose 'Look at all three . . .' campaign proved to be the sales turning-point for this automobile. As a result, J. Sterling Getchell, Inc. . . . named him Director of Psychological Research. . . ."

Well, it looks plausible: Dichter worked for Chrysler and for Getchell. And Getchell's "Look at all three . . ." is perhaps the most famous single advertisement for an automobile. (It was not a campaign; the ad ran only once.) But Dichter could not have had much to do with it, because it ran in 1932, six years before he came to the United States and probably before he had ever heard the word "Plymouth." Also, incidentally, it was an ad wrong from top to bottom, in "motivational" theory.

Be that as it may, advertising men buy Dichter for stimulation. "You get a new lipstick account," says Richard Lessler of Grey, "and the danger is that your copywriter will look up everything ever written in lipstick ads, and start running on the old rails. Dichter will get the copywriter off the rails, off his ass, give him new ideas and start him really thinking."

Dichter can reasonably claim to have performed this service for the advertising research business as a whole—he has jolted virtually everybody out of the old ruts. Unfortunately, the jolting has been accomplished by means of exaggerated publicity, for which Dichter himself is partly to blame. Whether he could have conquered the often unintelligent and sometimes malicious opposition to him without such publicity is a question neither he nor anyone else can answer.

2.

Dichter and most other "motivational researchers" claim to use psychological tools to find basic human attitudes toward a product, a brand, a package, a color; they would say that without a knowledge of these attitudes no valid answers can be found to a company's marketing problems. But psychological tools are not necessarily restricted to measuring the universe: they can also be applied to the measurement of particular situations, without regard for the over-all "motivational" background. Thus, while Dichter wants to know all about lawns, Jim Vicary (whose research firm is usually but erroneously bracketed in the same category with Dichter's) will want to know as much as he can about the problem facing the grass-seed company. "I'm fundamentally a marketing researcher," Vicary says. "I'll use the obvious tools when I can. But when the obvious tools fail, and a manufacturer is screaming that the goods aren't moving, I'll use whatever I find. You must understand, though, that this thing works only when you have a *demonstrated problem*: a competitor is doing something very good—what is it? Then you can pull together materials that contribute to an answer. What the researcher does is to give the entrepreneur a better risk position in his conflict with his competitors. Or, simply, the research gives him confidence in his decisions, so he can really *move*."

A tall, casual, graceful man in his early forties but looking younger, with deep-set eyes and a square face that photographs badly, Vicary works out of a small suite of offices in a converted private mansion, most of which is used for the Cercle Français, just off Fifth Avenue in New

York's East Sixties. The office staff numbers only six people and, though the field staff includes four hundred part-time interviewers, the operation as a whole is a small one; it lives, mostly, off a single specialty, research to determine the best brand names for new products and company names for corporations. But Vicary will also undertake public opinion polling and standard market research jobs if he feels they are the sort of thing he is equipped to handle. Though Vicary really is eclectic about motivational research, with no strong convictions about the theoretical validity of any single tool as opposed to any other single tool, he almost always begins with cultural anthropology, a brief survey of what this sort of product has meant in legend and literature through the centuries.

Michigan-born, Vicary started off as a researcher from the sociologist's angle and picked up his training in psychology while on the job for the J. L. Hudson department store in Detroit, one of Gallup's subsidiaries, the Crowell-Collier research department, and Benton & Bowles. He founded his own firm in 1945, hoping to extend the English technique of "Mass Observation" to the American market, retired temporarily to take the Benton & Bowles job and keep eating, then returned to independent practice as a specialist in brand names.

Like any new, independent researcher using techniques which may seem dubious to potential clients. Vicary desperately needed publicity, but he refused to go after it in the established manner by making sweeping claims about complicated subjects. Instead, he thought up gimmicks. The first, which was only fairly successful, was associated with the "M-O" venture. Mass Observation, in which Vicary still believes, seeks to supplement standard public opinion polling by a national panel of volunteer diarists, who write down their reactions to each day's events, as observed locally or read in the newspapers. Vicary, in extending this plan to the United States, planned to add "trained observers"—newspapermen, barbers, county agents, police officers, and so on—plus a special children's panel, which would report in on what parents were saying. The theory was that children, without already assumed positions to maintain, would catch a drift of opinion in the family more quickly than their parents would, because the parents would require considerable time to rationalize a change of attitude.

The children's panel, though an interesting idea and seemingly newsworthy, brought Vicary little attention. His second gimmick, however, made the newspapers and magazines in a big way. This one was a clocking of customer eyeblinks in a supermarket, based on the principle that the eyeblink rate measures an individual's relaxation or tension. Vicary found that the normal eyeblink rate of 32 per minute dropped to 14 while the women (and men) were browsing through the supermarket shelves, and did not begin to approach normal again until they were nearing the checkout counter. (At the checkout counter, as the cash register rang up the figures, it went up to 45, indicating tension.) The conclusion was that women shopped in a trancelike state; but Vicary, typically, refused to go beyond this conclusion and draw up a list of prescriptions for marketers based on his new findings. He was supplying a fact; he would let others apply the fact to their own problems.

The third gimmick, "subliminal advertising," promises to make Vicary's name one of the best known in the business. Working again from a theory—that the conscious mind actually "sees" only a part of what the eye presents (just as the conscious ear overhears only what sounds interesting)—Vicary arranged with the owner of a northern New Jersey movie theater to install a second, special projector for an experiental purpose. Using this second projector, Vicary flashed onto a movie screen the words "Coca-Cola" or "Eat Popcorn." The words were either flashed so rapidly, or printed with such slight intensity, that the conscious eye could not notice the presence of the message superimposed on the movie scene. In fact, people who have been told that the message is going to appear cannot see it. Nevertheless, Vicary felt, the unconscious eye would perceive the slight difference and "read" the lettering.

Films treated in this manner were alternated with untreated films at the theater throughout the summer of 1957; and on these evenings when the Vicary-doctored movies were shown, Coca-Cola consumption went up about one-sixth, popcorn consumption by more than one-half. Vicary patented the idea, and organized a company to treat movie and television film with "subliminal" messages, gaining a good deal of publicity in so doing. Whether this venture in itself has a commercial future is another question; as Vicary points out, it is unlikely that so dim a stimulus can produce any response at all except when the prospective customer already has in his mind the idea of purchasing this product—as he does with a Coke at a drive-in movie. To Vicary's delight, however, subliminal advertising immediately raised a storm in the press (the head of Kenyon & Eckhardt, reacting with typical hypersensitivity, denounced Vicary for what he took to be an implication that people disliked television commercials). And, of course, the prospect has Orwellian overtones; if it developed that subliminal messages could change people's attitudes or implant unconscious prejudices, everybody (including Vicary, who was a conscientious objector during the war, and shows none of the traits of the power-mad psychological manipulator) would agree that it ought to be legally prohibited. For the time being, there is no chance that subliminal advertising will be used— except, perhaps, in movie theaters for the purpose already demonstrated. The television networks are in bad enough trouble without adding this accusation to their burdens. Vicary has already got what he wanted out of it, anyway.

In the money-making end of his business, the choice of brand names, Vicary relies mostly on free association, though he also uses sentence completion (such as "NATURAL FIBERS ARE —— ——" when looking for a name for a Goodrich synthetic fiber), recall tests, and what he has been forced by the trade to call depth interviews. "Though I've proved to my own satisfaction," he says, "that there isn't any depth in them. You might call them *breadth* interviews, if you chose."

The naming job begins with the submission by the client of all the names he, his staff and his advertising agency have been able to think up. "They've given us as many as nine hundred or a thousand names," Vicary said, "and we want them all. They'll tell us their stated aims of what they want to accomplish with the name when they give us the job, but by looking through *all* the names we can learn something about their unstated aims, too. And that's important. So we'll take your names, sort them out, add a few of our own and send back a selection of recommendations, based on our experience. You take these recommended names to your legal department, see if you can use them; and take them to top management, to see if there's a name *we don't want*, good as it may be, so I don't have to waste my time proving it out. The list of recommendations goes through, some names are added. The president of the company may have a pet name, nobody wants to bell the cat, so that goes in the hopper, too.

"When the list comes back, we'll take the names they say they like best, ten of them, type them out on index cards, all caps, and show them to respondents here in New York. We show them one at a time, ask respondents to pronounce the name and say anything that the name brings to mind. Free association. We go through all ten, then ask them a few filler questions, where they shop, things like that, useful but not revelatory. Then we tell them it's going to be a product, show them another ten cards, and ask them what kind of product they think it will be. Finally, we take the cards away and ask them which names they remember. Some come through beautifully, some come out distorted. Do you mind if I lie down on the couch?"

Not at all.

Vicary took the two steps across his narrow office from his desk to his couch and stretched out. "Thank you," he said. "I don't know why I'm telling you all this, somebody's likely to set up a business in competition with me. But I guess we have the reputation, now. Anyway, we feed distortions of the name back into the hopper, or our investigators may feel that certain *syllables* in the distortion are valuable, and incorporate them in new names. We might add some other names by running a free association test on the product itself. A day's work comes back, results from ten or twelve respondents, we throw out some names, add others, and the next day we go out again. There can be any number of reasons for rejecting names, there may be patterns of difficulties in pronouncing, or bad connotations." For example, when

Vicary was testing Haven Homes for Lumber Fabricators, Inc., a pre-fabricated house company, he found the suggested new name associated with old folks' homes, funeral parlors, cemeteries.

"We come down to a final group of eight or ten names," Vicary concluded, "and send them out for a national study, four hundred cases. If you try to do more you get researcher fatigue, four hundred is enough. This stuff about twenty thousand cases is just to impress somebody." The questionnaires that go out into the field will include a free association test on words other than the proposed product name but related to the product or to the marketing situation (for Goodrich's new fabric, for example, the list included *soft, Goodrich, light, warmth, rubber, orlon, wool, Du Pont*). Some words are included to give the bones of a psychological classification of the respondents according to Jung, and a tentative further classification may be attempted in the sentence-completion test ("OLD THINGS ARE —— ——"; "PARENTS' ADVICE TO THEIR CHILDREN —— ——"). These questions are present mostly to make sure good names are not rejected because of an unfortunate free association by an odd-ball respondent who might free-associate *everything* unfortunately. In the Goodrich problem, which Vicary considered particularly difficult, respondents were told finally that the names they were looking at on the index cards were to be used for a new fiber and asked which they thought would be best for a "new, soft and luxurious" fabric.

The word Vicary came up with was Darlan, but he does not think it automatically conveys the idea of a soft and luxurious fabric. "We sat around when all the results were in," Vicary says, grinning, "and we finally decided we had to tell Goodrich that you couldn't build a feeling of quality into the name, you'd have to build it into the fabric. We thought about that for a moment, and then we realized, hell, that's where the quality ought to be, anyway."

3.

To Alfred Politz, the findings of the "motivational" researchers are interesting; but they don't prove anything. He stated the case most thoroughly in an article for the October, 1956, *Public Opinion Quarterly*:

Any one specific piece of consumer behavior goes back to a multitude of psychological and mechanical causes. It is the specific combination and the relative strength of the various causes which lead to a specific purchase. To take Coca-Cola [a Politz client] as an example, everyone will agree that the taste of the drink contributes to the purchase. Taste, thereby, is a reason for buying and drinking, a reason of such magnitude that a change of the taste may destroy the whole brand. However, there is the taste of Coca-Cola's competitors. The taste of a competitive drink may pull customers away from Coca-Cola or drive them to Coca-Cola. What is the real reason for drinking or not drinking Coca-Cola?

It is obvious that the price of Coca-Cola and the price of competitive drinks both constitute new reasons. There is the fact that some people are strongly motivated to drink Coke because they are thirsty. There is the social symbolism of a Coke among teenagers. There is the relative strength of the attraction Coca-Cola offers as a social catalyst when boy meets girl, the convenience of obtaining Coca-Cola, the convenience of obtaining other drinks, the convenience of carrying, storing and serving the liquid from different bottle sizes. There is the feeling of a "lift" connected with drinking a Coke. There is a feeling of relaxation, of rest, connected with drinking a Coke. Each of these causes is sufficient in strength to raise or lower the frequency of purchases. It is the privilege of the non-researcher to talk loosely about the real reason or the reason why. It is the obligation of the researcher to recognize that a multitude of causes (some of them may be called reasons) lead to the effect: the consumption of Coca-Cola. If we intend to discover the relative strength of the contributing causes we have to measure them. . . . Causes act in different directions, partially benefitting and partially retarding sales. If we do not know the relative strength of these causes we cannot compute the effect of a practical marketing action. One can perform a useful function in marketing by getting a good idea. But not everything that is good must be called "research."

To this central analysis of the research problem Politz adds the concept of the "controllable cause." From the welter of reasons for buying—motivations and attitudes of the consumer, qualities, distribution and price of the product—the manufacturer must select those reasons which he can, in fact, influence. He must not assume that wherever he finds a reason for buying his product he can increase his sales by advertising that reason; instead, he must be careful to concentrate his promotion work on those relatively few reasons for buying which can be magnified by advertising.

In Politz's terms, the ideal advertising campaign would have three characteristics: it would be unique (nobody else using the argument), believable, and important (touching on the "main issue"). "There are products where the main purpose of using the product has the main issue value and therefore sells," Politz says. "With anti-histamines the purpose is to remove cold symptoms, and that's the issue. The main purpose of Camay is to clean your skin, but that isn't a selling issue."

This approach bears a certain resemblance to Bates's Unique Selling Proposition, but Politz does not demand all three; he sets up a hierarchy of values. "Uniqueness," he says, "is not so important as believability, which is not so important as touching the main issue. In all these things there is a question whether you approach from the positive or the negative side. I say, 'The motor is the most important part of the car.' Somebody says, 'What good is the motor without the wheels?' That is negative. We operate in an infinite causal chain which produces our effect; take out any part of the chain, you do not get the effect. To determine the relative value of two causes you must start arguing from the positive side—the motor is more difficult to make than the wheels, a man who can make a good motor can also probably make good wheels. From the negative logic, of course you must have uniqueness. But not when you compare."

Among Politz's services for his clients (he has only eight to ten of them, all big—like Chrysler, Socony-Mobil, Du Pont, U. S. Steel, Coca-Cola, Bristol-Myers, Kimberly-Clark) is the development and comparison of advertising "issue values." He may go after it in a wholly straightforward way: asking people what they think a toothpaste should do, then dressing up these opinions as advertising slogans and asking another panel whether they believe a toothpaste really could perform what these slogans claim and whether they've ever seen such claims before. Or he may step a small distance out from standard procedure, going to one panel of respondents and asking them which brand of a product they use and why they think it's best, then going to a matched panel and asking those who have switched brands to say why they switched. On such a test for Kotex, a Kimberly-Clark subsidiary, he found that the same percentage of Kotex and Modess users gave one reason for their preference: "more absorbent." But when he went to the switchers, he found that seven times as many women had changed from Modess to Kotex as had gone the other way because they found the old brand "insufficiently absorbent." Politz then went to his client's production people and told them (they had never told him) that Kotex was more absorbent than Modess, a fact they admitted. They had never advertised the advantage, however, because they felt that the added absorbency in Kotex was a reserve strength rather than a true product feature, that women would not notice it. Politz told them quite a number of women were noticing it: it was an "issue."

It is a common experience at the Politz shop for consumer research to reveal actual product differences which the engineers had never thought to mention to anybody. Chrysler, for example, was disturbed by the common belief that other cars had a far faster pickup than the Chrysler line, which Chrysler engineers said was simply untrue. Politz, given the problem, reasoned that the public could not *know* how good an automobile's acceleration was: few people can judge the speed at which they are traveling, let alone the *rate of increase* in speed. At this point, a researcher who placed his main emphasis on theories would have explained to Chrysler the importance of the symbolism of an automobile and the subterranean ways in which symbols influence people's opinions about specific details of performance. Politz, while regarding the public's error as a psychological phenomenon, thought the source might lie in the human animal's tendency to measure something which he cannot, in fact, judge by some extraneous but real physical quantity which he *can* judge. He sent interviewers out to ask car owners whether they thought their car had fast acceleration or not, and when the results were in he measured the tension of the spring under the accelerator pedal in each make of automobile. He found that wherever the accelerator spring was tight, and considerable pressure was necessary to drive the pedal to the floor, people thought the car had slow acceleration; wherever the spring was loose, people thought the chariot was blessed with get-up-and-go. Chrysler loosened the springs under the pedals.

It is an interesting and rather ironic note that the researchers who apply predetermined formulas to find the "real reason" for buying all come out of those academic subjects which have deduced their formulas from isolated insights: psychology and sociology. Politz, the complete empiricist, comes out of an academic discipline largely induced from general principles: mathematics and physics. German by birth, he went to Sweden in the mid-thirties to get away from the Nazis (quite literally, since they were looking for him: he was deeply involved in an underground organization). In Sweden he "fell in love with advertising" and began experiments with it which have not yet ceased. He started by setting himself up in the aspirin business. Aspirin in Stockholm could be sold only through a small number of licensed druggists, none of whom kept stock on hand; instead, suppliers sent messengers over with fresh pills three times a day. Thus, Politz could easily measure the pulling power of the ads he ran for his brand of aspirin, simply by counting up the number of pills sold by the messengers on the days when the different ads appeared. When he came to this country shortly before World War II he found out about mail-order testing and Claude Hopkins, the direct route to "scientific advertising," and cursed himself as a ninny for all the money he'd thrown away in Sweden. Later he found out what was wrong with mail-order advertising, too, but he still uses split runs occasionally to test the various approaches to a sales argument. He also likes to keep his hand in with his own business, where he can experiment without worrying about what people may think; for some years he ran a retail hardware store in Tampa, and he is now fooling around with a mouthwash which he distributes throughout the state of Florida and uses as a private laboratory for advertising ideas.

A short, athletic man who could be graphically represented by three triangles (broad forehead to jutting chin, big shoulders to narrow waist, hips to small feet), Politz at fifty is one of the most forceful people in advertising. Didactic by temperament, he teaches his clients and their agencies as well as his associates and fellow researchers; when he feels that the lesson is not going well he can become exceedingly scornful. He still speaks a slightly pedantic English with a marked German accent, which adds a perhaps unintentional force to his scorn. Since opening his own office in 1943 he has devoted himself to eliminating the illogic from consumer research, especially in the areas of sampling, questionnaire construction and "project design"—a term of his own invention expressing his belief that no single survey can be more than one part of an over-all research project.

When Politz takes on a new client, which happens rarely, he wants to know whatever the client knows about his sales, distribution, share-of-market and general standing in his product field. He also wants to know the client's business philosophy. "We call it 'the client's religion,' " said Lester Frankel, then Politz's vice-president, now moved on to his competitor Audits & Surveys, Inc. "We feel there's no point coming out with recommendations that go contrary to the client's feelings about himself." Each survey is preceded by "the development of ideas and hunches," which grow out of conversations with client or agency people ("We work with the agency people," said Frankel, "when they're very good and they have a lot of ideas"), out of "projective" testing and "unstructured interviewing" à la Dichter, out of the results of previous surveys, or out of what the formal Politz flow chart calls "the researcher's observation of self." Frankel says, "That's a very important source, especially with Politz himself."

These ideas or hunches serve merely, in Frankel's words, "to pinpoint the area of investigation." Once Politz has decided what subjects should be investigated, the serious job of questionnaire construction begins.

Here Politz feels most strongly the need for applying rigorous logical tests, to eliminate the possibility of erroneous answers. He is full of examples of questions which seemed all right, and drew honest answers, but gave cockeyed results. One of his favorites sets up the hypothesis that there are three brands of gasoline sold in a town, and only two customers (or sets of customers). Brand A has 40 per cent of the business, while brands B and C have 30 per cent each. But consumer research, honestly conducted, shows B and C to have 50 per cent each, and A to have no business whatever. The question asked the two customers is, "Which brand do you usually buy?" Customer 1, as it happens, buys 60 gallons of brand B and 40 gallons of brand A every week; customer 2 buys 60 gallons of brand C and 40 gallons of brand A. Though brand A sells 80 gallons to 60 gallons for each of the others, brand A is eliminated from the market by the question, "Which brand do you *usually* buy?" As Politz points out, the difficulty here is not one of semantics (everybody understands what the question means), but one of formal logic.

Finding the right questions requires great experience and almost inhuman cleverness. "The answers should show," Frankel said, "whether your hypotheses are true or false. Often in research, even good questions can merely tell you that the hypothesis is true. If the hypothesis is false, the questions produce 'insufficient evidence.' Alfred likes to tell the story about the man who found out by research that soda makes you drunk. He changed all the other variables—used rye, Scotch, bourbon, brandy, and others. But he got drunk every time. Since the soda was the only constant, it had to be the soda that made him drunk." Cleverness can enter into questioning designed simply to give a plain fact, rather than to prove a hypothesis. To find out which of the new-model automobiles have been making the most impression on the public, Politz does not go around and ask people their opinions. Instead, he asks them which of the new cars they see most often around their neighborhoods.

Before the questionnaire goes out to the nation at large, Politz tests it in a pilot study near New York, to make sure that the answers which come back will actually provide usable information. Then the call to arms is sounded, and Politz's six hundred steady interviewers (there are nine hundred others used occasionally) begin to beat the bushes to find the households specified in the area probability sample. Usually, Politz's samples are quite large—even up to Vicary's twenty thousand —because he wants to be able to "cross-ruff" the data: that is, to find out the extent to which his hypotheses are true not only on a national basis but also regionally and within demographic classifications.

Like most researchers, Politz finds repeatedly that his survey has raised almost as many new problems as it has settled old ones. Factors unforeseen when the questionnaire was drawn up appear from analysis of the answers, leaving the client company with a better knowledge of its position than it had before the survey started, but still unsure in large areas where decisions must be made. So Politz does not undertake one-survey jobs (except for media, which are handled in a separate division). He insists on one-year, preferably three-year contracts, which will include a number of different surveys, each handling some new matters, each solving some of the problems that came up in the preceding job. In return for this assured continuing relationship he agrees not to do any work for his clients' competitors (and competition for this purpose is defined very broadly: Politz would not do any work for a beer company, because he works for Coca-Cola). But the expense of the total job is very great; it is doubtful that any of Politz's corporate clients get out for less than $200,000 a year. Only the giants can afford it.

Politz regrets this situation but can see no help for it. "Small firms," he says, "have justifiable problems, but I don't think they can necessarily use this kind of research. To a large extent, they must use judgment. . . ."

4.

Since the early 1950's Politz has devoted almost all his public appearances and printed articles to attacks on motivational research and its procedures—attacks which are devastating from the Politz stand-

point but somewhat vitiated in effect by his inevitable admission that
the motivationists do turn up good ideas, even though they can't prove
anything, and that his own sort of highly verified research can be
carried only by very large companies. There seems no good reason why
a smaller company which cannot afford Politz must rely solely on its
own judgment when it can buy Dichter's help cheap. While Politz's
attention was concentrated on the bright butterfly of Dichter, however,
a juggernaut came rolling up on his rear. Motivation research, as the
fad of the industry and the darling of its most "advanced" practitioners,
has already seen its best days. The new fad, already gaining adherents
from those agencies like Y & R which have been in the van of every
new research venture, is "operations research."

Briefly, the new idea, which neither calls for nor can be given
extended discussion, assumes that all marketing problems can be reduced to mathematical formulas which can then be solved by mathematicians and their faithful servants, the electronic calculators. The
leading practitioner at present is Arthur D. Little, Inc., a Cambridge,
Massachusetts, firm of physicists, mathematicians and engineers, which
undertakes any kind of research at all (the same people who work on
marketing problems, for example, will be studying golf balls for the
United States Golf Association, which is concerned about the way the
pros are hitting the ball beyond the traps and making golf courses too
small). Little's mathematicians have great experience in reducing complicated questions to the yes-or-no variety which can be handled by
electronic calculators, and they are masters of the Theory of Games.
They have constructed "mathematical models" of marketing situations,
and their contention is that they have already reached a stage where,
once all the relevant data is appropriately placed in the model, they
can predict the sales results of an advertising effort.

The appeal of this procedure to the advertiser is obvious. Motivation research can promise him merely a psychological or sociological
certainty, and these are two notoriously inexact disciplines. Little can
promise a mathematical certainty, a guarantee to dutch the book. One of
Little's mathematicians has already made a speech foreseeing the day
which advertisers have dreamed about for decades: the day when ad-

vertising copy will actually be written by electronic machines. (Shepherd Mead, formerly a vice-president of Benton & Bowles, had already placed just such a vision into his futuristic novel *The Big Ball of Wax*; the narrator visits an advertising agency and notes "the copywriter machines, resting under their tweed covers.")

What is wrong with operations research is equally obvious: as Little admits, the model can be set in motion only by assuming a given value for the effectiveness of the advertising. (And assuming a rate of decay of effectiveness; Little claims to have proved that advertising campaigns must decay at a predictable rate, but the experience of the industry is to the contrary.) Once the specific effectiveness of the advertising is assumed, it is doubtful that the enormous complexities of operations research are really necessary to tell the advertiser what he needs to know.

Yet, in precisely this area, it is at least possible that operations research will make a major contribution to advertising knowledge. Though it may never be able to predict sales results from advertising plans, a properly designed mathematical model, fed correct information, should be accurate in working *backwards*—that is, in deriving the effectiveness of the advertising from the final sales results. Perhaps by the employment of this roundabout, cumbersome machinery an advertiser will finally be able to learn exactly how much good his advertising does him.

CHAPTER 16

AND THIS IS HOW WE KNOW WE'RE RIGHT:

The Proofs

"I know half the money I spend on advertising is wasted, but I can never find out which half."

John Wanamaker

1.

The offices of Daniel Starch and Staff are located on a high-traffic corner of the Boston Post Road in Mamaroneck, New York, in a two-story white building with a mock-classical façade and an odd, almost triangular shape. Inside, there are no walls to separate the offices, tabulating rooms, bullpens and libraries; instead, free-floating room dividers in startling colors establish areas and break up possible vistas, and an acoustically treated ceiling works to establish privacy of conversation. From the ceiling the symbolically interesting shapes of a sprinkler system intrude on the offices, providing the key to the odd décor: this building was a department store before Starch took it over. Which is fair enough, since the Starch operation is the department store of the research business. Anybody can buy, and the prices are low.

What Starch measures is the basic question of print advertising: readership. The work of the organization is based on an apparently simple but at the time revolutionary insight which Daniel Starch first published forty years ago. In essence, Starch proclaimed that the mere presence of an ad in a publication does not mean the readers of the publication have noticed it, that an advertisement can influence only the people who have actually seen it, and that people will be likely to remember whether or not they have seen an ad if it is shown to them, recalled to their attention, during the course of an interview. The psychological principle involved is "recognition"; the question asked the respondent is, basically, whether or not he recognizes the advertisement.

Starch developed his theory of advertising research during the course of an unusually distinguished academic career. Born in La Crosse, Wisconsin, in 1883 (in an area so thickly settled with German immigrants that he still speaks with a very slight accent), he won his Ph.D. at the University of Iowa and taught as an instructor at Iowa and Wellesley, as an associate professor at Wisconsin and Harvard, and as a full professor at New York University and the University of Washington. In 1928 Starch made the first study of the mushrooming radio audience, and in 1931 he began the first continuing study of magazine readership. Today, a slight, rather bent old man with wrinkled skin pulled tight over a fine skull, he exercises a benign, soft-voiced supervision over the four hundred permanent and seven hundred part-time employees of Daniel Starch and Staff.

The basic data for Starch reports is gathered very simply. Interviewers are sent out with copies of a recent issue of a magazine (for weeklies, the interviewing ends no more than ten days after the issue hits the stands), and they ring doorbells until they find someone who says he has read the issue. The interviewer then leafs through the magazine, page by page, asking the respondent if he saw this ad, if he noted the product it advertised, if he caught this picture or that picture, the headline or the subhead, and if he read more than half the advertising copy. Except on special order, no questions are asked about advertisements less than one-half page in size, and no respondent is ever asked to commit himself on more than 100 ads. The interviewer starts each session at a different point in the magazine, so that every ad will catch an equal proportion of fresh and tired respondents. Should the respondent fag out to the point where he quits in the middle, his interview is thrown away and his interviewer trudges on to find another reader.

Interviewers are scattered throughout the country, and the number of interviews each performs on a magazine is determined by the geographical distribution of its circulation. The interviewers are under instruction to go into every kind of neighborhood and to reach people of every economic class. In all, the Starch interviewers will flip through a single issue of a "general" consumer magazine with 300 readers—150 men and 150 women. If the magazine is aimed primarily at one sex, the other will be eliminated from the interviewing pattern.

No fewer than twenty-four magazines, eleven of them weeklies, are studied by Starch every time they appear. Included on the list are *Life*, the *Saturday Evening Post* and *Reader's Digest*, all three of the big women's magazines, both major chain store magazines, the nationwide Sunday newspaper supplements and such others as *Time*, *Seventeen* and *True Story*, *Capper's Farmer*, *Coronet* and *Ebony*. Six other consumer magazines are studied occasionally—eight specified issues of *The New Yorker*, for example, twelve of *Look*, six of *Better Homes and Gardens*. A separate service studies some twenty-seven business publications and still another service looks at most ads in certain issues of seven newspapers scattered across the country.

Part of the expense of the Starch service is borne by the publications themselves, which are that much more attractive to advertisers because ad readership measurements are available. The cost to advertisers and agencies is thus extremely low: anyone who subscribes to as many as six Starch reports a month can have them for only $25 each, while the top price to infrequent buyers is only $50.

For this small sum the advertiser receives an envelope stuffed with statistics. Enclosed is an actual copy of the magazine, with a set of paper stickers on each advertisement, announcing what percentage of each sex of the circulation saw the ad as a whole and each of its component parts. The meaning of the little numbers on these stickers is then refined in a tabular summary covering all the ads in the issue. The summary applies the percentages of readership in the sample of three hundred to the magazine's total circulation, then divides by the cost of the space used to show the number of readers of the ad per dollar of expenditure on it. Now the advertiser has all the elements necessary to compare the fruits of his effort with the readership results gained by other advertisers in the same issue of the magazine—but Starch, in another tabulated column, saves him the trouble. Here each ad is assigned a "cost ratio" measuring its readership per dollar against the average of all other ads in the magazine: 100 is average, so an ad with a cost ratio of 150 has secured half again as many readers per dollar as the average ad in the issue, while an ad with a cost ratio of 25 has done only a quarter as well as the average. So that he who runs may read, Starch further analyzes its figures to give each ad a ranking —this ad ranks 32nd out of 118 ads in this issue—on the basis of the cost ratio. For each of the three central Starch measurements—how many people saw the ad, how many associated it with the brand name, and how many read more than half the advertising copy—this cost ratio and rank order material is separately broken out of the raw statistics by electronic tabulating machinery.

This data is printed up in separated sections, each devoted to a single product group—Ads for automobiles and ads for soaps are, in the cliché of the business, apples and oranges—you can't compare them. (Commenting on the cliché, Thompson's Art Porter notes that a number of advertisers "are beginning to become curious about the fruit store we run in this business.") Moreover, automobile manufacturers and soapmakers are not really in competition with each other. What is important to the automobile advertiser is how well his ad did when compared with the ads of other automobile companies; one look at the sheet of yellow paper, and he knows.

So runs the theory. Following the theory, many advertising agencies have bragged to their clients about the high Starch ratings their ads were receiving; almost all of them have lived to regret the brag. The day inevitably comes when a campaign about which the agency feels strongly shows up badly in the Starch reports, and a client conditioned to accept Starch figures as a branch of gospel begins to think that his agency does not know its business. In fact, some advertising campaigns that are universally regarded as highly successful have never pulled particularly strong Starch ratings, and some that show up well on Starch have been rapidly abandoned because they failed to seduce customers. Against the Starch theory, many advertising men pose a simple question: after the student has examined all the stickers on all the pages and read all the numbers in the tabulation and analyzed all the figures on his yellow sheet, exactly *what* does he know? Is the sample large enough? And what (if any) is the relation between readership and selling effectiveness?

"Well, a bigger sample is always better," says Howard Stone, a brisk, Harvard-trained businessman who has worked for Starch since 1937 (with two years off as research director for Campbell-Ewald, the Chevrolet agency), and is now president and part owner of Daniel Starch and Staff. "But we report on a great number of advertisements in a great number of magazines, and we feel you learn more from small samples on fifty issues than from a big sample on one issue." Actually, outside tests of Starch's accuracy have given the service a remarkably clean bill of health. In 1955 the Advertising Research Foundation's PARM (Printed Advertising Rating Methods) Committee hired Politz to duplicate Starch interviews with a probability sample of six thousand families, and the correlation between the Politz percentage figures and the Starch percentage figures for ads in the same issue of *Life* was very high, indeed. (It was .85; exact correlation, complete identity in the findings, would be expressed statistically as 1.00.) The Starch part of the ARF study cost about $40,000, more than ten times as much as Starch received for its work on this issue, and Howard Stone feels strongly that the cost of improving the accuracy of Starch reports would far outweigh the benefits to Starch subscribers. "The watches you and I use so satisfactorily in our daily lives," he told a 4A's meeting in 1951, "are only approximately correct. A really good watch costs so much that most of us reject it as economically unsatisfactory."

Obviously, however, readership in itself does not guarantee sales effectiveness. "If an agency finds that a client is taking Starch figures too seriously," says John Caples of BBDO, "it has an easy way to beat the game. Instead of showing a big picture of the car, you show a big picture of Marilyn Monroe and a little picture of the car. If that doesn't work, you take some clothes off her." Rosser Reeves puts the matter, as usual, in an even more pointed manner: "You can get very high recall by passing wind loudly at an elegant dinner party. But you may not improve your social standing." On the other side of the advertising fence, the motivationally minded will argue that an ad can deposit a favorable impression of a product in the customers' minds without leaving any recollection whatever of the ad.

"You ask me," says Howard Stone, "whether I think such things have ever happened. Yes, I think they have. But you're talking about exceptional cases. We have done tremendous amounts of experimental work in trying to relate sales with exposure to ads. One step of the work was to have interviewers ask respondents about recent purchases of brands before or after they go through the readership questions. With rare exceptions, we find high readership and high purchases, low readership and low purchases, going together. That doesn't prove our point, because it can work backwards, too—people are more likely to read ads for the brands they use. But we think it's significant.

"What advertising does is to 'move you closer'—that's what we always say—to buying the product. If you use a big picture of Marilyn Monroe to advertise spark plugs because pictures of Marilyn Monroe have high readership, you aren't moving people closer to buying the product. But you've recognized a real problem. Spark plugs are a dull subject, low in readership. So you don't advertise spark plugs, you advertise cars, a high-interest subject *related to your product*. That's exactly the sort of thing you can learn to do from readership research."

2.

Starch readership figures can tell an advertiser which ads are drawing attention, but they do not directly say *why* the high-rated ads are doing well and they give no hint whatever about the message that the customers actually receive from their reading. Spotting the factors that produce high readership is one of the great parlor games of the advertising business (Marion Harper, Jr., and Herta Herzog of McCann-Erickson have crept through mountains of Starch data and emerged with no fewer than 178 factors which influence the readership of a magazine ad; thirty-odd of these factors are applicable to any given product problem, and McCann's creative people are supposed to weigh them all in constructing ads for the agency's clients). And the Starch organization itself has been offering since 1956 a "Reader Impression" service in which forty to sixty readers of an ad are subjected to "clinical or probing type interviewing" to determine what they thought about while looking at the ad. To facilitate their recollection, the interviewer spreads the ad out before them once again while asking his questions. This service is new and expensive, and its acceptance by the industry is still in doubt.

Among the obstacles which the new Starch service must surmount is competition from the somewhat similar "Impact" service which the firm of Gallup & Robinson has been offering since 1951. Opinion researchers primarily, George Gallup and Claude Robinson have always regarded readership measurements as merely a foundation for further research. Their reports are designed to show which current ads succeed best in getting *and holding* the attention of readers, why these ads are remembered, and what sales message comes across from them. The service is for sale to advertisers only, though agencies are almost always invited to sit in on the presentation of the reports. Within the trade, Gallup & Robinson is usually regarded as directly competitive with the standard Starch readership service, but whenever a client buys the Impact reports his agency, anticipating the need for a counterweight, buys Starch.

Gallup's technique involves a more serious challenge to the respondent who is being interviewed. As in Starch, the respondent is shown a copy of the magazine and asked if he has read this issue—but Gallup will not take a simple yes for an answer. The respondent must further "qualify" himself for the interview by describing some article or feature which he read in this particular issue. After he passes this test, the magazine is put aside and he is shown a deck of cards on which are printed the products and brand names advertised in this issue (plus, he is told, several brand names *not* advertised in this issue; "to keep him on his toes," Gallup says). Looking at the cards, the respondent announces which brand names he remembers as advertised, and the interviewer writes each of them at the head of its own sheet of paper.

Then the interview itself begins. "We make him describe the ad," Gallup says, "tell us what it looked like. Then we put him through a catechism—what did the ad say, what went through your mind when you saw it. We find out what stayed in his mind, what impression the ad made on him. Then we ask a series of questions to find out how favorable the impression was. The interviewer writes everything down verbatim. If there are any emotional overtones in the subject's reaction to the ad, we'll find out about them with these questions."

The technical word for Gallup's approach is "recall," as distinguished from Starch's "recognition." Since a deck of cards is used as a prop to memory, the method is "aided recall." Gallup says, "This way of doing it has several advantages. A lot of people can look at an advertisement and be completely unaware of who the advertiser was—a good third of all ads are looked at by people who remember the picture and can play it back to you beautifully, but they don't remember whether it was an insurance company or a food product. Even if they do remember who the advertiser was, there's the question of what idea came through, if any at all. They see a picture of a baby carriage in the ad, what they think about is, they wonder what kind of brakes it has. The ad is for a breakfast food." At the end of the interview the respondent is asked if he uses this sort of product, which brand of it he bought most recently, and whether the ad in question had made him want to buy this brand.

Since Gallup's interviewers do not show the respondents copies of the ads (except for checking purposes, after the meat of the interview has been taken from the carcass), the Gallup & Robinson procedure is easily applicable to television commercials, too. The same steps are followed: the respondent "qualifies" by describing the show and then tells what went on in the commercials—"the same catechism," Gallup says. "What they did, what they showed, what they said." All comments (however worthless) are supposed to be written down by the interviewer. Verbatim transcription is more difficult, though, when the respondent is talking about television commercials: the interviewer does not have a copy of the ad with him to help him figure out what the hell the man thinks he's saying. To solve this problem, Gallup has recently been sending his people out with battery-operated tape recorders concealed in specially built clip-boards; the interview comes into the office in *spoken* form, and secretaries transcribe it directly into typescript.

Virtually everything Gallup takes from the respondents goes back to his clients in the bulky final report. The advertiser learns what percentage of people who remember something about the television program or the editorial content of the magazine also remembered something about his ad, what percentage had a favorable reaction to the ad, and which sales arguments came through to the most people. Attached to this summary of the data is a complete set of the transcripts of what the respondents said about the ad, an obvious mine of suggestions for improving its content or its execution or both. "But this is only half the job," Gallup says. "The other half is factor analysis."

Because Gallup has conducted interviews on competitors' ads as well as his client's own, he can tell the client which sales arguments used by the competition are making the strongest impression on the customers. "As soon as you can in any field identify the successes and the failures," Gallup says, "you can determine the factors. If you wanted to start a chain of restaurants it would pay you to take two years to study the great successes and the great failures in chains of restaurants. We've, tried such analyses in fields as far removed as medicine—you can use them in any field. Our question is, What factors or principles are common to the ads which come out with the highest scores as opposed to those which come out with the lowest scores? We've been working at it six years, systematically analyzing our experience. We can tell the advertiser in any product field what the good ones are doing."

Gallup's qualifications for making such analyses grow out of more than two decades in the field. His is the only name in advertising which is known to most Americans; it precedes the word "Poll." There was a Gallup, however, before there was a poll. Like Starch, he comes out of an academic background, but his field was journalism rather than psychology. His doctoral dissertation was a readership study of the Des Moines *Register & Tribune:* "The question was, what did people read? Well, you ask them and they say, the editorials and the national news, everything that reflects glory on themselves, never the comics or the sports. But if you show them the paper, make them focus their minds on what they actually read—what did I read *on this page*—they can't keep thinking of what they ought to have read." This dissertation on readership research was followed by a pioneering study which extended such research to magazines, and then Gallup went on to teaching. He was a young professor of journalism at Northwestern when Raymond Rubicam of Young & Rubicam snatched him away to New York in 1932 to head the first fully staffed agency research department. In 1935, while at Y & R, Gallup founded the American Institute of Public Opinion, and in 1947 he left the agency to concentrate his efforts on his own firm.

A large man in his middle fifties, Gallup has that vast informality of dress and manner which only the midwestern American (he was born in Iowa) can properly carry off. Talking about his business, he jams his hands in his trouser pockets and wanders around his rather small, square, conservatively furnished office in Princeton, New Jersey. He addresses everyone who works in his organization by his or her first name (the business is now so large that he doesn't always get the name right, which rather shocks everybody in earshot). In addition to the Institute of Public Opinion and Gallup & Robinson, he operates a third service, Audience Research, Inc., which measures the probable popularity of movies, books and television programs not yet exposed to the public. Gallup is proud of the fact that he has done so much of his work in fields where his results can easily be verified—predictions of elections, attendance for movies, sales of books.

The central tool of Audience Research, Inc., is a theater (called "Mirror of America") in Hopewell, New Jersey, about ten miles from Princeton and convenient to people living in several large cities, any number of small towns and farming areas in New Jersey and Pennsylvania. The theater is a remarkably pleasant place, with individual wicker armchairs instead of the usual banks of theater chairs, a brilliant gold curtain, spanking-clean silver wallpaper and a wood-paneled lobby including an elaborately equipped open kitchen which serves homemade baked goods, coffee, ice cream and sodas to the invited audience. Reactions to the films shown in the theater are measured on an electronic device called the Hopkins Program Analyzer. Each member of the audience has a dial to turn indicating degrees of individual pleasure or displeasure at each moment of the program; electrical impulses run from each of the dials to a central box which draws a continuous graph of total audience liking or disliking. When the show is over, the audience participates in a discussion which is recorded and then analyzed to explain the squiggles on the graph. It is always somewhat discouraging to new television advertisers to find that the graph dips heavily into an area of disliking every time a commercial breaks in on the entertainment.

Gallup & Robinson uses the Audience Research theater to screen commercials which have not yet been broadcast; interviewers call on members of the audience the next day and put them through the standard catechism, thus "pretesting" the commercials before the advertiser spends his money on air time. Much the same technique is used to pretest print advertising: Gallup puts together a magazine (called *Impact*), prints in it the ads to be tested, and distributes copies to a selected sample of homes. The next day the interviewer calls to ask the usual questions about what the householder got from his reading.

Gallup's respondents can play back to the interviewers, of course, only that part of the sales message which has stuck in their conscious minds. Though emotional overtones in their reactions to the advertised product may come through in their replies, their attention is focused primarily on the sales points in the commercial rather than on the mood. Brand-image and motivationally oriented agencies therefore tend to have more than the usual distrust of the Gallup & Robinson data, and Gallup repays them in kind—somewhat sadly, since Ogilvy used to work in his shop. "David was my strong right arm for years," he says, "but this brand-image argument is just the current craze. It's wholly unimportant in most cases. People will give you a full and faithful report of what went through their minds when they saw the ad, and that's what you want to know, that's what's important. The direct relationship."

3.

"We know nothing about print advertising," says Horace Schwerin. "This is our eighth year of trying to measure it, ha?, and we're still without a single effective test." As a result, the Schwerin Research Corporation attempts merely to measure—very specifically—the selling power of television commercials. Schwerin works with theater audiences placed in a controlled situation which is supposed to simulate the mental processes of shopping. If his tests are valid he has an immediate measurement of relative advertising effectiveness. Since few advertising men are willing to admit even the possibility of exact measurement, most of Schwerin's claims are heavily discounted in the trade. Those agencies which use his service most heavily are quick to say that they don't "agree with all of it." But a number of his clients—such as General Mills, Miles Laboratories, RCA, Campbell Soup and Toni—have retained his organization for more than ten years; and, as he says, "when you work with an organization over ten years they learn whether what you say is true or not, ha?"

Horace Schwerin is a burly, cheerful but argumentative statistician and sociologist who became interested in reactions to broadcast messages before the war, when the only broadcast medium was radio. During the war, as an officer working on training camp morale problems, he had an unrivaled opportunity to try out his theories on captive Army audiences. "They would broadcast a message to all the men at breakfast," says Henry Newell, one of Schwerin's vice-presidents, "urging them to change to their other pair of shoes when they returned to barracks. Meanwhile, Horace's people were putting chalk marks on everybody's second pair of shoes. When the men went out again for the morning's work, Horace's people would go back and find out how many of the shoes in the barracks had chalk marks on them, and you knew exactly how effective the broadcast argument had been." After the war was over, Schwerin went to work for NBC, testing proposed new radio programs and estimating their potential popularity. At the end of 1946 he got his first outside client, who wanted Schwerin to tell him how well people *liked* his commercials. By 1950 the business had grown to the point where Schwerin moved out of the NBC studios and bought the Avon Theater, a floundering movie house on Sixth Avenue at the edge of the Times Square honky-tonk, to use as the laboratory for his work.

At first Schwerin and his assistants worked along the lines that Gallup & Robinson were to follow—the percentages of the audience who could remember what the commercial had said, and their attitudes toward what they recalled. Attitude measurement, however, can never be more than second best in advertising research. Product advertising seeks to influence people's behavior, not their attitudes, and the relation of attitudes to behavior on any fixed basis is a feat beyond even the claims of the social scientists.

A number of researchers have had a crack at the problem. In the largest single project, RCA, Ford and Atlantic Refining went out together specifically to determine how accurately people's attitudes foretold their purchasing behavior. People who thought they might buy a television set within the next year or so were given cards with the names of television set manufacturers on them and asked to place one card aside as the brand they liked best and were most likely to buy, to place four cards in a separate box as brands they regarded highly and thought they might buy, and to put the rest away as most unlikely or out of the question. Later, these respondents were checked on their actual purchases, by interviewers who came in and looked at the new television sets in their homes. Fifteen per cent of them had bought the brand they thought they were most likely to buy; 22 per cent had bought one of the four brands they regarded as possibilities; 59 per cent had bought a brand which they had set aside in the interview as most unlikely or out of the question. This inability to foretell purchases is not restricted to big-ticket items, either. In 1954 Du Pont stopped 5,200 women on their way into a supermarket and asked them to check the brands they were going to buy when they got in among the shelves; then the interviewers took a look in the ladies' shopping baskets on the way out. Three out of ten had purchased the brands they expected to buy; seven out of ten had changed their minds in the store.

Such phenomena do not particularly surprise advertising men, who have learned the hard way about the fickleness of brand loyalties. Foote, Cone & Belding, when it had the Frigidaire account, stressed in its new business presentations the fact that annual surveys of the appliance field always showed more prospective purchasers for GE refrigerators than for any other brand, while the statistics on actual sales at the end of the year always showed Frigidaire as the biggest seller in the field. Such results are among the reasons why old-timers in advertising are highly suspicious of research in general; as Maxwell Sackheim says, "the public does not know what it wants." The true advertising researcher, however, loves nothing more than a barrier on the main road: it gives him a chance to explore in the back alleys.

The route Schwerin found was even more direct than the old highway of interviewing. What he needed, he felt, was a simulated sales situation, to show how people change brand preferences under advertising pressure. The only way to simulate a sales situation in a theater was to offer product gifts *with a choice of brands*. By choosing one brand as against others for a gift, the consumer would be forced to go through a decision-making process quite similar to that involved in a purchase. Now, an audience which had gone through this decision-making process could be exposed to a television commercial and thereupon asked to choose *again,* on the same terms, for a second round of gifts. Then a comparison of the number in the audience choosing the advertised brand *before* they saw the commercial (the "pre-choice") with the number choosing it *after* they saw the commercial (the "post-choice") would measure the selling power of the sales pitch. In his first experiments, Schwerin offered everybody in the audience a pack of cigarettes or a sample of baking powder both times around, but he found that such gifts were too unimportant to stimulate the kind of thought that goes into a real purchase. They produced a bias toward new products: since it's free anyway, let's try something new. So he changed to a drawing, a ticket stub pulled out of a revolving drum, the prize to the winner being six months' supply of cigarettes or $25 worth of baking powder. "People think twice," says Henry Newell, "when they know there's going to be a closetful of the stuff around the house."

A Schwerin test begins with the mailing of free tickets to about 350 names chosen at random from the phone books covering New York City and the five surrounding counties. (For two weeks every year Schwerin takes his show on the road to verify the New York results, and in 1957 he set up a continuous "control" operation in Kansas City.) Each name receives four tickets, and a letter inviting him and his friends to the Avon Theater to see the films of two new television shows and to participate in testing which will help "improve television programs and commercials." As a further inducement, the letter announces that valuable prizes will be awarded to the winners of a drawing to be held at the theater. Seven or eight such sessions are held every week—four or five at night, with a mixed audience; one or two ladies' matinees; and a children's show every Saturday morning.

Each ticket has three stubs, one of which is retained by the spectator. The other two are taken at the entrance to the Avon, a rather worn theater with a tiny lobby and a long, narrow auditorium seating 420. Each spectator receives a mimeographed booklet which he will fill in during the course of the show. The evening opens with a young, personable emcee telling a few jokes and describing what is about to happen. Then the audience is requested to fill in the first page of the booklet, which asks questions about sex, age, education, occupation and rent or mortgage payments (to indicate income; in Canada and in England, where Schwerin has separate organizations, a direct income question is asked, "but," says executive vice-president Leonard Kudisch, "you couldn't do it here"). The following page lists half a dozen brands of some product, and each spectator checks the brand he would like to win if his ticket should be the one pulled out of the drum. Price differences among brands are eliminated by offering a dollar value rather than a number of pieces. Then the first drawing is held, the winner rises from his chair, and an assistant comes to find out which brand he has chosen for his prize (it is never announced to the audience). There may be as many as three drawings, each involving a different kind of product, before the screening of film and commercials begins.

The show itself is a half-hour television program with three one-minute commercials embedded in it at the usual places. At natural intervals while the film is running a number flashes beside the screen and the spectators are asked to make a pencil mark in their booklet on one of three spaces opposite that number; the spaces indicate liking (or interest), neutrality, and disliking (or boredom). When the show is over, the spectators are asked to recall each of the commercials, to note down the brand name if they remember it, and anything else that came through to them from the commercial. "The idea," says Leonard Kudisch, "is not so much to get playback data as to focus attention on the commercials." Then comes the second set of drawings and prize awards, with each spectator noting his "post-choice" on still another sheet in the questionnaire. The meeting is then thrown open for a brief but lively discussion, with members of the audience making points about both the program and the commercials. (These points, incidentally, are often highly knowledgeable—especially in the children's shows.) An assistant beside the stage notes down the points as they are made, and selects half a dozen of them which he rephrases (to eliminate the personality of the person who made it) and then puts to a vote; each spectator votes by marking yet another page in his booklet.

The pattern is then repeated, on an ordinary night, with a new half-hour television show and three new commercials.

If possible, Schwerin sets the commercials to be tested into shows which have never been seen in the New York area. One show may be used over and over again, as Desilu's pilot film for *A Date with the Angels* was used in the spring of 1957, while the producer was trying to peddle the series to a network. (The peddling operation was successful, forcing Schwerin to find another program for his purposes.) Sometimes the tests are held to find out what type of program provides the best context for this sort of commercial, and then Schwerin may be reduced to showing programs which members of the audience may have seen before. At no time, however, will he use a show which has ever had a prominent sponsor identification. A few of Schwerin's sessions are held to test new programs alone, with no interest in response to the commercials. (Almost all new NBC program series go through the Schwerin sieve, though NBC does not always pay attention to Schwerin's verdicts.) Discussions after the film ends are much more prolonged and, according to the theater staff, much more interesting when the purpose of the test is to judge a program. In analyzing program potentialities, Schwerin has never missed on predictions of a big hit or a flat failure; "but," says Henry Newell, "there's that big gray area where you can't be sure."

The most remarkable statement that can be made about the Schwerin tests is that they seem to work—i.e., people *do* change their brand preferences as the result of seeing commercials in Schwerin's theater, any given commercial will produce about the same percentage change every time it is tested, and many commercials will not produce any change at all. An analysis of the first 5,400 tests on "independent" commercials (those delivered by announcers or obscure actors, not by a well-known personality) showed that about half of them had failed to influence brand choices by Schwerin's spectators. A few commercials had actually *decreased* the percentage choosing the advertised brand (one, for an electric razor, produced a drop of nearly 10 per cent). The rest were effective, drew spectators toward the advertised brand but in widely varying degrees. The size of the shift produced in a Schwerin test depends not only on the commercial itself, but on the product area—commercials for washing machines are regarded as no better than fair if they produce an increase of 10 percentage points from pre-choice to post-choice, while a 5 per cent jump would be spectacular for a cigarette. In those product areas where, as vice-president Ray Maneval puts it, "the same arguments are ridden over and over again," Schwerin will double the size of his sample—running the same program and the same commercials two nights in a row before two different audiences—to verify the inevitably small shift in choices.

If Schwerin's technique is valid, it must work on all aspects of television advertising. It can determine the kind of program in which a commercial pulls best (generally, Schwerin says, commercials show a better score when they are set in "high-type" programs as opposed to junk). It can provide measurements for the comparison of "reason-why" selling arguments as against a brand-image or mood-provoking approach (Schwerin feels that either method is fine, provided it stays on its own side of the fence: if the commercial is full of hard-hitting arguments, high choice scores will correlate with high recall of the selling points, while mood commercials score highest when the viewer can recall nothing but a snatch of slogan or a scenic setting). It can determine precisely where the commercial should be slotted within the context of the program (commercials at the very beginning or end generally do less well than those surrounded by entertainment). It can indicate the sort of person who should present the sales pitch on the screen (a celebrity, an announcer, or an actor playing a part: RCA did particularly well in the Schwerin scores when the arguments for its television sets were presented by a juvenile actress playing the role of a baby-sitter). Only one factor can be tested at a time, so a number of sessions may be necessary before Schwerin's analysts are prepared to make recommendations. For one especially thorough client, Miles Laboratories, Schwerin once ran twenty-six separate tests of what was basically a single commercial.

Obviously, Schwerin's tests of a single commercial cannot measure the cumulative power of a campaign. But, he says, "to the very best of our knowledge, ha?, a stimulus that tests strong will grow more than a stimulus that tests weak. We've never seen a contrary result." All researchers are professionally prejudiced against the very idea that an individual ad (which they can measure, maybe) is only part of the larger whole of the campaign (which research cannot hope to measure until it is over). "Cumulative effect," says George Gallup, "has historically been the rationalization for bad advertising—'Nothing is happening now, friend, but just wait and keep spending your money. . . .'" Nevertheless, the history of advertising is full of campaigns which started slowly and gathered power. Many of the most effective sales arguments are more than slightly unbelievable on their first presentation, but become acceptable through the power of simple repetition. Most of the important brand images become part of the public consciousness only by the slow, careful construction of a product aura. "Take our work for Ohrbach's," says Alan Greenberg of Doyle Dane Bernbach. "How could you pretest a six-year campaign on the basis of a single ad when the campaign is to change people's image of a store? When people see an ad they see it in terms of a Gestalt, and the next time they see it it's in terms of another Gestalt, and the campaign itself is a Gestalt."

Basically, however, Schwerin's tests seem to be distrusted because the whole idea seems too simple to men who have learned over the years that advertising is an immensely complicated subject. Several research men have tried to disprove Schwerin's theories on his home grounds, clipping apart films of commercials which have done well on his tests and substituting sections from commercials which have done badly (this sort of tampering with copyright material is, of course, wholly illegal). But nobody has yet found a way to dutch Schwerin's numbers game, to explain in terms other than Schwerin's own why it is that certain commercials never work and certain commercials always work when fed into the Schwerin roulette wheel. Still, the feeling that Schwerin's service is just too silly for words is very widespread among experienced advertising researchers—and the strength of this feeling is a ponderable obstacle to the Schwerin procedures.

CHAPTER 17

AND THIS IS HOW WE KNOW WE'RE RIGHT:

Certainty Begins at Home

"Well, I'd hate to admit at this stage in my life, as a young man with maybe three or four more good years in this business, that we'll never be able to measure all the variables. There are lots of variables, I suppose, in the making of an atom bomb, but some son-of-a-gun was smart enough to figure it all out."

Paul Gerhold, director of media and research, Foote, Cone & Belding (New York)

1.

Virtually all market research firms put some of their time into measuring the effectiveness of advertising. The Nielsen Food and Drug Indices and Sam Barton's Market Research Corporation, both devoted to the measurements of actual product purchases, have over the years developed ways in which their clients can correlate sales data with advertising effort. Though Alfred Politz is primarily concerned with measuring market potentials and the factors behind consumer attitudes, none of his clients would think of approving an advertising campaign before Politz had looked at it. Ernest Dichter of the Institute for Motivational Research has even launched his own testing service (available to companies which are not otherwise clients of the Institute) to measure television commercials. He gathers a group of half a dozen people in a living-room setting and shows them a program, with commercials. During the show, a hidden camera takes pictures of the audience through a hole just above the television screen. Then Dichter's interviewers hold a long, long round-table discussion with the people in the living room about what the commercials meant to them, and how closely they felt *integrated* into the commercials ("if it was a food product," Dichter says, "could they taste it?"). On the basis of this discussion and the photographic record of individual reactions during the show, Dichter's analysts assign the commercial a *numerical rating* which is supposed to indicate its effectiveness as a sales weapon. This service was first offered in 1957, and it is far too soon to say whether its measurements will become part of the permanent table talk of the advertising business.

Several big client companies have thought up their own advertising testing procedures. Procter & Gamble has a particularly elaborate set of tests, performed mostly by Burke Research of Cincinnati and guarded by the company and its agencies with security precautions that would do credit to the Atomic Energy Commission. Men who have worked closely with P & G, however, report that the tests are different from those performed elsewhere only in the thoroughness of their application. Among the more ingenious testing devices developed by a manufacturer is a Philip Morris test for print advertising, based on the assertion that an individual smoking two brands of cigarettes at once, taking alternate puffs from each, cannot tell the difference between the two. If he is shown advertising for each while he smokes, and asked which cigarette *tastes* better, a change in taste preference will reflect the selling power of the two advertisements and nothing else. By gathering separate, "matched" samples of respondents, using the same ad for the competition's brand in every test while changing the ad for the Philip Morris brand (which may be Benson & Hedges, Parliament, Marlboro or Spud as well as the namesake), the company can measure the relative efficiency of alternative advertisements for its products.

Every agency does some advertising testing on its own, submitting its ads to panels of respondents, asking them questions, tabulating and analyzing the answers. Sometimes this testing will be as simple as sending a boy down to Grand Central Station to ask the people in the waiting room which of two advertisements they like best. Sometimes it will be fantastically elaborate, involving 5,000-home samples and lengthy questionnaires drawn up by practicing psychiatrists.

At a few agencies, most notably BBDO, the employees of the agency itself have been marshaled into groups (unmarried girls, parents of young children, and so forth), and their opinions will be asked when somebody wants an ad tested but the job doesn't seem to justify the expense of a real research project. Such incestuous question asking, while probably better than nothing, often produces remarkable cases of intellectual hemophilia. Allen Funt, the Candid Camera Man, recalls an occasion when the then-agency for Pabst Blue Ribbon Beer asked him to take his recording equipment into streets, offices and bars and ask people the simple question "What'll you have?" The agency's officers were convinced that upwards of 90 per cent of the population, asked such a question out of the blue, would automatically parrot back the words "Pabst Blue Ribbon"; then Funt's material could be put together to make a wonderful presentation to the client. Funt was somewhat skeptical about the project, and asked the agency why it was so confident of the results. "Oh," came the answer, "just try it on anybody around the office here, you'll see, it's a kind of running joke." Since a job is a job, Funt abandoned the argument and went out to do the agency's bidding. He gathered quite a number of interesting answers to the question "What'll you have?"—but two days of steady work failed to turn up anybody who replied, "Pabst Blue Ribbon." The agency paid his bill and wrote off the expenditure to experience.

Nobody can say as a fact what percentage of the work that the agencies do along these lines is self-serving and essentially dishonest; estimates range from one-quarter to three-quarters of the total. (Drawing up a research questionnaire which would elicit this information might make an interesting experimental assignment someday for some association of social psychologists.) Obviously, it is to the agency's benefit if the client can be convinced that his advertising has been meticulously prechecked and therefore *must* be wonderful. At the same time, however, the agency has a real stake in creating the best possible advertising for its clients, and if it believes in ad testing it has considerable incentive to do an honest job.

Most agencies try to pretest their advertising by duplicating or adapting the procedures used by the independent research firms. At Y & R, inevitably, these procedures are largely Gallup's. BBDO uses John Caples' mail-order copy testing and Schwerin's television service and its own internal panels, and pretests magazine advertising by means of an ingenious procedure which combines Gallup and Starch and eliminates the artificiality of strange, unfamiliar and ill-printed magazines like Gallup's *Impact* or Y & R's *New Canadian World*. By special arrangement with two of the major national weeklies, BBDO gets about a thousand first-off-press advance copies of coming issues. The agency's production department, working fast, removes some of the legitimate ads from the issues and "strips in" proofs of the ads which BBDO wants to test. Usually two alternative versions of each ad will be substituted for the existing pages, and then 700 copies of the altered magazine—350 with each of the ads to be tested—will be given away on the day the real issue hits the newsstands to two "matched samples" of people (same age, income, education groups, etc.) who do not ordinarily read this magazine. Two or three days later BBDO sends interviewers around to find out which ads members of each sample remember without prompting (unaided recall), which ads they remember after mention of a brand name (aided recall), and which ads they can recognize when an interviewer flips through the issue with them (Starch). The comparative ratings of the two ads on all three tests will guide the agency in deciding which advertisement to run; but the test is most useful in deciding technical questions—such as, shall we use one big picture of a cake made with Betty Crocker mix or two smaller pictures of two goodies made with two different kinds of mix?

Those agencies which rely on brand images and "motivational" sales arguments will pretest their advertising with techniques from the psychology laboratory. Ruthrauff & Ryan, which grew up out of mail order and always preferred direct approaches, once carried psychological testing to its ultimate reach, subjecting respondents to hypnosis after they had looked at an ad to discover how much of the message had penetrated into their subconscious minds. For all sorts of reasons, this experiment was dropped shortly after it had been started.

At some agencies testing is regarded as secondary to the following of rules for effective advertising which the executives have drawn up through their years of experience. Kenyon & Eckhardt has a thick book of such prescriptions for advertisements (known inside the office as "the Bible"), and ads will not even go out for testing if they break K & E's established rules. And there are a few agencies—Doyle Dane Bernbach and Earle Ludgin being the most important examples— which take a dim view of all ad testing. "I am not," says Bill Bernbach, "going to hire a man to make a survey which tells me that there appears to be salt in the sea." Nevertheless, the central argument in the Bernbach philosophy—the idea that the picture should express the sales pitch by itself—leads clearly to a test question, and the agency has done considerable picture testing. It will take a portfolio of different ads for different products to a respondent and, after he has had an hour to look through the portfolio, ask him which *slogans* he remembers. In each test there are several sets of portfolios, identical except for different versions of the ads Bernbach is testing, and the slogan is the same on each version; only the picture is different. The picture which produces the highest recall of the slogan will be preferred for use in the final advertisement.

2.

Three agencies, each in its own way, have done the most notable work in ad testing. Foote, Cone & Belding has been the most ingenious; McCann-Erickson the most spectacular; and Ted Bates the most thorough.

Foote, Cone—the successor firm to Albert Lasker's Lord & Thomas —can justly claim to have tried everything, from split runs through semantic differentials. This agency was the first to use what is still the most remarkable psychological research tool ever invented—a kind of lie-detector instrument which measures the sweat on the palm of the respondent's hand. The advertisement which makes the respondent sweat most is the one which most deeply arouses him, emotionally (run that one up on the flagpole, Manny, and let's see who salutes). Currently, Foote, Cone is experimenting with an almost equally mechanical device in the field of straight recall—the "Communiscope," which shows respondents a three-second or four-second glimpse of the ad to be tested, and then tries to find out what they remember from the flashed advertisement. And the agency has put some thousands of dollars of its own money into experiments on the "Mindex," a kind of game board on which the respondent plays by placing cards marked with brand names into boxes reflecting opinions ("one of best," "fair," etc.). A product's score on the Mindex measures its "share of mind," which must precede share of market. The device was invented by Cornelius du Bois, formerly research director for Time, Inc., now working for Foote, Cone.

The key to Foote, Cone's testing philosophy is supplied by Sherwood Dodge: "the real problem about measuring advertising effectiveness is costs; clients can afford to do it, and should, but not an agency." Dodge, a man in his early forties but seemingly younger still, is one of the few people in advertising born to the business; his grandfather was Claude Hopkins. In 1957 the Fletcher Richards agency bought him away from Foote, Cone, where he had been since his emergence from college twenty years before, serving as copywriter, researcher, account supervisor, marketing director and management officer. Behind a bland, round, inexpressively handsome face, the lively gray eyes concealed when necessary by horn-rimmed glasses, Dodge is, as Edsel's David Wallace put it, "a very savvy guy." In his ordinary work he is required to seem sober, cautious and highly responsible, so he channels a vast fund of cleverness into designing tests which will produce reliable answers at relatively low costs. Largely at his suggestion, Foote, Cone did a great deal of inexpensive mail research, single-answer interviewing and simple behavior measurement, with remarkable results.

One test that Dodge likes to describe at meetings was conducted to reassure a client who saw a competitor making inroads in his market with a new advertising slogan. The question to be answered was, "Is my slogan as good as my competitor's?" Foote, Cone had a number of batches of the product made up and packaged in plain wrappers. Half the samples were then labeled with a rephrasing of the client's slogan, the other half with a rephrasing of his competitor's slogan. One of each was given away to a number of housewives at the kitchen door, and a few days later an interviewer called to ask, simply, which of the two supposedly different products the housewife had liked best. Nearly 80 per cent of the housewives had a preference, and they voted two-to-one in favor of the sample with the Foote, Cone slogan on it. Since the two samples were otherwise identical, only the slogan could have created the preference, and Foote, Cone could safely report back to the client that his competitive position was secure.

Foote, Cone has pretested a number of campaigns, or sales arguments for campaigns, by mailing out alternative ads (or letters containing the arguments from them) to two matched samples of households. Since the agency believes strongly in cumulative effect, it does not send just one ad; instead, the household in the sample receives three or four letters over a period of a few weeks, each containing another ad from the campaign. About a month after the last letter is sent, Foote, Cone hires an independent research firm to go to these households and perform a routine market research job, asking the housewife which brand she bought most recently in a dozen different product classifications, only one of which interests the agency. (Precautions are taken to make sure that the respondent does not connect the interviewer with the ads she received.) Meanwhile, other interviewers go to still a third sample of households which have *not* received an ad mailing from the agency. A significant difference in brand purchases between the households which have received the ads and those which have not proves the effectiveness of the advertising; a significant difference in purchases between the two samples which have received the two different campaigns proves the superiority of one advertising approach to the other.

Perhaps the most ingenious behavior measurement Foote, Cone has ever attempted involved mailings alone, without any expense for interviews. Two different campaigns for a new product were sent to two matched samples of households, together with letters asking whether the recipients would like to participate in a consumer test for the product. Those who replied that they *would* like to participate were sent a letter of apology and a quarter; they were told that the quota for the test had been filled, but that some samples of the product were still available. If they were interested in trying the product, they should return the enclosed quarter, and the agency would be glad to send them a sample.

"It was a brilliant test design," says Paul Gerhold, the rather short, cheerful, professorial research director of Foote, Cone's New York office. "I can say that because it wasn't my idea. Disillusioningly, however, it produced almost exactly the same number of quarters for each of the two advertising approaches. I think it was because the two ad ideas were of equal merit, or equal lack of merit—but it's hard to sell that to the client. . . ."

3.

In 1948 McCann-Erickson, under the leadership of its new president Marion Harper, Jr., went looking for what vice-president Donald Armstrong calls "a creative research tool" which would be related directly to *sales*. "You take two toothpaste ads," Armstrong says, "and, obviously, one of them sells better than the other one. We wanted to find a measure that would tell us in advance which of the two ads will sell better, and *why*. We experimented for two years, using variations on split-run testing and consumer-jury testing, submitting the ads to panels of consumers and asking them questions." At the end of its experiments the agency found what it called, with that gift for controversy which has distinguished Harper from the start of his advertising career, "the relative sales conviction test." The words "sales conviction" are a bloody shirt waved in the face of McCann's rival agencies, who have not taken well to the idea of the test. "I've examined this thing," says the head of an agency which recently bought away one of McCann's research directors, "and I can assure you it's a fraud."

"Well," says Donald Armstrong with a wry grin, "it isn't black magic. Basically, it's a putting together of two ingredients—the best market research we can find, a quota sampling of product prospects, and then the application of what is commonly thought of as 'depth interviews.' First, we have to find what we call the 'heavy-user category,' there's one for every product. Thirty-two per cent of the people who use toothpaste buy 84 per cent of all the toothpaste sold. These 'core users' are the people you have to influence with your advertising if it's going to be successful. We have to know who these people are for all our advertising, so media research can find out how to reach them. Once we know who the members of this group are, we can apply the relative sales conviction test by interviewing them.

"Basically, we ask them one simple question. We show them two advertisements and ask, 'Which of these two would be most likely to convince you to buy this product?' We've tried all sorts of substitutions for the question, but this one is always the best. The respondent picks one of the ads, and the interview then goes on for forty or forty-five minutes more. We ask him how he came to his decision, if there was any part of either ad that boomeranged, that made him less likely to buy the product. Then there's the interpretation, going over all the transcripts, which is done by one person, who comes up with a rating score—which ad will do better, and how much better."

Each relative sales conviction test involves at least 1,800 interviews in New York, Chicago and Los Angeles and in a distant suburb of each. The final rating scores arise from analysis of the respondents' comments rather than from mere addition of their statements of preference for one ad over the other. Often the analyzer finds that the ad which most people *say* would be more likely to make them buy is actually a less effective selling instrument than its rival. Since the comments are not reduced to numerical form in the analysis, but are allowed to filter through the trained mind of the researcher (five such researchers have interpreted sales conviction responses during the seven years of testing), there is no important quantitative data to which McCann can point as proof that the test is accurate. It was therefore necessary for the agency to "verify" the test by applying it to situations where different ads had run and the sales results from the ads were easily measurable. Not the least interesting part of the relative sales conviction test is the ingenuity McCann has shown in verifying it.

Obviously, the test could be verified by the examination of split-run mail-order ads. McCann kept on the alert for the appearance of split-runs, and when it found an interesting example it sent out researchers (the agency maintains its own staff of 2,600 interviewers). When the relative sales conviction test had been completed, and rating scores assigned to the two published ads, the agency approached the advertiser and asked him for the actual sales results for the two ads. The same procedure was followed when the agency found pairs of different direct-mail sales letters going out to prospects (usually magazines looking for new subscribers).

Then there were department store ads, where the relative pull of the two halves of a split-run could be measured by counting sales in the store the next day. With department store ads, split-runs were not the only chance for testing, because a department store might advertise a shoe sale, with pictures of different styles of shoes; or a silverware sale, with illustrations of different patterns. Again, McCann's interviewers went out to test consumer reaction to the different styles and patterns, and the research analyst predicted which of them the store had sold in greatest quantity. And then the store was asked for the facts.

The possibilities were still not exhausted. *McCall's* magazine at one point decided to try and break away from its invariable cover illustration of a lady in a hat and to run a picture of a cake on the cover, instead. Since newsstand sales of magazines fluctuate for all sorts of reasons, *McCall's* did not feel that it could measure the success of the cake simply by putting out an issue with the new type of cover and counting the copies sold. Instead, the magazine ran a split-run on its covers, printing half of them with the lady and half with the cake. McCann again applied its relative sales conviction test to find out which cover would sell more copies. (In real life, both covers sold the same number of magazines.) Finally, the agency invaded the intellectual specialty market, going out with copies of two major theoretical books in the social sciences which Mentor was issuing in pocket reprint, and predicting which of them would sell better.

In all, by mid-1957, McCann secured verification on 143 relative sales conviction tests. The agency's prediction of rank order (which ad did better) was correct on 141 out of the 143 tests.

This impressive statistic is heavily discounted at other agencies. As observed, most advertising men do not feel that the correct mail-order ad is necessarily useful in general advertising. Department store advertising is news, one of the reasons people buy their newspapers, while national advertising is just advertising, people accept it because it's there. Magazine covers and pocket reprint books are scarcely items central to the general distribution scheme of branded products. But it is only with such material that sales results can be verified, and surely McCann's claims for its test are more believable because the results were right rather than wrong when the agency stuck out its neck to verify its work—at a cost which Armstrong estimates at $200,000.

Exactly how extensive McCann's claims have been is a matter of dispute between the agency and its rivals. Armstrong himself, at any rate, is relatively modest about the test. A dashing young man with long light hair and a ruddy complexion, Armstrong was an English major in college and went into the advertising business as a messenger boy at Young & Rubicam, hoping to become a copywriter; instead, as he puts it, "I fell in love with a guy named George Gallup." His basic interests remained in the creative end, however. "My excitement in research," he says, "is in this area of influence, how do you make people do things? That's the fun." Armstrong regards the relative sales conviction test as primarily a creative tool, a measurement of the relative technical quality of two different approaches to a sales proposition—"though the test could be used to measure propositions, too.

"It's very rarely," Armstrong says, "that we'll just take the ad which scores better on the test and run it. Usually, we'll take elements from all the tested ads. Or you might want to use all the ads as they stand, whatever their scores on the test. You can test four ads, and one of them receives a rating of only five per cent—but it selects an audience which the other ads don't reach. So you'll use that ad, too, to influence that part of the market."

4.

At Ted Bates & Company, inevitably, testing is a question of fundamentals rather than ingenuities. Bates operates from the premise that advertising works by giving the consumer a reason for buying the advertised product. If this premise is true, the effectiveness of a campaign can be judged by the answers to two factual questions:

1. What percentage of the population remembers what was said in the advertising for a brand?

2. Given the two groups, group A which remembers the advertising and group B which doesn't—to what extent are the people in group A more likely to use the brand?

"The penetration concept," says Clifford Parsells, vice-president in charge of media and research, "goes back to World War II, when one man at Colgate—Roy Peet—began pounding us with a question, a fundamental and very good question. He said, 'You are a man with a package goods problem, the merchandise is available everywhere and it's a good product. You spend one million dollars or four million dollars on ads—how do you know whether the ads are doing you any good? With all these modern techniques, isn't there some way we can go to people and get some reasonable measure of what a campaign accomplishes?'

"Now," Parsells continues, "there has been very little research—research of the kind a university might pick up—on this problem of what you get for your million dollars. We had to start from nothing. We tried a dozen different approaches, all aimed at solving the one problem—how do you siphon off from the minds of people the knowledge they may have?"

The answer, finally, was a direct question: the interviewer gives the respondent a brand name, and asks her what she remembers about the advertising for the brand. "In the early days," Parsells recalls, "we had this problem of handling the material. You ask five thousand women what they know about Palmolive soap. Some of them give the whole slogan, some give part of the slogan, others give you something which is the slogan all screwed up. We decided not to be arbitrary. If they have any idea of it at all, we accept it; they remember.

"All right, that's the first question—brand argument recall. The second question is, behavior. The interviewer asks, 'What did you clean your teeth with last night?' Then you relate the two. If they know what you're trying to tell them and they're not using the product, then what you're telling them is pretty silly."

This measurement of advertising "penetration" and "usage pull" is performed once a year on the eighty major brands in the product fields in which Bates works. The numerical size of the sample interviewed is a confidential figure, but it is obviously enormous; Rosser Reeves says it is "the biggest in America, bigger than Gallup or Roper ever used on a presidential campaign. We measure recall in 744 counties of 48 states, thousands upon thousands of people. The sample is so large because we get so much use out of it, we even cross-ruff it on media—if the Boston area shows less recall than other areas on one of our campaigns, we know there's something wrong with the media we're using in Boston."

The major use of Parsells' data, however, is in judging the extent to which remembrance of the sales argument appears to make people buy. "Let's say," says Reeves, "there are fifty people who *don't* remember the ads, and two of them use the product. We call that the level of usage. Then there are fifty people who *do* remember the ads, and four of them use the product. The ads increase product usage by two out of every fifty people, or four per cent. That's the usage pull. Well," Reeves continues, pointing at a bar graph on an easel card, "here's a campaign by another agency, one per cent of the people who remember it use the product. And here's a campaign of ours, twenty-five per cent of the people who remember it use the product."

Most advertising campaigns—even Bates campaigns—contain more than one argument, and nearly all products have used different arguments at different periods in their history. Generally speaking, Bates's penetration surveys show that people retain only one argument for a product. "If you ask about Palmolive," Reeves says, "a lot of people will tell you about the Dionne Quintuplets. Ask about Camels, and they'll give you 'I'd Walk a Mile for a Camel.' Well, Camels hasn't used that slogan since 1944." Again, the usage pull enters, this time to measure the quality of the different sales arguments: obviously, the sales argument to pound at is the one which produces in the group of people who remember it the highest percentage of brand users.

The circle is closed by relating a campaign's penetration and usage pull to the money spent on it. (There are several services which supply statistics on the expenditures of the various advertisers, but none of them is notably accurate; Bates employs a special staff to estimate the advertising expenditures of its clients' competitors.) These penetration-per-dollar and usage-pull-per-dollar estimates answer Roy Peet's good question of what the advertiser is getting for his money. And the continuance of the survey year after year enables Bates's clients to measure changes in the efficiency of their own and their competitors' advertising. If such results are obtained, and Bates believes they are, then they justify the $1 million of its own money which the agency has spent on penetration studies since 1943. "Usage pull" is not really very significant in a single survey on a single brand, because users tend to remember ads for the brands they buy; but measured relatively, year after year, it must have some value.

"Yes," says Clifford Parsells, and clears his throat. Parsells is a big, ruminative man whose dignified and conservative mien is tempered by a fondness for loud Argyle socks. "You must understand that penetration is not as good as Reeves will tell you it is. We're taking off the surface of people's minds what's there when we're there. Now, you can't catalogue the human mind into conscious and nonconscious, but undoubtedly there is something under the surface. We simply don't know how to measure it, and we don't think anybody else knows how to measure it, either. Then, a housewife who doesn't remember the brand message when the interviewer is there may recall it the next day or the day after. [Once, to measure the effect of this time lag, Parsells sent interviewers back to a large section of the sample sixty days after the first interviewing session. He found that the percentages of penetration had remained stable—but that half the people who had remembered a brand argument on the first interview had forgotten it during the two months. Their place in the bar graphs was taken by people whose minds had been blank when the brand was mentioned during the first interview.] On the other hand, a woman in a grocery store merely remembers what she remembers at *that* moment. It isn't just interviews which happen at a single point in time.

"It all comes down to the role of research in advertising," continues research director Parsells. "Any agency can put together an ad and say, 'Beautiful ad—it says this and this and this.' Well, the research man says, 'Get a hundred people together, and let's see what the ad says to them.' That's fine. But to use research to tell you you should say this or say that is to assume that research, sociology and psychology are a hell of a lot more competent than they are. Personally, I'll take a good, experienced copy practitioner's opinion over any research, any day. . . .

"You know," Parsells finished up, "this is a fascinating business. It's a very educated business, educated by know-how, like a good bartender. You don't really know why you do it, you just know how to do it."

Part V | IMPACT

CHAPTER 18

ON POLITICS

"I am quite certain that if Dewey had known these things, and understood them, he would have been President."

Rosser Reeves

"In the 1948 campaign, Truman sat Ed Kelly and Jim Thompson down on the back of his special train, and convinced them he was going to win. It was one of the greatest sales ever made, and it didn't have anything to do with Madison Avenue. Election day the Kelly machine had every precinct worker out on the streets in Chicago getting out the vote, and Truman squeaked through in Illinois by 21,000."

former Senator William F. Benton
(cofounder, Benton & Bowles)

1.

Two men, one of them an acquaintance of the General's and the other a complete outsider, were primarily responsible for advertising by means of 20-second television spot announcements the presidential candidacy of Dwight D. Eisenhower in 1952. The acquaintance was

Alfred Hollender, a slight, rather shy man then a broadcasting station manager and now head of the television department at Grey Advertising, who had met the General while supervising the U.S. propaganda radio to Germany during the war; the stranger was Rosser Reeves of Ted Bates. Hollender had come into the campaign through a letter which he wrote the General, offering his services, shortly after Eisenhower had announced that he would accept the Republican nomination if it was offered. Reeves, too, was a volunteer, though the process in his case had been more complicated: good friends from the oil business had called him up from a country club locker room and asked him to come up with a slogan which would counteract what they considered the strong effect of the Democrats' "You Never Had It So Good." Reeves told them they didn't need a slogan, they needed a plan. "If you want to elect Eisenhower," he said, "you go after maximum penetration: use spots."

Radio spot announcements, cast very much in the form of regular commercials, had been used in national elections since the Liberty League spots for Landon in 1936. Their purpose, however, had been strictly supplementary, and they were concentrated in areas where the candidate's formal speeches were broadcast at low-audience hours. If they presented any personality, it was usually a local figure endorsing the candidate rather than the candidate himself. The idea of spending a large part of the campaign budget on spot announcements, with the candidate himself as featured player, and using these spots to some extent as a substitute for broadcast campaign speeches, had never been formally suggested by anyone until 1948, when E. H. Little, chairman of Colgate-Palmolive, had the Bates agency prepare sample radio spots for Thomas E. Dewey. With the full approval of BBDO, which had handled the New York State Republican party advertising effort for some years and was planning the advertising program for the 1948 national campaign, Dewey turned down Little's suggestion.

The three basic arguments in favor of spot announcements to promote the Eisenhower candidacy were the low cost per thousand homes reached; the fact that spots, unlike full-length programs, would reach people not already prejudiced in favor of the candidate; and the opportunity to concentrate fire in the relatively few critical states which could not certainly be counted in either candidate's column. Using these arguments, Hollender had convinced the General and his brother Milton Eisenhower that spots should be employed and had put together from newsreel clippings a few spot announcements for use in the Republican primaries, even before Reeves mentioned the idea to his friends. But it was the telephone call from the clubhouse that closed the deal: Reeves's companions, among them oilman James Snowden, promised that they would raise the necessary money for the campaign if Reeves would handle the advertising end.

A few weeks later Reeves gave a dinner in a private room at "21" to show suggested scripts and story boards to his friends and a few of their friends. The next step was formal contact with Citizens for Eisenhower, the secular arm of the Republican party for 1952, at which point Hollender and Reeves came together. A second dinner at "21" sold the spots approach to Walter Williams, chairman of C-for-E, and to John Hay Whitney, who was C-for-E's chief fund raiser. A committee including Williams, Whitney and Reeves then waited on Sherman Adams, chief of staff at central Eisenhower headquarters, and convinced Adams that the General himself should appear in the spot campaign. The formal Republican 1952 "Campaign Plan," presented to Eisenhower and Nixon and their staffs on August 7 by Robert Humphreys, Republican National Committee public relations director, stated that "The use of radio and TV station-break 'spots' during the last ten days of the campaign is a *must* for stimulating the voters to go to the polls and vote for the candidates."

By that time Reeves was already at work on the spots. Though he had arranged for assistance if he needed it (several agencies offered "the whole copy department"), in the event he wrote all the scripts himself, without help. "Every word of them," he says today, "and very tedious work it was." Taking a six-week leave of absence from Bates without pay, he established himself in a suite at the St. Regis Hotel, and researched by reading the newspapers. "I took Eisenhower's speeches," he recalls, "and read them all. He was talking about three thousand things, and you don't do that in advertising. You lose penetration." In the end, he picked something more than a dozen over-all themes out of the Eisenhower campaign argument and set up an appointment for himself with George Gallup, whom he had never met. He asked Gallup what issues were most important with the public, and received the reply that people were most disturbed about the Korean War, corruption in Washington, taxes and the high cost of living, in that order. Reeves prepared a few scripts and had an artist draw story boards for spots on each of these themes. He used in all the spots the same introduction, an announcer saying, with suppressed excitement, "Eisenhower Answers the Nation!" Then the voice of "an ordinary citizen" would ask a question, such as, "Mr. Eisenhower, what about the high cost of living?" And the General would reply, in this instance, "My wife, Mamie, worries about the same thing. I tell her it's our job to change that on November fourth." A formal disclaimer from the television station (of the "What you have just heard is a paid political announcement" variety) would end the spot and in each home the television set would then return to its usual fare.

As an advertising man, Reeves felt that just one issue should be chosen, and should be hammered home in all the spots. He presented his arguments to Walter Williams and representatives from the Republican National Committee at a meeting in the Hotel Plaza toward the end of August, and was turned down. Instead, the Republicans told him to hit at all the issues Gallup had described as important, and to get all the scripts ready for September 13, when Eisenhower would be in New York, and would be able to take a day to make his part of the films. Reeves had hoped for more time to get the spots written, and more time with the candidate to get the films right—one does not make fifty television spots in a single day, even with professional actors—but he was destined in this venture to work under orders.

By the time September 13 came Reeves was just as pleased he had just the one day with Eisenhower before the cameras: only twenty-two spots were ready, approved by Citizens for Eisenhower and waiting for the General. Reeves and Eisenhower met, for the first time, at the Transfilm studios in midtown Manhattan, and the Bates make-up department prepared the candidate for the cameras. Reeves was particularly anxious to have Eisenhower appear in the spots without his glasses, but without his glasses the General was unable to read the prompt cards. The head of Bates's radio-TV department personally took a brush and hand-lettered huge prompt cards for Eisenhower to read without glasses.

The first few spots went like the wind, and Reeves realized that Eisenhower probably could go through the planned fifty in a single day. So he sat down at his typewriter and wrote twenty-eight spots in a few hours, under forced draft. As he finished each spot he would take it to Milton Eisenhower, who would either okay or reject it. Sometimes Reeves, who was pulling most of Eisenhower's lines straight out of already delivered speeches, would protest against the rejection; to which the invariable answer would be, "I don't care if he said it in Texas in June, the General isn't going to say it now." Accepted scripts would be read quickly by the candidate, then passed on to be lettered on the prompt cards.

Eventually, $1,500,000 were spent to put these television spots on the air, and echoes of the controversy which they caused can still be heard. They were regarded as an important and in many quarters as an undesirable innovation in American political campaigning, and they will be worth a footnote in the history books someday. Part of that footnote should be a vignette of the scene in Transfilm's studios as recalled by Reeves: Hollender working with the camera crew, Reeves himself pounding a typewriter in a back room, a high-priced executive hand-lettering prompt cards, and Milton Eisenhower keeping up the spirits of the next President of the United States, who sat in a hard chair between takes, shaking his head and saying, "To think that an old soldier should come to this!"

2.

Advertising agencies work for political parties under the usual financial arrangements of the business, collecting their pay on media commissions rather than directly from the client. (The media, however, do not maintain the usual financial arrangements in their dealings with political parties; payment for commercial advertising is due ten days to a month after the ad is published or broadcast, but political parties must pay in advance, cash on the barrelhead.) Since the services of an advertising agency cost a political party nothing—the party would have to pay the same media rates if it placed its ads directly—every political campaign these days employs the services of an advertising agency. In a national campaign, when the commissions begin to run to hundreds of thousands of dollars, the agencies will do all sorts of work for the candidates without extra charge. But the fact that advertising men are doing a certain job of work does not mean that this job has thereby become "advertising" instead of "politics."

In 1956, for example, Walter O'Meara, head of the copy group for the Democratic party's advertising campaign, persuaded Adlai Stevenson to use a teleprompter (which he had never been willing to use before) to make sure he got his cues correctly during the filming of the television spots called *The Man from Libertyville*. Once he had experienced the convenience of watching his words run in front of him, Stevenson could not be parted from the device; before a speech in Albany, he complained to his staff that the rostrum was too high, blocking a clear view of the teleprompter—could they have the rostrum lowered, please? But Stevenson did not need an *advertising* man to sell him the value of the teleprompter—indeed, a speech consultant could probably have convinced him much more easily. Senator William Benton recalls talking to Bruce Barton about one of BBDO's contributions in the 1952 Republican campaign: "Bruce Barton told me about the chaotic conditions that prevailed in the TV campaign until Ben Duffy took charge. Duffy, he said, was the man who went backstage, got

Eisenhower to lie down for a while before a speech and to read it over a little before delivering it. I've no doubt he did. But that isn't what you would call great Madison Avenue technique; any newspaper publisher or strong-armed manager could have done the same."

At the end of the 1952 campaign, Roger Pryor of BBDO staged a television spectacular for Eisenhower, featuring film clips of the "Crusade" with cutbacks to the appreciative and confident candidate. In 1956, Norman, Craig & Kummel cut apart a newsreel film of the Republican National Convention to present a run-down on the "Joe Smith" story before Stevenson's first televised speech. Both these jobs were theater work, not advertising; it was merely an accident of organization that they were done through advertising agencies rather than by the movie directors who used to set up rallies for candidates. In the same line, in 1956, Alan Jay Lerner, author of the book and lyrics of *My Fair Lady,* suggested the distant shots of the crowd, spotlights sweeping over them, which helped build an aura of excitement about Stevenson's entrances for his speeches. And actor and director Robert Montgomery drew the schedule for the Republican National Convention. There is no *advertising* technique involved in the staging of a political show.

Again, advertising agencies have taken over most of the work of planning a candidate's arrival and departure—what routes should be followed, what signs should be carried by the crowd, and what cheers the populace should cheer, which people should be admitted into the same room with The Presence. Such work was done in the past by former newspapermen; it could easily be done by any good circus press agent. Advertising agencies may organize these matters more thoroughly and think of special gimmicks to make them more convincing, but the participation of agency people does not transform the work of the old-fashioned advance man into advertising work.

The line must be drawn also between advertising and public relations. Advertising, whatever its faults, is a relatively open business: its messages appear in paid space or on bought time, and everybody can recognize it as special pleading. Public relations works behind the scenes; occasionally the hand of the p.r. man can be seen shifting some bulky fact out of sight, but usually the public relations practitioner stands at the other end of a long rope which winds around several pulleys before it reaches the object of his invisible tugging. The fact that both advertising and public relations work with the "mass media" has concealed the more important fact that they look at media in different ways. Advertising supplements the content of the media, by means of advertising pages or paid commercial announcements; public relations seeks to direct and if necessary distort the media's supposedly undirected and undistorted content. The advertising man must know how many people he can reach *with* the media, the public relations man how many people he can reach *within* the media. An advertising man ghosting an article on a candidate's behalf is not doing advertising work any more than a college professor writing a speech for another candidate is teaching students.

Only three of the jobs performed by advertising men for a political campaign can be regarded as advertising work: the preparation of actual print ads or broadcast announcements, the selection of media for these commercial messages and for the candidate's speeches, and the measurement by research of how well the candidate's message is coming across. The last two of these are purely technical contributions, to which there can be no reasonable objection. The first of them, however, raises a number of serious issues on which intelligent men may disagree; and Rosser Reeves's spot announcements, though they were a relatively minor factor in the 1952 Republican campaign, are the perfect case in point.

3.

The most common objection to the use of advertising to magnify political issues is that advertising oversimplifies. A good part of the technique of advertising has the single purpose of simplification, of finding from the welter of causes which make people buy a product the one or two or three which can be refined down to a "reason" and then blown up to a slogan. Applied to branded products, the technique at its worst can do little harm to society as a whole, because product purchases are trivial matters and because people do not buy even the most heavily advertised product a second time unless it has given satisfaction. Applied to political issues, however, the technique must partially misinform, create undesirable emotions, and distort the realities which, in theory, underlie the decision of the electorate.

A convenient description of what is wrong with the injection of advertising into politics was given (quite unconsciously) by Morton B. Lawrence—president of an advertising agency which bears his name and which drags behind it a subsidiary called Political Campaign Associates—in a 1956 article for *Printer's Ink* entitled "Political Campaigns—new source of agency profits." Writing of the "campaign theme," Lawrence claimed that "it is in this area that an agency can be of greatest help to the candidate. A broad theme must be developed, based on the issues and personalities involved. It may be a positive theme stressing the accomplishments of your candidate or a negative one attacking the record of the opponent. After the theme is developed, it should be condensed into a simple form that can be used as a campaign slogan." Later in the same article, Lawrence gave a short list of "*dos* and *don'ts*" for the preparation of a brochure. Rule 2 read: "Make it attention-getting. In a recent campaign for political office, the literature we prepared portrayed a tiger embracing a building, with the caption, *Keep Tammany out of the courts.* How much more effective it was than the usual *Elect Wilson Jones!*" Rule 5 read: "Don't attempt to write a thesis [*sic*] on all of the issues."

The written plan prepared to help Reeves sell the idea of television spots to Citizens for Eisenhower proposed that "The spots would be the height of simplicity. People . . . would . . . ask the General a question. . . . The General's answer would be his complete comprehension of the problem and his determination to do something about it when elected. Thus he inspires loyalty without prematurely committing himself to any strait-jacketing answer."

It is clear enough that elections which are seriously influenced by the sort of thing Lawrence proposed or by the kind of spots Reeves actually produced would depart a great distance from the democratic ideal of an informed and responsible electorate making intelligent and sober decisions.

To which the answer from Reeves (Lawrence apparently does not understand that there is a real problem) runs along these lines: The electorate is uninformed and irresponsible before advertising enters. Politicians in their speeches, and partisans writing about the campaign in the press, do not attempt to present the issues of an election in their full complexity. Like the advertising man, they go searching for pat phrases, for slogans. They take the moles off their own faces and fling disfigurements at their rivals. As Charles Michelson, then Democratic party public relations director, said in the 1930's, people "vote for or against a picture that has been painted for them by protagonists and antagonists in a myriad of publications, a picture that must be either a caricature or an idealization." Oversimplification is the vice of the politician as well as of the advertising man.

Reeves reports on a dialogue between himself and his next-door neighbor Harlan Cleveland, now dean of the Maxwell School of Citizenship and Public Affairs at Syracuse University but then executive editor of *The Reporter* magazine, which had run an article highly critical of the Eisenhower spot announcements. (The two men came together not because of the article but because "it turned out he was the father of the little Cleveland girl who was always around the house.") "I asked Cleveland what his objection was," Reeves recalls, "and he said it was selling the President like toothpaste. I said, 'The essence of democracy is that people be informed of the issues. Is there anything wrong with a twenty-minute speech? Or a ten-minute speech? Or a five-minute speech? No. Then what's wrong with a one-minute speech or a fifteen-second speech?'

"Cleveland said, 'You can't say anything in a fifteen-second speech.' I told him, 'As a man who has been responsible for five hundred million dollars' worth of advertising I know more about that than you do.'" As it happened, Reeves had watched the opening of the Republican National Convention on television in a group that included the columnist Drew Pearson, who thought General MacArthur's keynote speech was "great. I thought," Reeves says, "it stank. I sent out a research crew at my own expense, asked 250 people if they knew what MacArthur had said. Only about two per cent of them knew. Two reasons: a) he covered too many bases; b) there was too much purple prose. Later I picked out three passages from that speech and photostated them on big boards, and showed them to a hundred people who had heard the speech. They read the three boards, and then I turned the boards around and asked them what MacArthur had said. They couldn't say. Once I took a Stevenson speech, tape recorded, and played it to 150 people. I got maybe eight per cent recall. You know the Calvin Coolidge story about going up to a farmer who'd been listening for two hours to a politician's speech, and asking the farmer what the politician was talking about. The farmer's answer was, 'He ain't said.'

"What I did with the Eisenhower spots," Reeves says, "was to apply the mechanics of advertising to the expenditure of money. It's a question of two mathematical factors. First, spots versus network speeches; you get a larger audience with spots. Second, recall; you get eight per cent on a Stevenson speech, 91 per cent on an Eisenhower spot. You have X dollars to spend. One way thirty per cent of the people know what you stand for, the other way sixty per cent of the people know. Cleveland said, 'This can lead to demagoguery.' I said, 'An uninformed electorate can lead to demagoguery faster.'"

It must be recognized from the beginning that Reeves's position is wholly defensible. Rosser Reeves, sitting in a hotel room and rephrasing quotes from Eisenhower's speeches to make them immediately comprehensible for any fool who might be listening, is not to be compared with public relations man Jon Jonkel, coming down from Chicago to Maryland and for $1,250 a month capitalizing on what he called "a very, very big doubt . . . in the minds of the people of Maryland" with a campaign which concluded in the famous composite photograph of Senator Millard Tydings apparently in intimate converse with Earl

Browder. Nor can Reeves be compared with campaign specialist Morton
Lawrence, regretting that the scurrilous attacks thrown by Thomas E.
Dewey and Irving M. Ives against Averell Harriman "came too late to
be effective." Advertising works in the open: there was nothing under-
handed about the Eisenhower spots.

And there is a good answer to all the specific criticisms. In his
excellent book *Professional Public Relations and Political Power*, from
which some of the information in this chapter has been taken, Stanley
Kelley, Jr., emphasizes the absence of the concept of *debate* in the
political thinking of the public relations or advertising man. "What
he conceives to be sound principles of strategy," Kelley writes, "usually
make it desirable for one side or the other to avoid [debate]. He is
engaged not only in trying to gain acceptance for a point of view, but
in attempting to gain for it a differential advantage in distribution."
But Kelley in this section of his book is comparing contemporary
political activity, involving advertising and public relations techniques,
with the American ideal of the town meeting, which was never capable
of expansion to the national scale. One party or another has always
had technical advantages in the presentation of its points—a better
speaker, who holds his audience, or simply a better ward organization.
The shifting of technical advantage from the party with the better
local organization to the party with the better advertising help might
seem highly objectionable to a partisan, but it cannot be condemned
as unethical.

Again, it is easy to criticize the specific Eisenhower spots which
Reeves wrote on the grounds (aside from their awesome vulgarity)
that they did not, in fact, present issues. Instead, they presented situations which were disturbing partisans of both candidates and then
offered as a solution, to quote the Plan, "the General's . . . complete
comprehension of the problem and his determination to do something
about it." Nevertheless, it is precisely on this level that politicians do
their campaigning, with or without the advice of Madison Avenue. As
the Plan for the spots said, "This was a technique that Roosevelt
certainly employed, and was certainly successful."

Even when one concedes the legitimacy of the honest employment of advertising techniques in a political campaign, however, the prospect provokes a queasy stomach. What is disturbing about this monster is not the spots on its skin, though these are aesthetically displeasing, but the idea in its head. Reeves works on the assumption, shared by the great majority of Americans, that a heavy vote is a good sign in a democracy, and that it is socially desirable to arouse people about political issues and to get them to the polls. This assumption, despite its popularity, is at the least suspect. Illiterates are not allowed to vote anywhere in the United States; it can certainly be argued that political illiterates, who pay no attention to political questions from one end of the year to the other and have no great interest in their voting rights as citizens, ought not to be encouraged to vote. These people are not reached at all by conventional campaigning techniques; if they happen to tune in a speech during the campaign season, they tune it out. But they can scarcely avoid spot announcements. Democracy does not benefit when their political apathy is disturbed by emotional slogans presenting simplified and one-sided views of the complicated affairs of state.

Apathy undoubtedly risks rule by political bosses, who command a loyalty independent of the issues in a campaign; and we believe in the rule of law rather than the rule of men. But rule by law does not necessarily imply rule by issues, and dishonest issues are more dangerous than dishonest men. Carried to its extreme, political bossism results in Hagues, Pews and Prendergasts; carried to the other extreme, public relations and advertising techniques may promote Joe McCarthys. Confronted with a choice between the two, most intelligent people will opt eagerly for Prendergast.

4.

These horrors do not, however, confront us. It is by no means certain that advertising techniques in politics are as powerful as Reeves believes them to be. William Benton, who has been a United States senator

and was cofounder of the firm in which the young Reeves discovered
his career, believes that the political values of advertising are highly
overrated. He does not pitch in with the Democratic party advertising
effort at campaign times because "I'm too busy campaigning"—which
he regards as a far more important activity.

"The problems of political propaganda are vastly different from the
problems of advertising," Benton says. "With advertising, you want to
win X number of people to buy Chesterfield cigarettes; and if the people
who smoke Camels don't like you, they won't bother to protest and you
don't care. In politics, if you disturb anybody, he can be vociferously
against you, which can stir up trouble and lose a lot of votes. Just one
vociferous protest in each community can upset your political organization. Suppose you put on a series of TV shows as I did in Connecticut
in my second campaign, the most imaginative television shows ever done
in politics—they haven't dared to do anything so original on a national
basis. The shows were immensely successful. When I went through the
factories, people's faces would light with *joy* at recognition, from having
seen me on television. But the programs offended some people, and I
had a recoil impossible in advertising."

Nor does Benton think that a political party always stands to gain
from hammering home a few simple issues, over and over again. "People
can just get sick of the issues," he says. "Keeping everlastingly at it
doesn't necessarily bring success in politics. There are people all over the
country who have kept everlastingly at it and are dead, politically. Herbert Hoover has kept everlastingly at it for more than thirty years, and
he couldn't get elected dog catcher, anywhere."

Walter O'Meara, who was Reeves's boss at Benton & Bowles and
copy chief for the Democratic advertising effort in 1956, believes that
television is vastly overrated as a political medium. (So does Morton
Lawrence.) "I think the newspaper reports of the television speeches
were more important than the speeches themselves," O'Meara says.
"There's something *solid* about headlines. In fact, I think radio was
more effective than television in lots of ways. Television tends to
deglamorize the candidate. When Roosevelt was coming over the

radio, that disembodied voice gave what he said an extra importance."

Actually, the disagreements between Reeves and his former employers are not so great as they might seem. Although Reeves has weaker moments when he feels that Stevenson could have won in 1952 with the correct employment of spot announcements, his enthusiasm never carries him to the belief that spots would have helped Stevenson much in 1956 or that Hoover or Landon could have upset Roosevelt with the best advertising in the world. Benton, on the other hand, would be willing to concede that in a narrowly decided election, like the Truman squeak of 1948, advertising techniques might swing the balance the other way. (Benton believes that the advertisements in his first campaign, especially one written by O'Meara, more than accounted for his narrow margin of victory.) Their disagreement arises, as disagreements in advertising so often do, from different measurements of effectiveness.

Advertising is essentially a surface phenomenon, a wind that can stir still water. But, as the poet observed, there are tides in the affairs of men. When the wind blows with the tide, it seems to create an elemental motion; when it blows against the tide, it blows in vain. The attitudes which a national electorate takes to the polls are more fundamental than the surface "issues" which are the apparent cause of victory and loss. As Bill Benton puts it, "Nobody even knows the relationship between a good campaign and the result in the election." And advertising can never be more than a single element in an over-all campaign.

CHAPTER 19

A PREMISE FOR A THEORY AND SOME MODEST PROPOSALS

"Well, you know, economic theory assumes that everybody acts rationally, and that rules out advertising right from the start."

Associate Professor, University of Chicago School of Business

----

"And then, Mr. Gumbrill, even suppose you could somehow get rid of the necessity of working, suppose a man's time were all leisure. Would he be free then? . . . I say he would not. Not unless he 'appened to be a man like you or me, Mr. Gumbrill, a man of sense, a man of independent judgment. An ordinary man would not be free. Because he wouldn't know how to occupy his leisure except in some way that would be forced on 'im by other people. People don't know 'ow to entertain themselves now; they leave it to other people to do it for them. They swallow what's given them. They 'ave to swallow it, whether they like it or not. Cinemas, newspapers, gramophones, football matches, wireless, telephones—take them or leave them, if you want to amuse yourself. The ordinary man can't leave them. He takes, and what's that but slavery?"

Antic Hay, by Aldous Huxley (1923)

1.

Economic theory—even its subsection business theory, which touches on the subject more closely—has never been able to handle advertising with any great conviction. Historically, demand for a product has usually been considered as a given quantity at a given price, on a boomerang-shaped curve influenced by concepts of "elasticity" and "substitution at the margin," useful in theory but inapplicable in practice. Economists have concentrated their attention on the problems of supply and the allocation of resources, or the problem of consumer demand as a whole throughout the economy. Occasional brave spirits have attempted to analyze (most often, mathematically) the factors influencing demand for a product; but they always stumble on advertising. There is no general theory of what advertising is, or how it works.

Advertising is also a great embarrassment to the exponents of the new "science" of business management. They write very specifically about the subject in such a way as to sweep it under the rug. Thus, Albert Wesley Frey of the Tuck School of Business at Dartmouth, in his book *How Many Dollars for Advertising*, gives a check list of 113 elements that must be considered in planning an advertising program. One of the 113 is, baldly, "Effectiveness of media and copy." A quarter of a century ago, before this subject was agitating the business schools, George Washington Hill of American Tobacco wrote, "It has been our experience here that advertising that produced results and increased sales, regardless of its expense, is inexpensive. On the other hand, advertising that does not increase sales, no matter how cheap it may be, is a drag on a business." Hill's statement is undoubtedly naïve; but it is a lot less naïve than Frey's check list.

Inside the advertising business, talk about advertising inevitably stays close to the trade questions of which campaigns are selling goods and which campaigns are failing, the newest tricks of r-o-p color in newspapers, how best to tie in a television commercial with a personality. When advertising men talk about how advertising works, they go down only a single layer, to research theories. Dichterisms, brand images, reasons why. Only rarely does anyone try to probe for a basic explanation.

"We need a theory," says Ben Gedalecia, BBDO's young research director, who came to the agency from the State Department only a few years ago. "We've been able to do good research tapping in places—but we can't follow the continuum, we don't know what happens all along the line."

There is no general theory and no map of the continuum. But it seems at least possible that so elaborate a construction is unnecessary, that many of the confusions which have beset economists and business-men in their dealings with advertising can be traced to their habit of looking at the problem from the wrong end. They assume that adver-tising "creates a want" in the consumer; but this assumption does not help to explain what actually happens in the market. It is suggested, with some diffidence, that people inside and outside advertising would think more clearly about the subject if they worked from the premise that advertising, in addition to its purely informing function, *adds a new value to the existing values of the product.*

This added value is most obviously apparent in the case of a soda pill, a placebo, which is advertised as a headache cure. The pill itself has virtually no value; but it will actually cure the headaches of a num-ber of the people who take it. The suggestion power of the advertising has created a value for a worthless product. Again, two identical lip-sticks marketed under different brand names may have very different values for a teen-age girl. Wearing one of them, she feels her ordinary self; wearing the other, which has been successfully advertised as the highroad to romance, she feels a beauty—and perhaps she is.

The value of a product to the person who buys it is not limited to the physical use he makes of it. The food faddist who drinks a recon-stituted nonfat dry milk solid receives the value of his belief that he is guarding himself against a heart attack; the careful young mail boy who twists a lemon peel into his martini receives the value of his feel-ing that he is doing the thing which is done in the circles to which he aspires. Whenever a benefit is promised from the use of a product, and the promise is believed, the use of the product carries with it a value not inherent in the product itself.

Except in the extreme case of the placebo pill and the cosmetic, the value added by advertising is small in relation to those values which inhere in the product without benefit of advertising. And the consumer will ordinarily perceive the added value in terms of an existing product feature: that is, given two identical cigarettes under different brand names, and shown different advertising slogans for them, he will say that one "tastes better" than the other. But the fact that the value is fictitious as *perceived* by the consumer does not mean that it is unreal as *enjoyed* by the consumer. He finds a difference between technically identical products *because the advertising has in fact made them different.*

In terms of this premise, it is possible to explain a number of otherwise puzzling phenomena in the market place—not least the fact that advertising actually sells goods, in the face of almost everyone's proud insistence that it never influences *him.*

The puzzle of how advertised brands, identical in fact, select different sets of customers is explained by different tastes. Some people like lobster and some people don't; some people like lobster well enough, but would rather have a steak. Different approaches to the advertising problem and utterly different advertising appeals may all work equally well because the values they create please different tastes. "Brand loyalty" results from the appreciation of the added value (perceived, again, in product terms); but since the added value is slight the loyalty is fickle, and value added to another brand, by a product improvement or a new advertising campaign, may end a long-standing patronage.

The concept of a slight added value also solves the old enigma of why a consumer can be persuaded by advertising to pay a higher price for brand A when it is in reality identical with brand B—but cannot be persuaded to buy brand A at the same price as brand B if A is in fact an inferior product. The added value is great enough to make a brand seem worth a little more money, but it is not great enough to overcome an observable deficiency in the product.

Finally, the premise of a small added value explains the often-observed fact that advertising is highly effective in good times and relatively ineffective in bad times. Money has a value, too, aside from what it can buy. In boom times, when money grows on trees, a slightly more attractive product may shake it down; in hard times, when money is precious for the security that it alone can offer, the incremental values of advertising will seem slight indeed if a similar, less advertised or even unadvertised product can be bought for less. Again, advertising is of little use in combating a trend against a kind of product—brewers, for example, spend more than $100 million a year to advertise their beer, backing the ads with the full panoply of motivational research, but per capita beer consumption goes steadily down—because advertising cannot add values great enough to overcome primary factors which lead consumers to find less and less satisfaction in using a product. Here, as on the political scene, advertising is the wind on the surface, sweeping all before it when it blows with the tide but powerless to prevent a shifting of greater forces.

The fact that advertising cannot reverse a major trend in national consumption or in the consumption of a product group as a whole does not, of course, mean that individual advertisers are wasting their money when they fight a trend. Advertising may add sufficient value to an individual *brand* of a product to enable it to resist the trend; by increasing its share of a declining market a brand may actually show a gain in sales even though industry-wide sales are falling. A case in point is the Bert and Harry Piel campaign which slightly (*very* slightly) increased the sale of Piels in the New York Metropolitan Area at a time when total beer sales in the city were slipping fairly rapidly.

It must be observed that the concept of added value is merely another, more accurate and more useful way of expressing the thought which is behind the phrase "creating a want." The value of a product to a consumer lies in its fulfillment of his desires for that product; increased desire must be reflected across the equation mark by increased value. The difficulty with the old idea of created wants is its implication that the increased value is somehow "artificial," not truly of benefit to the consumer, and that the observed phenomenon of brand loyalty must reflect the consumer's stupidity and malleability. But the consuming public, whatever its failings in the kingdom of abstract ideas, has repeatedly shown itself to be remarkably shrewd in its evaluations of competing products. Advertising which has been spectacularly succesful in selling an inferior product once fails utterly to sell it a second time to the same people.

As a matter of strict logic, advertising *must* somehow change the product to which it is applied. In recent years, some advertising research psychologists have gingerly approached this question, via Burleigh Gardner's concept of the "brand image." But the psychologist's habits of work lead him to assume that the image is something present in the consumer's mind, rather than something pervasive in the product itself. It is remarkable how many people who readily see that a new package or a new brand name will change a product fail to see that advertising inevitably has a very similar effect.

Within the advertising business, acceptance of such a premise might open new and perhaps more fruitful fields for research investigation (though, in fact, some researchers have been working along these lines for some time—on the assumption that the advertising does something to the consumer which distorts his rational judgment) and might restore the creative intuition to its rightful place as the value-creator in advertising. And, among its other blessings, the assumption of added value would work to rid the business of two of its worst nuisances: the advertising man's apparently insatiable need for self-justification and the advertising critic's apparently unceasing attacks on the business for its alleged fraud, deceit and "hidden persuasion."

None of the usual self-justifications of the advertising man will stand up very well under logical analysis. The contention that advertising operates to cut prices by making possible the economies of mass production is true, if at all, only in a very long-term sense (in the jargon of Joel Dean, writing in the *Harvard Business Review,* "empirical findings for industries whose production is mechanized indicate that incremental production costs are usually constant over the range of output that is significant for determining advertising policy in the short run"). The contention that advertising cuts distribution costs by pre-selling the consumer is contradicted at every turn by monstrosities such as cellophane-wrapped bananas and fresh frozen meat balls. The contention that advertising works to create progress by enabling manufacturers to profit heavily on new product features is rebutted in large part—not entirely—by the visible triviality of the new features that hove into view each year, created to meet the demands of advertising. The educational service performed by advertising in introducing new products is quickly subordinated to advertising's continuing role as a competitive weapon. There is, of course, no need for the advertising man, or for anyone else, to justify what he does for a living; society by and large is willing enough to accept each legal occupation on its own terms. But if the advertising man feels a need for justification, the concept of added value should be a very satisfying one.

And, meanwhile, it would still the loud voices which continually denounce advertising as dishonest, and the consumers who buy advertised products as a collection of bamboozled nincompoops. The notion that advertising can "manipulate" people into buying products they should not buy was always both arrogant and naïve, proved false by advertising's inability to keep an inferior product afloat or to sell against primary trends. It may be true that branded products do represent sexual symbols, and that the psychological researcher can show an advertiser a way to use these symbols in his selling effort. But a product which satisfies the sublimated sexual drive gives its consumer a high order of tertiary value. By inflating the consciousness of this value, the advertiser has increased the consumer's pleasure in the product—has delivered, in short, the added value which his advertising promised.

Where status symbols are concerned the case is even more clear. The pleasure of driving around in a new car, or of serving unsalted caviar to company, cannot be understood as a bare use value. The admiring eyes that follow the car, the heightened respect of the company, are satisfactions not likely to be missed by the consumer. To the extent that advertising can increase these satisfactions by building a "brand image," the consumer receives the added value which was his reason for buying this particular brand. He has not been "duped" by advertising; on the contrary, he has taken sensible (if unconscious) advantage of what advertising offers.

Many people will object that advertising creates "false" values for a product, but in an economic context it is unimportant whether a use value enjoyed by a consumer is true or false. Outside standards of judgment cannot be applied to assess the reality of private gratifications. The history of human vice indicates that values most widely regarded as false will always seem real enough to command a price in the market place. The truth or falsity of advertising values is a matter of individual opinion, not a subject for objective analysis.

2.

And there seems to be only one civilized cultural opinion on advertising and most of its work: A rousing, roaring thumbs-down. The great bulk of advertising is culturally repulsive to anyone with any developed sensitivity. So, of course, are most movies and television shows, most popular music and a surprisingly high proportion of published books. When you come right down to it, there is not a hell of a lot to be said for most of what appears in the magazines. A sensitive person can easily avoid cheap movies, cheap books and cheap art, but there is scarcely anyone outside the walls who can avoid all contact with advertising. By presenting the intellectual with a more or less true image of the popular culture, advertising earns his enmity and calumny. It hits him where it hurts worst: in his politically liberal and socially generous outlook, partly nourished by his avoidance of actual contact with popular taste.

Successful advertising, which must create massed sales, cannot rise too far above or fall too far below the cultural level of the people at whom it aims. Even if an advertising man suspects that he could win results with a more intelligent ad or television program, or a presentation on a higher cultural level, he is restricted by his position as a servant, spending someone else's money. He may dare a new approach in an advertising theme; but he cannot be asked to dare a cultural standard which may cut him off from his client's market.

Though most advertising must retain the cultural standards of its audience, advertising can and does work small changes in public taste. On balance, these changes are probably in the direction of increased sensitivity. Advertising copy and headlines have frequently done the devil's work, marching in the van of the general debasement of the English language. Advertising requires extreme simplification of complicated subjects, and the advertising writer must therefore stretch previously precise words to cover large areas. But advertising is a visual as well as a verbal phenomenon, and the first purpose of advertising art is to catch the attention of the consumer, in such a way that he is favorably inclined toward the message. Generally speaking, originality in art is more likely to win attention than the same damn thing all over again, so advertising art has kept within reaching distance of advanced design. Via advertising, the public has become familiar with what sensitive people usually regard as "good design"; and familiarity in this area breeds acceptance. In the more general sense, and on its own terms, advertising as a whole seeks in a modest way to heighten public sensitivity, because a more sensitive perception will be more likely to recognize the values of slight product differences.

The culture must be seen, of course, in a wider focus than aesthetics, and in this more general view advertising's intellectual critics denounce it for poisoning wells. "Advertising has concentrated," writes *Fortune*'s Daniel Bell in the *New Leader*, "on arousing the anxieties and manipulating the fears of consumers to coerce them into buying." Stripped of its emotional language, and rephrased in the terms of an added-value concept, the accusation is that advertising creates insecurity in the culture for the purely commercial purpose of increasing the value of a brand. Reduced to cases, the charge is that Listerine and Colgate, for example, force people to worry about mouth odors in order to make them conscious of the benefits they would receive from using a product which, it is claimed, eliminates mouth odors.

And there is no way around it: the accusation is true. A weasel word may be said again about the relatively minor influence of advertising on fundamental attitudes, the fact that the fears and anxieties are real and exist before advertising stimulates them further, that advertising cannot create a fear or an anxiety not already present in the consumer— at least in the latent form of an experience not fully considered—before he comes upon the ad. Yet the fact of the matter is that advertising often does magnify the pains of modern existence to sell a product which is supposed to assuage them.

Taken by itself, the act seems morally unjustifiable. But the product very often *does* assuage the pains—not infrequently, in those areas of health and beauty where the fear appeals are most commonly used, because of the power of suggestion of the advertising itself. The poor old crock who feels tired every afternoon at three, from a complicated set of physical and psychological causes, may be persuaded to believe that what ails him is Tired Blood; and a dose of Geritol, though his condition may be such that it doesn't help what ails him, may cure him of the symptoms which disturb him. The girl who is ashamed of her pimples may bear them with more grace after she buys and applies a product which is advertised as the greatest pimple destroyer in history—even if the product is actually nothing more than second-rate cold cream, aerated (with lanolin added). Most of the products advertised as cures for such ills are not completely worthless, either; they actually will produce something of the benefit claimed for them.

In real life, advertising does not plummet untroubled people into a pit of anxiety, for the single, vulgar result of an advertiser's profit. Advertising probably does increase the number of people who feel some concern about their physical or social failings. But it offers to all people, those who felt the concern before they saw the advertising and those in whom it is newly aroused, a solution (a guaranteed solution, in the context of the advertising) to their troubles. For a considerable proportion of those who try it, the product actually *is* a solution, and drinking it down frees them of their anxieties. Measuring the damage done to the national psyche by the increment of fears created by advertising, as against the soothing of the national psyche achieved by removing the same fears from a number of people who previously suffered them, is a task for a subtle metaphysician indeed.

Finally, there is the relationship between advertising and what a large number of people who parrot each other call "conformity." This relationship is difficult to discuss, because the alleged "conformity," as a new development in society, does not exist outside the imaginations of the people who talk about it. It is true, of course, that a large mass of citizens drawn at random from within a single culture will have more things in common than not. It is also true that modern communications have produced some breaking down of old and perhaps valuable regional distinctions. And it is true that developments in the past thirty years have raised the economic condition of the nation's lowest tenth and lowered the economic condition of its highest tenth; raised the educational level of the lowest tenth and lowered the educational level of the highest tenth. The community appears to be more homogeneous, from a distant look. But the same developments which have created the appearance of homogeneity have also brought about an astonishing increase in the variety of entertainments, of housing and furnishing possibilities, of hobbies, of consumer goods—even of intellectual pursuits, for those so minded. "Conformity" is the burden of impoverished communities, where people work to exhaustion and have neither the leisure nor the disposable income to express their tastes. A prosperous middle-class community may feel, more strongly than a poor community, that it does not like people who rock the boat; but within broad limits its members are free to indulge their individuality as they have never been before.

And advertising's contribution here is, on the whole, to increase diversity. Advertising lives by the product difference, real or asserted, by appealing to different tastes in values. It is axiomatic in the toothpaste business, for example, that a brand with 30 per cent of the market may throw a fresh $10 million into advertising to gain perhaps a 5 per cent increase in sales; while the same $10 million, devoted to advertising a new brand, may give the new brand a 20 per cent share-of-market. If advertising looks like other advertising, as so much of it does, the fault lies in the limited skill of many practitioners (and in the fact that advertisers, knowing that their competitors are smart, insist on ads similar to the competition's ads). The purpose is not to make anyone "conform."

What lies behind the cry of "conformity" and the blast at advertising for allegedly promoting it is the deep disappointment following upon the arrival of the millennium. We have achieved the nineteenth-century dream: everyone has enough to eat and decent clothing, by any standards but our own nearly everyone is well housed, the workday is short and leisure is ample. But the millennial culture turns out not to be very interesting; the average man remains a mediocre fellow, and pleased with himself, to boot. Which is, of course, well within his rights. Perhaps advertising *ought* to do something for the culture, but it won't; says it can't; says it shouldn't be asked; in its most defensive moments says the majority is *right* to like garbage, simply because it buys so much garbage. Holding up an inescapable mirror which reflects disappointment, and refusing for reasons of trade to comment on the picture in the mirror, advertising asks to be disliked by that element of the community which aspires to a higher culture. It is.

3.

The most interesting cultural phenomenon created by advertising is the advertising community itself, with its strange blend of assertion and obedience, prosperity and insecurity, flamboyance and timidity. In the agencies, especially, at the heart of advertising, endless confusions of purpose, functions, organization and status create a nervous, overworked and overstimulated internal society. At the root of it all lies the problem of professional standing. Organized as a profession, as a number of independent firms which offer their clients nothing more nor less than the developed skills of the staff, advertising has not been able consistently to establish the long-term client relations which are the

economic foundation of professional practice. In the absence of stable
agency-client relations or accepted ethical standards to govern the
solicitation of clients, the agencies must compete with each other as
businesses, although what they offer is a professional service.

Competition among businesses is conducted in many ways, but
it revolves around a concrete product about which, in the last analysis,
a rational judgment may be made. The "product" of a professional
service, however, is an elusive substance, and laymen are not equipped
to judge its quality. (Though Ned Doyle likes to quote Alexander
Woollcott to the effect that you don't have to be a chicken to tell a
rotten egg.) When professional services aggressively compete with each
other for clients, the weapons they find in their hands are flattery, boastfulness, scorn and servility. These are the vices of advertising.

They come in pairs: servility with flattery and boastfulness with
scorn. The servility is the most disturbing, and there are examples of
it all over the business—the expensive entertainment, the unnecessary
"services" of procuring hotel accommodations and tickets to hit shows,
the willingness to buy supplies from the client's sister's husband's
niece, or to find a job in the agency for the son of the client's biggest
customer. There is the willingness to drop important work and run
over to the client's offices to hold his hand if he feels he wants his
hand held. Most visible and distasteful of all, there is the insistence
that every employee at the agency buy and consume the client's brand
—and no other.

Not every agency makes such a demand on its employees. It would
go against the grain at Thompson, for example; Bill Bernbach says that
his people are not expected to use the client's product, "just to make
better advertising for him." And, of course, there is some justification
for a client who requests that the people who actually work on his account should be sufficiently sold on his product to use it themselves.
But the notion that everyone in an agency must fit his personal consumption pattern to the agency's list of clients is an appalling indignity
for the agency and for the people who work at it.

At BBDO, which is the worst offender in this line, signs appear periodically on the announcement boards: "Confucius say, Advertising men who use product advertised by rival agency should draw paycheck from rival agency." When BBDO advertised Lucky Strike alone, the cigarette machines contained no brand but Lucky Strike (now they contain Hit Parade, too). Alex Osborn once went so far as to plead with his employees to use BBDO-advertised brands exclusively, even at home, on the grounds that "BBDOers" and their families accounted for nearly ten thousand people, a large enough market to have an influence. (Albert Lasker, when his agency had the Lucky Strike account, once found a copywriter smoking Chesterfields, listened patiently to the man's explanation that he had taken his wife's cigarettes by mistake, then commented: "Your wife, I presume, has an independent income.") There have been rumblings of revolt against this tyranny at BBDO: a pair of mysterious signs on the cigarette machine, one labeling it "THE RUSSIAN POLLING BOOTH," the other quoting Bruce Barton's well-publicized statement that "the people's right of free choice—in their food, their clothes, their books, their homes—is the very essence of Democracy." But overriding the irritation of employees is the agency's fear of what the client might *think* if he found people at his agency buying a rival brand.

Though no other element of agency servility is so degrading, other aspects create more serious friction among the staff. The account executive who takes the work of the account group to a client conference and sells it down the river when opposition develops is a stock figure in the conversation of agency people; and this servility, rarely discouraged by agency managements, inevitably embitters the people who must do the job over again, hunting painfully for their second-best thoughts. Worst of all is the willingness of agency heads who do not believe a word of it to accept the "science" of business management, to agree with clients that advertising ought to be scientific and that the agency will somehow transform itself from a professional creative consultant to a machine turning out guaranteed advertisements, guaranteed media schedules, guaranteed marketing plans. The growth of research and marketing departments is often cited by agency heads as an example of the increasing maturity of the advertising business, and in part it is; but in another part it is merely a new facet on the old limestone of pandering to the client.

This common willingness to make over the agency into whatever image the client would wish it to have may be complemented in an agency sales talk by the recitation of what this agency gives that no other agency could possibly offer, and the denunciation of rival agencies for their incompetence. In no other trade do practitioners cry to the world their low opinion of their colleagues. Many lawyers believe that the average level of competence at the bar is not very high; many doctors feel that the medical profession could stand considerable improvement in personnel; many plumbers do not think much of other plumbers. But they all maintain a professional *espirit,* keeping their opinions for their wives or for a few intimate friends, and concealing such thoughts from the customers. In advertising, even an agency as thoroughly ethical as Young & Rubicam will think nothing of running an advertisement for itself, showing empty chairs around a television set, implying that other agencies turn out television commercials which drive the customers out of the room. (The equivalent would be a General Motors ad showing Plymouths by the score overheated and steaming by the side of a road on a hot day.) Advertising men who denounce their rivals as incompetent fakers should not be surprised at the public belief that advertising is full of incompetent fakers. This, too, results from the need to sell professional service as though it were a business.

It would not be too strong to say that advertising today *needs* to establish its professional status. Claiming an indestructible permanence for the agency system, Marion Harper of McCann-Erickson says that "we have something a manufacturer can't have—a creative society who choose to work together this way. They don't choose to work for General Motors or Colgate." But if McCann-Erickson is a business, as Harper says it is, there does not seem to be any profound reason why creative people should choose to work in one business rather than in another. Few occupations are as dependent as advertising on the quality of the incoming talent, and nowhere else does the absence of talent show so plainly. (As the old saw says, lawyers hang their mistakes, doctors bury theirs, but the advertising man must publish his.) Without professional status, advertising cannot offer much to the young talent on which its future depends. Other fields of endeavor can easily outbid it in respectability and security; the money is good but the hours are lousy and the work is unhealthful; glamour repels as many as it attracts; and the challenge of the job can be seen only in professional terms.

Historically, advertising has offered a quite remarkable inducement to its best practitioners: the opportunity to be paid for continuing their education to the end of their lives. Somewhere in the creative advertising man's work there turns up, adding effectiveness to the whole, all the experience, all the random bits of information, all the academic disciplines he has mastered. "Every good creative person in advertising whom I have ever known," Jim Young said in his often-reprinted lecture *A Technique for Producing Ideas* (to which the introduction was written by no less than Reinhold Niebuhr), "has always had two noticeable characteristics. First, there was no subject under the sun in which he could not easily get interested—from, say, Egyptian burial customs to Modern Art. Every facet of life had fascination for him. Second, he was an extensive browser in all sorts of fields of information. For it is with the advertising man as with the cow: no browsing, no milk."

Here and there in advertising one finds people whose joy in their work easily overcomes the irritations of the agency business and flows out around them, into their associates and into the pages they write. Jim Young is one, BBDO's Jean Rindlaub is another. Both of them had to give up formal education at an early age and go to work for a living; both have found in advertising an opportunity to educate themselves that no other trade could have given them. "Of course," Jim Young wrote in a chapter of "afterthoughts" to his lecture, "if you consider that your education was finished when you left college, and wouldn't be caught dead with a copy of, say, one of Jane Austen's novels under your pillow, go no farther. . . ."

No other trade calling for the exercise of a developed intelligence was open to a Jim Young or a Jean Rindlaub, who held no college degrees. Today advertising cannot count on pulling fine practitioners out of the ranks of the unschooled: anyone who seriously desires formal education will get it. Advertising must compete with the professions for the intelligence of the graduating classes; to compete successfully, it must be a profession itself, and it must stress the breadth of intelligent interest which it asks from its practitioners.

Several agencies are already organized on a thoroughly professional basis. A client cannot turn down a Doyle Dane Bernbach advertising campaign any more than he can turn down a lawyer's brief; if he doesn't like it, he can go get himself another boy. Bernbach has a rule that it will not solicit any account unless invited to do so by the principals; in 1957 the agency turned down one of the nation's largest advertisers on the grounds that it didn't like the way the company did business. David Ogilvy, too, has turned down large billings because he distrusted the account. Similarly, every account executive at Ted Bates is empowered to resign any account on the spot; J. Walter Thompson and Y & R will never make a speculative presentation. Bill Bernbach likes to say that advertising is an "art," but lawyers will use the same word in the same sense about their work. To Bernbach, to Stanley Resor, to George Gribbin, to Reeves, Ogilvy and others, advertising is a profession based on the creative intelligence of its practitioners. And advertising can, in fact, claim that dignity, when it breaks the bounds of servility.

The future of advertising must lie in this direction. With the conception of himself as a professional offering a trained creative intelligence, the advertising man can face his critics calmly. He can face his clients courageously. And he can face himself in the morning.

INDEX

TITLES OF INTEREST IN
ADVERTISING AND SALES PROMOTION

For further information or a current catalog, write:
NTC Business Books
a division of *NTC Publishing Group*
4255 West Touhy Avenue
Lincolnwood, Illinois 60646-1975 U.S.A.